PRAISE

TRUTH DE.

T0357122

"This book is the voice of the U'wa in the words of Abby, and these memories of the truth are a primary source of respect, help, and coordination for the defense of Mother Earth."

> —JUAN GABRIEL JEREZ TEGRIA-KUANAKUVO (U'WA NATION), legal advisor for international affairs at AsoU'wa, the Association of the U'wa Traditional Authorities and Cabildos U'wa

"As I entered the very powerful space of *Truth Demands*, I began to do a drum beat against my leg, a beat that made it possible for me to keep reading. It will take many readings to fully absorb the impact of this book. It couldn't have come at a better time as we humans navigate so many upheavals and make necessary decisions about our climate future."

> —DONNA CHAVIS (LUMBEE NATION), founder of the RedTailed Hawk Collective and program manager of Climate and Energy Justice, Friends of the Earth US

"Today's catastrophe of climate change is preceded by more than a century of atrocities based on the dig, burn, and dump global economy of fossil fuels, mostly on Indigenous lands like that of the U'wa. *Truth Demands* is a single searing thread connecting one story of murder and grief to the story of climate change, and all we need to organize, imagine, and fight for collectively to overcome it; it is a story as big as our world can contain. . . . *Truth Demands* allows the U'wa to tell their own story, while connecting us directly, simply, to it. This book does not make sense of the brutal murders of Terence Freitas, Lahe'ena'e Gay, and Ingrid Washinawatok—that is not possible. But it does help make meaning of their lives and blazes a path forward for all of us who remain."

> —MIYA YOSHITANI, co-director of Movement Innovation Collaborative, former executive director of Asian Pacific Environmental Network, and past steering committee member of the Climate Justice Alliance

"A wise and tender unfolding, demonstrating what real healing and transformation can look like in the face of unspeakable loss and ongoing destruction and devastation. This is a love story, both deeply intimate as well as vast and collective . . . [that] beautifully articulates the delicate dance between stillness and action and how we can hold space for both. Deftly weaving the personal and the political; Indigenous ways of self-determination and earth-based, grassroots activism; and interlacing the stories of local communities brilliantly rising up from the Philippines to Colombia to Standing Rock and beyond, this book is a compelling call to action that challenges oppression and domination without othering. It is essential reading, filled with exactly the kind of truth that this precarious moment demands."

—KAIRA JEWEL LINGO, author of *We Were Made for These Times* and *Healing Our Way Home*

"This remarkable book embodies Abby's brave, thoughtful responses to challenging and indeed tragic turns of events. She pulls the reader all the way through to what we need to continue life on Earth. And because of that, I believe this book will help many people."

—JOANNA MACY, PhD, root teacher of The Work That Reconnects and author of *World as Lover, World as Self*

"Sometimes grief blinds you; sometimes it opens your mind and your heart. This is the astonishing and brilliantly told story of a woman navigating a tragedy that is wrapped in a mystery and a geopolitical fight. It's a story of resilience and insight told in a voice that honors the young man and women whose lives were taken much too soon. *Truth Demands* is a story you should read to understand the healing powers of the deepest pain."

—NICHOLAS THOMPSON, CEO of *The Atlantic*

"Fierce, heartbreaking, and surprisingly full of joy, *Truth Demands* is the memoir of a young activist grappling with love and death amid the brutal politics of fossil fuel extraction in the global South. Abby Reyes's book is at once a suspenseful study in political organizing to defend human rights against corporate, extra-legal, and state-sponsored violence; a glimpse into one Indigenous community's long, patient work of survivance; and, last but not least, a look into the wounded heart of a lover and a mother who never stops demanding truth and justice. Written with the delicacy of a novel and the pace of a thriller, this book will find a place among memoirs of spiritual enlightenment as well as among classic stories of political education. Teachers of anthropology, sociology, gender studies, ethnic studies, and politics as well as law will find this an essential text."

—ANGELA P. HARRIS, JD, distinguished professor of law at Seattle University Law School, co-director of the Critical Justice Institute, and co-editor-in-chief of the *Journal of Law and Political Economy*

"As a Colombian, as a Latin American, as a lawyer, but mostly as a mom, friend, and daughter, I profoundly recommend this book. Advancing climate justice is not easy. It takes reinventing our societies and the world as we know it. The stakes for our children could not be higher. This story brings us more fully into the risks that environmental human rights defenders take to shape our collective future, risks that can often, as here, only be understood in the context of war and conflict. To work to end impunity while somehow staying a whole human being is a path of fierce feminine love and strength, one Abby generously reflects in this book. Reading *Truth Demands* created space for me to face my own fear and pain. To step toward my own healing, and in so doing, my country's healing."

—ASTRID PUENTES RIAÑO, UN Special Rapporteur on the human right to a clean, healthy and sustainable environment and professor at the Berta Cáceres Environmental Law Clinic at the Universidad Iberoamericana in Mexico City

"Heartbreaking and inspirational. . . . This book is not for the faint of heart, but it is a necessary read for embracing the reality of risk that human rights defenders face every day as they valiantly seek to protect Mother Earth. I applaud Reyes for this raw rendering, artfully crafted in a way that kept me spellbound from beginning to end. I have emerged from the reading as a better, more informed, and grounded person and advocate."

—JACQUI PATTERSON, executive director of the Chisholm Legacy Project Resource Hub for Black Frontline Climate Justice Leadership and a 2024 *Time* Woman of the Year

"Anyone who considers themselves a climate activist or wants to become one must experience this painful and beautiful story, an all-too-familiar account of the desecration that people living on the frontlines of fossil fuels have endured for too long. *Truth Demands* probes a tragic history—one that continues to shape so many of us—in a way that only this author could do. With the factual precision of a lawyer and the fierce love for the peoples and communities she brings to life, Reyes makes clear the true cost of oil in human, ecological, spiritual, and deeply personal terms. . . . This book is an important reminder to bring our fierce love for people and planet along with our smart climate strategies so that we have the potential and power to end the fossil fuel era. And that's what we all need, and what healing, justice—and science—demands."

    —KATIE REDFORD, JD, co-founder of EarthRights International, executive director of the Equation Campaign, and co-editor of *The Revolution Will Not Be Litigated*

"Our stories hold the keys to our liberation. This might be why many of us shy away from their telling. Abby Reyes's story (and the courage it has taken for her to open her throat to tell it) is a gift to all of us who long for the sovereignty of our bodies, our water ways, and our ancestral ways of being in relationship to the land. The price of unfettered resource extraction by the fossil fuel industry is often hidden behind by well-paid lies and distractions. Abby Reyes calls on us to see and feel it so that we may break ourselves free from the devastation of it."

    —ROSA ESPERANZA GONZÁLEZ, founder of Facilitating Power

"A gripping feat of storytelling. . . . Reyes's words are entrancing and skillfully weave together her personal [story] with the stories of those on the frontlines of climate justice. . . . It is a fiercely passionate book that implores us to consider how ecological activism is full of the very same markers of colonial injustices the world increasingly wrestles with. We are lucky to read a depiction here that gives those stories a name, a place, and most importantly, a heart."

    —SEEMA JILANI, MD, pediatrician, global health advocate, and frequent contributor to the *New York Times*

"In this extraordinarily moving piece of writing, Abby Reyes has beautifully captured the pain of loss, the difficulties of finding unity and strength among survivors of atrocity and, most importantly, the rediscovery of joy. I cried in parts, was angry in parts, and kept thinking of the very young Abby I mentored through the early years of this story. My own mentor, political economist Albert Hirschman, used to say that a true scholar knew about the relationship between the head and the heart. In *Truth Demands*, Abby advances a wise understanding of the integration of head and heart with stories of daring and courage to end our oil wars. This moving and gorgeous book is required reading for students of social transformation and those yearning to find their place."

—TERRY LYNN KARL, PhD, Stanford University Gildred Professor of Latin American studies and political science, author of *The Paradox of Plenty*, and co-editor of *Oil Wars*

"The key narrative of this century is about humanity's fight to overcome fossil fuel interests, and this book tells the story more completely than any I've read. Reyes . . . has mastered the art of seeing beyond our current constraints. She hasn't just crafted a basic whodunit about the murders but has delved profoundly into underlying inquiries of who among us engages in such actions and why. If you're keen to understand this struggle, to grasp our evolution toward better versions of ourselves and the transformations required to turn the unsightly caterpillar of 20th-century extractivism into this century's splendid butterfly, read this harrowingly beautiful book. Within its pages, you'll discover stories of justice, the lighthouse of integrity from the U'wa, and larger truths that we must confront."

—DANNY KENNEDY, founding CEO and venture partner at New Energy Nexus and author of *Rooftop Revolution*

"*Truth Demands* is many things—a reflection on healing, a practice in accountability and solidarity, and a call to action for a just transition in right relationship with Mother Earth. And the bright thread running through it all is a love letter to Abby Reyes's many teachers and mentors. Reading it made me think back on the lessons of my own with gratitude."

—AMY LAURA CAHN, JD, climate and environmental justice lawyer

"Abby Reyes has written a raw, honest, and wise memoir of healing—of the intertwining of the U'wa people's generous and costly work to defend and heal their territory from the ravages of petrocapitalism and colonialism with Abby's own inner journey toward healing a heart broken by the same demons. Like the Mantra Pushpam, the Vedic hymn that sings that 'she who understands the source of water understands herself,' Abby's emotional narrative returns again and again to images of water: literal rivers contaminated by oil and blood and inner waters calming external waves. In sharing her journey to self-understanding, Abby—and, through her telling, the U'wa—charts a course for all of us across waters roiled by personal and systemic trauma."

> —MARTIN WAGNER, JD, former managing attorney of the International Program, Earthjustice

"This graceful work of politics and art is a testimony to resistance and strength. *Truth Demands* offers an essential source of inspiration and support for those ready to put our collective shoulders to the wheel for a livable climate future for all."

> —ANNIE LEONARD, former executive director of Greenpeace USA and author of *The Story of Stuff*

"*Truth Demands* is a story of reckoning for our times. Abby shares her journey such that we receive critical tools and ideas for transforming ourselves in order to transform the world. This book is a powerful invitation to co-create the world we so desperately need."

> —JODIE TONITA, leadership coach and strategist and former director of the Social Transformation Project

"... beautifully written, totally engrossing ... It drew me in from page one and never let me stray . . . an incredibly timely reading for anyone who wishes a wise political overview of standing in alliance with Indigenous peoples and their struggles to protect Mother Earth's waters, lands and air, and cues and clues about ways to walk that path."

> —NINA SIMONS, co-founder of Bioneers and author of *Nature, Culture, and the Sacred*

Truth Demands

Truth
Demands

a memoir of murder,
oil wars, and the
rise of climate justice

Abby Reyes

North Atlantic Books
Huichin, unceded Ohlone land
Berkeley, California

North Atlantic Books
Huichin, unceded Ohlone land
2526 Martin Luther King Jr Way
Berkeley, CA 94704 USA
www.northatlanticbooks.com

Cover design by Jasmine Hromjak
Cover photos © Vitalii, noppharat via Adobe Stock;
EduardHarkonen, StreetFlash, and ablokhin via
Getty Images
Book design by Happenstance Type-O-Rama

Printed in Canada

This book is nonfiction memoir. The substance of the events, experiences, and conversations detailed herein have been faithfully rendered as the author remembered and interpreted them, to the best of her ability; they are not intended to be definitive representations. Some names, identities, and circumstances have been changed to protect the privacy and/or anonymity of various individuals involved.

Truth Demands: A Memoir of Murder, Oil Wars, and the Rise of Climate Justice is sponsored and published by North Atlantic Books, an educational nonprofit based in the unceded Ohlone land Huichin (Berkeley, CA) that collaborates with partners to develop cross-cultural perspectives; nurture holistic views of art, science, the humanities, and healing; and seed personal and global transformation by publishing work on the relationship of body, spirit, and nature.

Rainer Maria Rilke, "I Am Too Alone," Poem 7 From *A Book for the Hours of Prayer,* in *Selected Poems of Rainer Maria Rilke,* trans. Robert Bly (New York: HarperCollins, 1981), 25; Alexis Pauline Gumbs, *Undrowned: Black Feminist Lessons from Marine Mammals* (Chico, CA: AK Press, 2020), 153; Tracy K. Smith, Lecture, City Arts & Lectures, San Francisco, November 10, 2023.

North Atlantic Books's publications are distributed to the US trade and internationally by Penguin Random House Publisher Services. For further information, visit our website at www.northatlanticbooks.com.

Library of Congress Cataloging-in-Publication Data

Names: Reyes, Abby, author.
Title: Truth demands : a memoir of murder, oil wars, and the rise of
  climate justice / Abby Reyes.
Description: Berkeley, California : North Atlantic Books, [2025] | Includes
  bibliographical references. | Summary: "Recounts the experiences of the
  author who, twenty years after her partner's murder, is called to
  confront the past when she finds herself a recognized victim-survivor in
  case 001 of Colombia's truth and recognition process"— Provided by
  publisher.
Identifiers: LCCN 2024043843 (print) | LCCN 2024043844 (ebook) | ISBN
  9781623175214 (trade paperback) | ISBN 9781623175221 (ebook)
Subjects: LCSH: Reyes, Abby. | Murder victims'
  families—Colombia—Biography. | Political
  activists—Colombia—Biography. | Fuel trade—Corrupt
  practices—Colombia.
Classification: LCC HD9502.C72 R49 2025 (print) | LCC HD9502.C72 (ebook)
  | DDC 333.7909861—dc23/eng/20250110
LC record available at https://lccn.loc.gov/2024043843
LC ebook record available at https://lccn.loc.gov/2024043844

The authorized representative in the EU for product safety and compliance is Eucomply OÜ, Pärnu mnt 139b-14, 11317 Tallinn, Estonia, hello@eucompliancepartner.com, +33757690241.

1 2 3 4 5 6 7 8 9 MARQUIS 30 29 28 27 26 25

The interior of this book is printed on 100 percent recycled paper, and the cover is printed on material from well-managed forests.

For Kiran and Julian: may you know
Kajka Ika, *the heart of the world*

For Pueblo U'wa, keepers of the
equilibrium in Kajka Ika: may your
song, and the song of all communities at
the heart of the movement for climate justice,
reverberate and strengthen .

For you and me: may the waters grow
still enough for us to hear this song,
take heart, and take heed

CONTENTS

Part 3

Part 4

I don't want to stay folded anywhere,
because where I am folded, there I am a lie.

—RAINER MARIA RILKE

There is something that I need, but I have to go so deep to find it. There is something I have to give, but I have to give it on my own time. There is something I'm going to tell you, but first I have to make a language for myself and the place I live that doesn't steal me from my purpose. Will you wait? There is something I'm going to tell you, just let me open up my mouth. See if I sing.

—ALEXIS PAULINE GUMBS

There is not a shelf life on clarity.

—TRACY K. SMITH

PREFACE

When I was twenty-five, my life became beholden to a set of murders near Indigenous territory in Colombia, land then coveted by a US-based oil company. My partner in work and life, Terence Unity Freitas, was slain, along with Ingrid Washinawatok and Lahe'ena'e Gay. I walked into adulthood through the gates of these murders. In those years, I felt pressed up against the machinery of fossil fuel extraction, tied there by the murders' known and unknown dismal facts. These circumstances sped up my training as a human being. I found myself unbidden in a wretched lineage of people paying the price of our oil wars and living with ambiguous loss. As with so many others before me, the murders forced me to learn basic practices for moving through grief and ambiguity that otherwise might have taken a lifetime to learn.

Here I share stories of learning these practices for survival. My hope is that they may be of use as we collectively navigate the climate catastrophe that is already baked in, dedicate ourselves to averting the worst, and co-create the course corrections we need.

I held fragments of these stories for years, awaiting resolution that never came. Shaping the fragments into this book changed my understanding of resolution. Questions about the murders may always remain unaddressed. Some stories may never be told. And the future will remain unknowable. To offer this telling, I had to acquiesce to these truths. Acquiescence led to acceptance, which stirred

my memory of agency. Finding agency in the telling led to my freedom, for it opened a back door to resolution.

These stories move between my ongoing work for both personal
and collective transformation. In my early adulthood, I was not only
concerned with securing justice for the murders in a narrow sense. I
was also committed to helping tip the scales toward social and environmental equilibrium in a global sense. As a strategy of collective
liberation, I diligently cultivated a vision of the future in which murders like this no longer happen.

For decades, I have worked for a vision of the future in which we
transition, as a species, from economies of extraction, milita-
rism, and exploitation—conditions that lead to murders like this
in the first place—to regenerative and resilient living economies
of interdependence. Multiple, coexisting, contemporary progressive social movements advance this vision. This vision is rooted
in long-standing work of place-based communities around the
world to assert dignity in the face of extractive industry aggression
against their lands, waters, bodies, and cultures—including that of
the Colombian Pueblo U'wa, indigenous to the territory where the
murders took place.[1]

Pueblo U'wa's ancestral and recognized territory in the rural
northeast is on the front lines of major installations of Colombia's
fossil fuel infrastructure. The U'wa contest this infrastructure as a
matter of territorial defense. They also contest its validity as a human
endeavor. They believe that keeping the oil in the ground is fundamental to the balance of the earth: "'If oil is taken from the earth,
our mother, she will dry out and will not produce what we humans
need to live. If we do not take care of the earth, then the earth cannot
continue to sustain us.'"[2] This understanding goes to the heart of
what the global consensus of earth system scientists tells us about
the deadly role that burning fossil fuels plays in accelerating climate
change. In walking alongside the U'wa during my youth, I listened as
their voice joined a global chorus of similarly situated frontline and
Indigenous communities showing us what it looks like to keep the

oil in the ground and to midwife our transition to climate justice. When social critic Arundhati Roy assured us that "another world is not only possible, she is on her way," I felt deeply in accord. On a quiet day, I believed I could "hear her breathing."[3]

Today, decades out, I watch as the children I raise and the university students I teach struggle to hear that breath. When my older son, Kiran, was twelve, he accompanied me to an afternoon lecture at the University of California Irvine School of Law, where I taught. The lecture was by Dr. Charles Sepulveda, an Acjachemen and Tongva scholar native to the land upon which the campus sits. Charlie told the story of the Santa Ana River, the main waterway that connects the ridgeline to the sea in that southern Californian bioregion. It is a story of a beloved river, vital to the daily life of his peoples. He told of the eventual channelization and disappearance of the river under the urbanized weight of triple colonization that Native peoples and the land have endured in the region over centuries.

Kiran was most familiar with these ghostly and industrialized riverbanks as home to an increasing number of hundreds of unhoused people in Orange County. The encampment was in the news as local officials used police forces to disband the makeshift settlement, an order later enforced with bulldozers. Charlie's lecture acknowledged this current state. He also took care to offer images and stories of local Indigenous people today reconnecting with portions of the waterway through visions of ecological restoration.[4]

As we left the lecture, ascending the stairs out of the law school into the gathering dusk, I put my arm around Kiran's broad shoulders and commented lightly about what a beautiful talk it had been. Kiran was silent. When I turned to face him, streetlight caught the tears welling in his dark eyes. "Mom," he said, "No. It was not beautiful. It was horrible, what was done to Native peoples and the river and the animals they cared about. There is no way it is going to change. Even if some people try to change it, everything will have to change, and there is no way enough people are going to change that much." His shoulders shuddered. "It's too late."

I touched him silently to let him know I heard him. I knew he did not want me to fix it for him. He did not, in that moment, want to hear about my yearslong path to resolve similar feelings in the face of the murders. Anything less than telling the whole story would have risked trivializing both of our experiences. So I said nothing. Instead, for the few minutes while we walked, we just let sorrow have a place.

With reverence and even awe, I am acutely aware that I don't know what our collective children will need to hear as we climb our way out of the debris of the present and live into the stories of the future that they will tell. But as "practice for a future to be possible" and as a hedge "against forgetting," I collected the stories I know.[5] I wrote the stories out to navigate the waters of grief, ambiguity, and the unknown. In the process, I swam in ponds, lakes, rivers, and oceans. In learning how to navigate these waters, I learned how to come home to the "island within myself."[6] The stories tell of this homecoming, of the teachers who guided me there, and of my faith in the practices that move us together toward the future that our collective children will author.

Several of these stories are part of a collective story of which I am only one custodian. As in any collective story, I can only tell it from where I stand. My telling does not attempt to summon one unified truth about what happened or its meaning. It is not an academic, historical, or legal rendering; it is memoir. These stories take written form but follow rules more akin to that of oral tradition, in which the freedom of the voice comes in part from a telling of one's own that makes space for multiple truths and multiple freedoms.[7] I stand on the shoulders of giants to offer this telling—the mentors, ancestors, and compañeres who bestowed the gifts of their own stories and teachings to me. Through this telling, I reciprocate.

In Part 1, I tell you about the heart of the world in U'wa territory and my invitation to Terence to make a home in my heart. I tell you about the day my heart flew away. I tell you what it was like to meet fear and sorrow and to realize there were thresholds I could not cross.

In Part 2, I tell you what the U'wa people were up against to pro-tect the heart of the world. And what it was like to meet and work with anger. I tell you about what I did when I realized I did not know how to call my heart back home. I share what I learned about foster-ing leadership in defense of Mother Earth and watering the seeds of climate justice. I share Terence's invitation from beyond the veil to unlock the door.

In Part 3, I tell you what I learned about calling my heart back home. And about staying intact as I crossed the threshold into Colombia's post–civil war Truth and Recognition Chamber.

In Part 4, I share our truth demands about the murders and what the truth demands of all of us as we call our collective hearts back home. I share what it can look like to keep "all under heaven intact," and take the leaps we need to change everything.[8]

I wrote to unfold my own voice. I opened my throat in a way that protects privacy, ceremony, and the lives of many other people involved in a manner that does not "steal me from my purpose."[9] Therefore, I have left some parts of the story untold. Some truths remain hidden.

PROLOGUE

Rainy Cow Field
Just across the Venezuelan Border

We Marked the Twentieth Anniversary

The email sat unread in my inbox. It was from Colombia. I knew what it said, but also knew I couldn't open it without more support. I shut the laptop. It was February 27, 2019. I was visiting Oakland, California, sitting in the living room of a musty ground-floor rental. Rain poured outside, surfacing the smell of the apartment's origins as a converted garage. Even so, the rain felt like a benediction.

I had traveled to Oakland to gather with a small group of friends to mark the twentieth anniversary of the murders of Ingrid Washinawatok El-Issa, Lahe'ena'e Gay, and Terence Freitas.

Ingrid Washinawatok El-Issa was native to the Menominee Nation in Wisconsin. Also known as Flying Eagle Woman, Ingrid had been the executive director of the Fund for the Four Directions, a private fund supporting Indigenous health, education, and language revitalization. Through sustained leadership in multiple intergovernmental commissions and committees over decades, her advocacy is credited with advancing us toward global recognition of the United Nations Declaration on the Rights of Indigenous Peoples.

Lahe'ena'e Gay was Native Hawaiian and the founder and president of Pacific Cultural Conservancy International, an organization dedicated to bolstering traditional Indigenous educational models. She was a renowned photographer, oral historian, and advocate for preserving cultural and biological diversity.[1]

Terence Unity Freitas was a white environmental and Indigenous rights advocate from Los Angeles. A few years out of college, he was an expert animal tracker, a second-degree black belt in Korean hapkido, and an instructor of women's self-defense—skills that earned him the trust of the U'wa. He was also my partner.

Together, Terence, Ingrid, and Lahe' had spent February of 1999 with U'wa women and elders walking the mountains and rivers of the eastern Colombian cloud forest, lands then sought after by US-based Occidental Petroleum Corporation (Oxy). Sharing stories and time, they were building the relationships and strategies needed to advance the U'wa people's self-determination goals.

They were kidnapped on the way to their flight home. A few days later, a farmer found their bound, hooded, and bullet-riddled bodies in his rainy cow field just across the Venezuelan border.

⤺

Twenty years later, a few of us visited a redwood grove in the Oakland Hills near where Terence had lived when I first met him. Danny Kennedy, Martin Wagner, and I walked among the silent trees. The mountain sky was heavy with fog, but our conversation was light. Danny, an environmental campaigner who was Terence's colleague at the time of the murders, recounted the whirlwind of energy and activity that Terence would generate. Martin, an environmental lawyer who had represented Pueblo U'wa internationally, described the uncanny way Terence presented as both wise beyond his years and so young. Martin recounted the hours Terence put in with him to communicate the legal arguments the U'wa were then beginning to articulate against the Colombian government.

I told them about our first morning together in Terence's one-room Oakland apartment, standing at the threshold of the open door. The dawn streamed in as Terence and I looked out into the street. I told them about turning back around toward his apartment and feeling Terence's hands firmly on my waist as I opened up to invite our first kiss. I remembered my finger tracing the silhouette from his temple, down his nape, and along the ridgeline of his shoulder. As I shared the detail with Danny and Martin, I couldn't quite let myself back inside the exquisite promise and vitality of that moment. Instead, we focused on our footing, picking our way up the trail to a damp knoll. The forest swallowed the words that we didn't need to remember our friend. We called Terence's mother, Julie, in Los Angeles, to mark the day. We walked back to the car.

Before getting in, I tapped my boots together to shake loose the moist forest duff. Then, from the back seat, almost as afterthought, I informed Martin and Danny about the letter I had received from Colombia.

Colombia Asked for My Truth Demands

The 2019 letter described the formation of Colombia's new, post–civil war Truth and Recognition Chamber. Translated into English, the legal writing was stilted and formal, describing the intention of the Chamber to conduct a "search of truth and . . . attribution of criminal responsibility."[2]

Back in 1999, within a few days of the bodies being found, the central command of Las Fuerzas Armadas Revolucionarias de Colombia, or the Revolutionary Armed Forces of Colombia (FARC), took responsibility for the kidnappings and murders. The FARC was a supposedly leftist guerrilla organization, standing for land reform and funding their operations in part through extortion of large landowners. By the late 1990s, the FARC was on the move and looking for new sources of revenue. Pueblo U'wa rejected and denounced increased FARC activity in their previously relatively peaceful corner of the country. By the time the FARC kidnapped and murdered Terence, Ingrid, and Lahe' in 1999, FARC's allegiances in the region were in question. In all the years since, with Colombia's internal conflict still raging until 2016, the facts surrounding the 1999 murders had not been clarified and justice had not been achieved.

By 2016, after almost sixty years of conflict, the FARC and other extralegal and legal armed actors completed a partial disarmament and agreed to participate in a transitional justice process with the Colombian state. The process is called the Special Jurisdiction for the Peace, or by its Spanish acronym, JEP. The Truth and Recognition Chamber is the body within JEP in charge of receiving information and acknowledgments of responsibility from participating ex-combatants regarding the conflict's most serious and representative cases of specific atrocities. It is a victim-oriented process aimed at clarifying the truth, as distinct from a truth and reconciliation process aimed at reconciling two armed groups. By 2019, the Chamber was ready to consider our case.

The invitation letter came twenty years *to the day* after FARC combatants kidnapped Terence, Ingrid, and Lahe'. The timing was uncomfortable. The letter invited the families of the slain into the Chamber to participate as victims in Case 001, a cluster of cases involving thousands of victims of kidnapping.

In the original Spanish text, they sought our demandas de la verdad, our truth demands. The letter communicated that:

They wanted to know our *stories.*

They wanted to know our *questions.*

They wanted to *put the voice of the victims in the center of the process.*

They wanted to discern how *to attribute criminal responsibility.*

They wanted to give ex-combatants the chance to *officially tell the truth or not.*

They wanted us to *use our rights to truth, justice, and non-repetition.*

I sat on the couch in the tiny rental thinking, Who are they kidding? The FARC murdered our friends and destroyed our families. The Colombian government waited twenty years, and *now* they're asking for our questions?

International oil companies had built and sought to expand oil operations in U'wa ancestral territory. The U'wa recognized the oil pipeline as a magnet for armed violence.[3] Twenty years later, the ex-combatants sitting in the Truth and Recognition Chamber were some of the people attracted to that magnet. When FARC guerrillas kidnapped Terence, Ingrid, and Lahe' on February 25, 1999, questions were already being raised whether the FARC, like the Colombian government, also provided protection to the local oil operations. It was the fingers of FARC soldiers that pulled the triggers in these murders. Multiple times. Firing into their faces, their chests, and their backs. I wanted to know whose hands pulled the trigger. But I was far more interested to know who ordered them to do it.

Agitated, I got up from the couch in the musty Oakland apartment, drank the last of my tea, brushed my teeth again, and applied lip balm. I did these actions through tears. I was familiar enough with weeping to recognize it as a reverberation of trauma, an unwelcome relative who comes and goes. I sat back down and fluffed the pillow that supported my lower spine.

I picked up the letter again and recognized what it offered. They were seeking the truth and wanted to know our demands for it. I watched the rain through the garage door.

Three Bodies Had Been Found

It had also been pouring rain that winter day in New York City in 1999 when we learned that three bodies had been found. During the kidnapping, we were methodically pursuing every lead we had. We activated our network on the ground. We opened up communication with the federal investigators in Bogotá. We readied delegations to stand by. We received word that the International Red Cross in Saravena had contacted the captors. The Red Cross had even instructed family members to prepare letters to Terence, Ingrid, and Lahe' for delivery by their local team.

I was picking up the phone to call Julie, Terence's mother, about preparing the letters for the Red Cross when we received the call from Ingrid's colleagues that three bodies had been found. One body held two of Ingrid's credit cards. For a surreal half hour, the gathering sat stunned. Ingrid's adolescent son came into the room, sat down, and asked me what was happening. I had no answer. The initial report was of two male bodies and one female. In our desperation we thought: This cannot be them. It doesn't match. Then one of us talked directly with the Venezuelan police. One woman with an eagle tattoo, the other with a triangle. And one young man, twenty-five to thirty, with dark curly hair. It was them.

Part 1

I am too alone in the world,
and yet not alone enough
to make every moment holy.

—RAINER MARIA RILKE

Sequential excerpts from Rainer Maria Rilke's poem "I Am Too Alone" open the four parts of this book. Shortly after the murders, Caroline Laskow introduced me to Rilke's poem, which serves me as both mirror and compass. Poem 7 from *A Book for the Hours of Prayer*, in *Selected Poems of Rainer Maria Rilke*, trans. Robert Bly (New York: HarperCollins, 1981), 25.

1

The Escalante River

I first came to know my "place in the family of things" on the Escalante River.[1] The Escalante River carves a narrow canyon through the Colorado Plateau in southern Utah. Humans indigenous to this land have walked this canyon for centuries. In the 1930s, the US government set up shop. Valuable minerals lay underfoot, and the waterways created easy pasture. The federal stewards were keen to facilitate the exploitation of these features, helping the US Bureau of Land Management earn its nickname as the Bureau of Livestock and Mining. The exploitation took its toll on the land, peoples, and waters. In the mid-1990s, outmaneuvering a massive mining company that had designs on property on the edges of this land, communities convinced President Clinton to give the Escalante some measure of protected status. While the campaign to protect the Escalante was heating up, I walked that red rock river canyon for a week. I had taken time off from Stanford University to join other students in learning about federal land management and energy extraction across the southwestern United States.

It was my first time backpacking through a river on a trail that was no trail. The trail was in the river. Far from the risk of flash floods, every so often the group encountered a sandbar or a cave and we'd stop to make camp, grateful for sure footing. The canyon was so narrow that, looking up from my sleeping bag, the night sky appeared only as a sliver between the thousand-foot monolithic and opaque black canyon walls. The stars moved through this slit as though upon a stage, from curtain left to curtain right. One night, at some point toward dawn, I awoke and peered up again at the ribbon of night sky. I saw two eyes. Two stars that looked like eyes. They were wolf eyes, and they were looking at me. I took in her gaze, staying with it. Our eyes locked in neutral and mutual recognition. She seemed to say: I see you. You are okay. You belong as I belong. Make a place for me. I am waiting for you to see your place. I closed my eyes and drifted back to sleep.

I awoke with a start to see that the night sky had shifted slightly, but of course she was still there, as any two stars can make a pair of wolf eyes. I locked in again with her gaze and drifted back to sleep. The wolf's accompaniment has endured for years.

2

The Sulu Sea

To Learn Many Ways of Seeing

After walking the Escalante River, I came back to college with a goal of studying conservation and community development. I consolidated this learning as a member of one of the first cohorts of Public Service Scholars at Stanford. Anthropologists Bill Durham and Renato Rosaldo advised my academic work. Professor Rosaldo and Afro-Caribbean theorist Sylvia Wynter showed me how to interrupt the violence of the Western canon and orient my budding scholarship south. Social change worker Nadinne Cruz taught me how to weave it together through the process of praxis, mentoring my development as a young organizer. In the early 1990s, Nadinne directed Stanford's Haas Center for Public Service and taught the community organizing class in Urban Studies. Her teaching drew upon theory and practice interwoven with stories of her own efforts in the Philippines to redistribute resources away from the elite, as well as stories from her family. She told how her mother, a doctor, survived the killing of two loves, a fiancé and later a husband, Nadinne's own father, who was killed right in front of her.

My father had come of age in the Philippines contemporaneously with Nadinne and had emigrated to the States around the same time as she did. My father chose assimilation, which for many years took the form of settling into the liminal space between the two cultures. He rarely spoke to me about the politics of either place. While I grew up visiting Pilipina aunties and eating Pilipino food, what I knew about Pilipino class struggle I knew from Nadinne and her books.

One day during my final quarter in fall of 1996, she pulled me into her office. Rows and rows of neatly shelved books about social, political, and economic change lined the vestibule. In borrowing from her private library over the years, I had come to understand why those walls held not only history and theory but also poetry and fiction. The latter offered visions of the future through which Nadinne taught me the skill of seeing beyond the constraints of our current conditions. She had introduced me to John Berger's *Into Their Labours* trilogy, his stories evoking agrarian villagers' strategies for surviving and thriving in resistance to class stratification and modernization.[1] On that day, she handed me another of Berger's books and said, "Abby, it's time for you to go to the Philippines." She wanted me to change my social location to experience firsthand how cultural consciousness determines our ways of seeing.[2] And so, I went.

I Cut My Teeth in the Rural Philippines

To get to the Philippines, I had a fellowship from the Henry Luce Foundation. The annual fellowship aimed to seed the consciousness of twenty emerging US leaders with a lifelong integration of the peoples, cultures, and priorities of the Pacific Rim. One of my fellowship peers was placed as a legislative staffer in Hong Kong during the year of the handover. Another of my peers apprenticed to manga artists in Taipei. A third worked for a national newspaper in Seoul.

I worked under the mentorship of Pilipina leaders who were working for social change in the same ways that I hoped to contribute back in the States.

I landed in Puerto Princesa, the capital city of the southern province of Palawan. Palawan is the constellation of Pilipino islands that runs between Manila and Borneo, dividing the South China Sea from the Sulu Sea. There, attorney Grizelda Mayo-Anda co-founded and directed the Environmental Legal Assistance Center (ELAC). In that rural outpost, she trained me along with several Pilipino recent college graduates from the Jesuit Volunteer Corps, which in the Philippines is akin to a domestic Peace Corps. The young people called her "Ate Gerthie," an affectionate and respectful title for a big sister.

Ate Gerthie and my other mentors were Jesuit human rights lawyers from Manila who, after the toppling of Marcos, moved to remote islands to help implement the then-new constitutional and sustainable development frameworks. While there, these lawyers began to see the legal overlap between environmental and human rights protections. Indigenous ancestral domain claims involve both sets of legal issues. Around the same time, similar analysis was coming out of other parts of Southeast Asia and around the world. EarthRights International, an emerging nongovernmental organization (NGO), was gearing up to lead litigation on behalf of the Indigenous Karen people of Myanmar against Unocal Corporation on allegations of rape, murder, and torture in the course of forced labor during pipeline construction. And in Nigeria, the Ogoni people were organizing in opposition to Royal Dutch Shell's pollution and human rights violations on their lands and bodies. This is the context in which I cut my teeth as a young legal advocate.

Where the Tagbanua People Met Shell

Toward the end of my time in the Philippines, Royal Dutch Shell and Occidental announced plans to build a gas pipeline that would weave through the Tagbanua Indigenous community's ancestral islands and fishing areas on the northern end of the province of Palawan.[3] On the day Shell arrived in Tagbanua territory, the ELAC team was there, too. I watched from the back of the gathering as the corporate representative disembarked from the bangka, a small wooden outrigger boat that ferried him to the island. I sat perched on the lowest branch of the mango tree that formed the shade for one of our outdoor classrooms, where we trained community members on techniques for community defense. We trained them about legal remedies, but also role-played how to conduct a citizen's arrest in the face of illegal hardwood logging or illegal dynamite and cyanide fishing. Sometimes the mango tree oversaw community discussions about what ELAC lawyers called "metalegal remedies" sought through direct action. In other words, ways communities could halt environmental harm in progress when legal remedies were not working or would be too late.

The man from Shell was Pinoy from Manila. Sweat stained his pink button-down short-sleeved shirt, which was tucked in tightly to contain his midlife paunch. Tagbanua men, women, and children sat on log benches and other branches of the mango. Some squatted near the ground. They came to hear his presentation and promises about the proposed project. During the presentation, most everyone's hands remained busy with daily tasks. Children peeling cashews. Men carving wood to make frames for goggles to use while spearfishing. Women weaving banig, or grass mats.

After the man from Shell finished his presentation, he was not invited any farther into the territory. He left on his boat and our Tagbanua colleagues asked ELAC for help. I started researching strategies for dignified community response and learned about Indigenous peoples fighting against the same companies in other parts of the world. That's how I met Terence.

When not with communities on the outer islands or in the forest, ELAC staff operated out of a small house on the main island in Puerto Princesa. There, in the mid-1990s, our dial-up access to email started to expose us to what it might feel like to be connected to communities all over the world who were facing similar challenges from extractive industries. A ragtag team of activists and journalists based in Berkeley, California, who called themselves Project Underground, started distributing *Moles,* a periodic email bulletin of just such stories. The Tagbanua, we learned, were definitely not alone.

Around this time, after two years, my role in Asia was changing— ELAC needed me to shift from being a visiting American fellow into a more deeply embedded role. I knew that I did not have the needed skill or experience. Also I was homesick. I was tired of living outside, sweaty and mosquito bitten. Most of all, I was tired of living alone. I wanted to have children. I knew I needed to go back to California to find someone with whom I could make a home.

In Colombia, the U'wa People Met Occidental

My octogenarian friend Bob picked me up from the San Francisco airport. Bob had lived on the Stanford campus for decades, first as a student, when the campus shut down for a spell during World War II, then as the athletics director.

Bob had retired into a modest redwood ranch home across from the student housing co-op that I had helped manage during college. He befriended co-op students with fresh-cut flowers from his garden and double-baked chocolate espresso cookies that he would bring out around 4 p.m. twice a week. He taught us how to manage cover crops in our vegetable beds and the massive volume of our fifty-person household's compost.

I became part of a decades-long lineage of fellow co-op students who took refuge in Bob's house. His kitchen table was reliably littered with newspaper clippings to discuss and photocopied cartoons and jokes to exploit. When I had left for the Philippines, I stashed my college belongings in the closet of one of Bob's spare bedrooms. And from his kitchen table upon my return, I looked up my route to Berkeley and Project Underground.

This was before cell phones, so I just showed up. Danny Kennedy, the director, opened the door. I explained to Danny my research mission and he walked me through a maze of desks to a small interior conference room. There I met Terence, who was using the conference room as his desk.

At that time, Terence intermittently operated under the auspices of Project Underground to support his work with the Indigenous Pueblo U'wa in Colombia. I learned that day that the U'wa were resisting the advances of the very same oil companies as the Tagbanua. U'wa leaders were the first people I ever heard call for humanity to simply keep the oil in the ground.[4] For them, it isn't about a "sustainable development" framework or "natural resource" management; it is about reestablishing the equilibrium between the world above and the world below the surface of the earth. To the U'wa, the world was created in layers of earth, water, oil, mountains, and sky. Below the surface of the earth where humans live our physical lives is a parallel world that sustains our spiritual lives. The two worlds balance and sustain each other. The equilibrium enables communication and direct connection between the material and the spiritual. The U'wa see oil as the blood of the earth and the earth as our mother.[5] They regard the cloud forests of eastern Colombia as Kajka Ika, the heart of the world.

In his role as a liaison between U'wa leadership and multiple NGOs based in the United States, Europe, and Australia, Terence was learning how to communicate the importance of making this shift to ways of seeing that centered the work of reestablishing equilibrium. I told him that I carried questions from the Tagbanua leaders. I asked him about how these companies were interacting with rural and Indigenous peoples in other parts of the world.

Terence told me that in 1983 Occidental was the first multinational company to develop a significant export-oriented oil field in Colombia—the giant Caño Limón oilfield in the Arauca province. The Colombian state oil company Ecopetrol partnered with Occidental to get that oil to the port on the Caribbean coast through the Caño Limón pipeline that flowed just north and east of Pueblo U'wa's state-recognized resguardo, or reservation.[6] He told me that the government did not recognize all the U'wa's ancestral territory as belonging to the U'wa. Rather, the state-recognized U'wa reservation is much smaller than their ancestral territory. Over time, as the U'wa asserted rights over all their ancestral territory and reclaimed land through various political and social processes, boundaries in flux were often vulnerable to shifting advantageously to exclude lands that the state sought to use for oil, mining, and gas extraction. International and Colombian law require consultation with and consent from Indigenous peoples before an entity commences an extraction project within their territories.[7] So the state chose to draw boundaries for the state-recognized reservation that excluded prospective extraction sites, making it easier for the government to skip tribal consultation and consent.

Amid Colombia's decades long internal armed conflict, non Indigenous campesinos, or farmers, and extralegal armed actors (both right-wing paramilitary and left-wing guerrillas) alike have regarded the U'wa people as the region's unarmed brokers and keepers of the peace. The U'wa are thus known as "the thinking people," or "the people that speak well."[8] While war ravaged other parts of Colombia, including areas close to them, the northeastern corner in which the U'wa lived had, to date, remained relatively peaceful.

But the Caño Limón oil pipeline cutting through the region attracted armed violence. Local guerrilla groups were claiming responsibility for an increasing number of pipeline bombings—hundreds of bombings that over the 1990s had spilled over 1.5 million barrels of crude oil into the wetlands and watersheds through which the pipeline cut.[9] By bombing the pipeline, guerrillas extorted oil companies to raise funds to support the armed insurrection—by making the oil companies pay a fee to prevent future bombings.[10] In other instances, by the time I had met Terence, locals in the region were beginning to question whether the guerrillas might have started to provide armed protection to the movements of the oil companies, just as the Colombian government and some of the paramilitaries did. Over the years, U'wa leadership has consistently, firmly, and publicly condemned any such tactics.[11]

In 1992 the Colombian government granted a new oil consortium led by Occidental and Royal Dutch Shell exploration rights to a large swath of territory that the oil industry called the Samoré block. The Samoré block covered U'wa ancestral territory in the departments of Arauca, Boyacá, and Norte de Santander. U'wa leadership objected to the idea that the government had given the consortium "rights" over oil extraction in the Samoré block. They tried every avenue available to them within Colombia to communicate this objection with the Colombian minister of environment and company representatives, to no avail. After a series of sham community consultations, on February 21, 1995, the Colombian government issued Occidental an exploration permit within U'wa territory.[12]

In response, U'wa leadership reached out to Colombian national Indigenous rights organizations and international environmental campaign NGOs to inform the world that, as an Indigenous pueblo, they were ready to commit mass suicide before they would ever consent to the newly proposed drilling. Berito Kuwar'U'wa (Roberto Cobaría), Terence's friend and then-president of the Association of U'wa Traditional Authorities and Cabildos U'wa (AsoU'wa), stated, "We would rather die, protecting everything that we hold sacred, than lose everything that makes us U'wa."[13]

Terence and others knew this was not an empty threat. It is told that when Spanish conquistadors first arrived, the U'wa retreated deep into the mountains to avoid enslavement, eventually pushed to the edge of the livable forest. Ultimately, this strategy proved untenable. The U'wa were being starved out. Many U'wa families chose instead to die with dignity by jumping off a 1,400-foot cliff together, family by family, unwilling to succumb.[14] The cliff, now called the peñol de la gloria, or the crag of glory, is near the municipality of Güicán de la Sierra, in the department of Boyacá. It is told that so many bodies piled up at the bottom of the cliff that they altered the course of the river there.[15]

Five hundred years later, the U'wa now faced a renewed threat—that of oil extraction. Once again, they were ready to assert their right to self-determination. The U'wa had the moral authority, growing popular support, and strong legal arguments. Their firm objection to oil extraction led to an impasse in Colombia. By early 1998, Shell Oil—just coming off a Nigerian human rights debacle with poet Ken Saro-Wiwa being hanged for demanding compensation for environmental destruction of Ogoni lands—was especially nervous about another public relations nightmare. The oil consortium faltered.

In the weeks before I met with Terence at Project Underground, news broke that Occidental was seeking to renegotiate their contract.[16] It appeared that Oxy had given up their drilling "rights" to most of the Samoré block to focus on one remaining key site of proposed exploration called Gibraltar in the department of Santander. The oil company heralded this development as a generous solution to the impasse, claiming that Gibraltar was outside the disputed area and therefore not subject to U'wa consultation and consent. The U'wa disagreed. What the oil company called Gibraltar, the U'wa called Shobar-kajka, a sacred site within their ancestral territory.

In this context Terence worked as a go-between, attempting to meet the U'wa leadership's core near-term demand, which was to speak directly with the Colombian government and US corporate leadership.

Terence Met the U'wa

Back in Berkeley, I asked Terence how his role started. In 1995, after graduating in environmental studies from the University of California, Santa Cruz, Terence returned to his hometown of Los Angeles to pick up environmental defense work with a communications outfit and to continue training under Great Grandmaster Ho Jin Song, from whom he had earned a second-degree black belt in hapkido. At the hapkido studio, he befriended a University of Southern California doctoral student in international relations named Leslie Wirpsa.

Leslie had spent over a decade as an independent investigative journalist, first in Bogotá and later as West Coast bureau chief for the
National Catholic Reporter. Shortly after Terence met her, she began
her dissertation on the U'wa struggle.[17] She provided Terence with a
political education.

Terence and Leslie shared the same birthday, twelve years apart,
both in the year of the tiger in the Chinese zodiac. They also shared
key childhood experiences and moved in the world in similar ways,
their instinct to defend honed with discipline through the martial
art they shared. They saw themselves in each other and got close.
Their romance was short-lived. Nonetheless, they worked together
in support of the U'wa people.

In May 1997 a group of international NGOs brought Berito to
Los Angeles to meet with Occidental executives and engage in a
series of interviews and direct actions in front of Oxy headquarters.
Berito, an oracle and interlocutor for the U'wa people, had by that
time decades of experience representing the U'wa externally before
Colombian governmental agencies.[18] By 1997 he was the pueblo's
international liaison, making his first international visit to give voice
to the U'wa people's rejection of Oxy's oil drilling project. During
the meeting with Oxy, Berito sang a song that U'wa parents use to
teach children about respect. He challenged the oil executives over
their claim to the oil running underneath U'wa territory and underscored the need to keep the oil in the ground to maintain the balance
of life on earth.[19] Terence was an official observer during the meeting
with Oxy, a role that began his accompaniment of Berito.

Terence and I Got a Glimpse

As Terence spoke, I scribbled his words in my spiral notebook. I
noticed he was also scribbling; doodling on the edge of his page.
I noticed that we wore the same Swiss Army watch that was popular
at the time. I noticed his hands, the tensile strength that seemed to
run up his forearm, disappear under his rolled-up shirtsleeve, and

reappear again in the curve of his neck. I noticed the long, tanned nape of his neck just below a head of dark curls not unlike my own. I was hearing him talk, but I was also listening to his body language. He stopped doodling. His hands rested and he held my gaze as he described Berito and the quiet clarity of purpose with which Berito moved, even during his first visit to Los Angeles, a discombobulating metropolis worlds away from the steady mountains and rivers of his home.

Terence told me the twists and turns that his U'wa accompaniment had taken since he first met Berito, and some about his experiences meeting more U'wa people from different communities during periodic trips to Colombia. He told me about a report he was co-writing based on research during these trips that would be called *Blood of Our Mother*. To protect Terence, Project Underground would publish the report later that summer without disclosing Terence's authorship. He started to tell me about the scarlet ibis, his favorite bird, and the ancient trees deep in the uplands of the territory. But then he stopped.

In the middle of his story, Terence asked me out on a date. That night. I laughed and pulled my notebook closer to me, sitting up. He wanted to go to a musical performance by John Seed, an Australian environmental activist who, together with Buddhist scholar Joanna Macy, had popularized some Western practices of what was then called deep ecology. Joanna was the first teacher I heard say to go ahead and let your heart break for the earth, that touching into the pain was vital to inform action that could make a difference.[20] I hadn't seen her or John since I was in high school. So I said yes.

Terence Unity Freitas. I didn't know who this person was. But I was curious. My yes conveyed that curiosity, and both of our bodies acknowledged a shift in the energy of the room. My shoulders let down. He seemed to widen his peripheral vision.

There was a sense that there would be time. That we could continue the stories. That this meeting wasn't a one-off. That the notebook could wait. Because something had begun.

Making our way back through the front office desks, he introduced me to the rest of the Project Underground crew, whose smiles betrayed that they, too, had been listening. I pretended like I had somewhere to go. I can't recount what occupied those interim hours or where we met up later that evening. I do recall Terence rolling up in a blue hard-shell jeep, stepping out to open the door for me with a gentlemanly air that finessed the fact that the door was broken.

On the short ride over to the makeshift musical venue, I let my finger trace a line over his wrist as he shifted gears. He registered the touch with the sharp exhale of restraint. During the performance, we sat in folding chairs in the back row, not touching. A silent army of senses sat like a third body between us, busily conversing, mapping out the histories, the points of pleasure and pain, taking note of what was on offer.

Later that evening, he took me to his studio apartment in Oakland. The building was nestled in an anomalous thicket of underbrush and redwoods next to Glen Echo Creek behind the car dealerships of Auto Row. Inside the room, along one wall, bookshelves held a sparse collection of ceramic bowls he had thrown and glazed. Along the other, a reading lamp sat next to his single bed. I stood in the doorway, waiting for it to become clear where I should sit. From the kitchen area, Terence was already chopping away, setting up the vegetables and salmon to steam over rice. He gestured to the floor. Perched upon meditation cushions, we ate dinner and talked late into the night. Without much fanfare, we acknowledged that I had missed the last train back to Stanford.

We Moved around the Men with Guns

Pushing a button on his answering machine, Terence played me a saved message. It was one word in Spanish, "veintidos," which means "twenty-two." He wondered whether the message was a hasty threat, referring to a .22 long rifle. He was still adjusting to the risks of his new work in rural Colombia. He was jumpy.

Listening to Terence talk about the different ways that his U'wa colleagues navigated daily security threats, I tried to calibrate what he was saying against my own limited experience in the Philippines. The attorneys who mentored me routinely navigated death threats for their policy advocacy on behalf of small fishers and farmers, a trend that had only worsened over time. But in the two years I lived in Palawan, I could point to only one instance in which a gun was on display. And our ragtag group of environmental defenders was the one passively harnessing the power behind it.

A forest-dwelling community south of Puerto Princesa had come to ELAC for legal assistance after a wealthy city dweller from Manila had bought up the mangrove forest along their town's coastline to build a commercial fishpond. Mangroves are comprised of trees in the intertidal zone, and their elongated web of above-ground roots provides natural filtration and an essential barrier to shoreline erosion on islands like Palawan. The intertidal flow through the roots provides nutrient-rich breeding grounds for fish and other marine life. To put a fishpond on a mangrove forest is not sustainable for the forest or the marine life that it shelters; fishponds and mangroves are not compatible.

Soon enough, the new landowner had fenced off the area, blocking the community's access to their fishing grounds. He then built six-foot-high mud barriers around the mangrove forest to keep the water in. He planned to drown the trees to clear the area for his fishponds. Ate Gerthie and team used every legal and political strategy available under provincial, national, and intergovernmental environmental law to stop the fishpond development. But those laborious and time-intensive methods were failing because of weak governance. In the meantime, the trees were, indeed, drowning.

During this time, the Philippines was still in post-dictatorship transition. The new Pilipino constitution devolved much power to local governments to regulate the use of land, water, and the coast under the broad umbrella of the Philippines' participation in the United Nations' new articulation of sustainable development goals.

Human rights lawyers like Ate Gerthie, who had come of age fighting against the Marcos dictatorship in Manila, pivoted to continuing the work at the local level. She and her peers played key roles in teaching and advising provincial and local governments across the southern Philippines how to codify and enforce the new environmental protection framework. She also built ELAC on the principle that, in rural and Indigenous communities, "developmental legal assistance," or direct legal aid combined with legal and political education, can be a critical engine of social change. She firmly anchored her primary allegiance with community-articulated priorities and at the same time made herself indispensable to governmental environmental agencies, including the enforcement agencies.

Because legal and political remedies at the mangrove forest were failing, one Saturday morning, Ate Gerthie gave the ELAC team a crash course on metalegal remedies. At dawn, we headed out in two large vans to the mangrove forest. On the way, we stopped at the local university. There our vans filled with ELAC's environmental science student volunteers and their friends. At that point, a military jeep also joined our caravan. Ate Gerthie hopped out of the van. She knew these particular young soldiers—she had taught them environmental law enforcement. After some kwento, or talking story, she had convinced them that they should join us at the mangrove forest to protect our metalegal actions there.

We arrived with bolt cutters in hand, donned our hiking boots, wrapped cloths around our heads to keep the bugs out of our ears, and picked up our shovels. We walked along the packed earth berm that the new landowner had erected to fence in the waterlogged mangroves. At each key intersection in the patchwork of proto fishponds, a team of us started to dig. For hours that day, the men with guns stood at attention to prevent the new landowner, or his collaborators from the local government, from entering and disrupting our work. At certain points in the day, the soldiers, too, picked up shovels to help. When the guns moved, I moved like a magnet repelled in the opposite direction, finding work in another part of the berm.

By afternoon merienda, a time for snack and rest, we had enabled the water to flow out and the tide to return. While the metalegal, legal, and political actions to stop the fishponds continued for months to come, that Saturday was my only direct experience of men with guns in the Philippines.[21]

To the Home That Was Waiting

Sitting there on the floor of Terence's studio, I had noticed that looking over my shoulder, which had become habit abroad, was not needed anymore now that I was back in California. *I* wasn't being noticed anymore—my halfway light, halfway dark complexion was unremarkable in the Bay Area. I did not want to be thinking about the side eye, death threats, and men with guns. In coming back to the States, I sought a reprieve. I wanted, perhaps, to sit on a couch somewhere and watch the new season of *Friends.* Terence, in contrast, was at full tilt in his accompaniment of Pueblo U'wa in Colombia.

I knew how to have that conversation; we were of the same ilk. But I was tired. I moved myself up onto his bed, my hand making a pillow for my cheek, and let myself reluctantly listen.

He tucked me in and laid his own body on a bedroll on the floor next to me. He turned off the reading lamp and fell silent as I fell asleep. A few minutes or hours later, he asked if I was awake. He asked if he could join me on the bed. I rolled onto my back. I said no. He made his case. I said yes. Catlike, he nimbly arched over off the floor and up onto the far side of the bed, settling in with the length of his back stretched along the wall and head propped up on one arm. His head was slightly above my head. He was trying to keep distance between our resting bodies. Our purportedly resting bodies.

The space between us once again filled with energetic aliveness. The index finger of his free hand lightly traced my silhouette from my hip bone down to my ankle, along the outer edge of my foot, firmly dipping once into the space between toes. As he made his way back up my other leg, my back arched slightly. He hovered his flat hand above my pelvis, not touching, as though focusing and transmitting the heat that was building between us. I drew his hand up to my chest bone, using both of my own hands to direct it to rest there between my breasts. We breathed. He tilted away from the wall slightly, making contact finally along the full length of our bodies. I felt the firm source of the heat between his legs and drew myself to it, curling my back body into the curve of him around me. Our hands stayed at the heart center, communicating everything that needed to be said. We moved gently, slightly, and slept.

The next morning, we were in the logistics of getting out the door to await our ride when I stopped us at the threshold. The dawn streamed in through the studio door in rich morning yellows. Terence and I stood facing out, him behind and towering over me. I turned back around to face him. That's when my finger traced his temple and the outline of his jaw, down his neck, moving along the architecture of his shoulder. I raised my chin toward him. He read the yes and kissed me. I moved the backpack off his shoulder, and it slid to the floor. I wanted his hands to be free. I slipped his right hand onto my belly. He looked at me, searching my eyes. I guided his fingers down. I wanted him to feel what I was feeling. I wanted him to feel the silky warm home that was waiting for him. He did. We breathed together. Terence's friend's car rolled up; we gathered our things and were off.

3

The East River

We Moved to Brooklyn

In the weeks after meeting Terence in the summer of 1998, I moved to Brooklyn to begin a social change network. My friend Jacinda and I were developing a global cohort of women working for change. While in the Philippines, I had shared our idea for Women Working for Change with Fran Peavey. Fran was a social change mentor from San Francisco whose teachings weave into several stories that follow. Fran introduced me to Polly Howells in New York. Polly is a feminist political strategist, writer, and therapist. She was Fran's lifelong friend, champion, co-conspirator, and funder, who then became mine. Polly emailed right back to say, "I want to help you realize your dreams." With that, she created a yearlong, funded internship for me in memory of Lela Breitbart, a young women's rights advocate who should have been a peer but instead had recently been killed in a hiking accident.

Polly arranged for my internship to be housed in Manhattan at her friend and former Congresswoman Bella Abzug's organization, the Women's Environment and Development Organization (WEDO). She helped me make the rounds at feminist and international NGOs in the city. Best of all, she arranged for me to sublet her friend's studio apartment near Grand Army Plaza in Park Slope, Brooklyn.

After wrestling with the sticky lock of the second-floor walkup, I opened the door that led immediately into the kitchen area and put my bags down. I walked the few steps from the door to the bank of windows. I tried to open them, but they were stuck. I tried the window in the bedroom nook, and it reluctantly rose. Immediately, I understood why the windows didn't budge. Cars below labored to make their way up the Union Street hill to Grand Army Plaza, and the studio was coated with exhaust. My mother and I spent the weekend attempting to lift the accumulated soot and grime. When we finished, we opened the windows for a spell to let in the evening's cooler breeze, and the studio felt like mine.

Soon thereafter, Terence joined me. His work with the U'wa was shifting. Instead of being housed at Project Underground, in Berkeley, he was negotiating a partnership with the Rainforest Foundation in New York, a rights-based forest protection organization founded by Sting and Trudie Styler. He arrived with an explosion of detritus built up during months of travel. Piles of receipts, spiral-bound journals scribbled with notes, and tangles of cords from various photographic and video recording devices littered the coffee table and spilled over onto the futon. Before and after my own work at WEDO, I spent the next several weeks helping him sort it out.

In September 1998 Terence accompanied Berito to a ceremonial gathering with traditional elders from across the world hosted by the Mirning Aboriginal whale-dreaming people of the Nullarbor in South Australia. After the ceremony, Mirning elders called in the whales to enter a state of communion with the humans. Terence described the presence of the whale with awe. Berito was in awe. Berito also came away from the gathering having fostered relationships with a newly global set of Indigenous peers.

Berito and Terence continued this trajectory in the United States. In October 1998 they were invited to the State of the World Forum in San Francisco, an annual gathering initiated a few years prior by Mikhail Gorbachev for the purpose of bringing together political and spiritual leaders focused on solutions to critical global challenges. Ingrid Washinawatok El-Issa organized sessions at the Forum.[1] There, Berito and Terence met Ingrid and Lahe'ena'e Gay for the first time. In their exchanges, it became clear there was work to do together.

Following the Forum, the U'wa leaders continued their conversation with Ingrid, Lahe', and Terence, braiding their hopes and dreams together. They articulated a plan for accompaniment in wholly new and powerful ways. I think of this type of accompaniment as the practice of putting into action one's critical political analysis together with one's understanding of interdependence, the protocol of deference, and love. It is compassion in action. It is rooted in a sensibility of mutual liberation. They would begin with a visit to U'wa territory in northeastern Colombia in February 1999.

We Learned Early Lessons in Movement Strategy

From the beginning, Berito and Terence, with the permission of AsoU'wa, the association of U'wa governing entities, conceived of the U'wa Defense Project through which they envisioned collaborating for years to come. As the U'wa Defense Project was still taking shape, Terence located himself inside a solidarity NGO—sometimes Project Underground, sometimes another organization. Institutional form was not the most pressing matter. What mattered then was to continue to mobilize the transnational advocacy network that had rallied to meet the call of U'wa leadership for international support. From his base in the nascent U'wa Defense Project, Terence co-convened this network as an U'wa defense working group comprised of eight or so additional NGOs from the US-based mainstream environmental movement and, at times, human rights organizations from Colombia and Europe. Embracing principles of nonviolent social change, the purpose of the working group was to coordinate international NGO response to Pueblo U'wa's call to action. Their call to action was for self-determination, reclamation of their traditional territory, and protection of their culture without fear of violence or repression.[2] These objectives were long-standing; Occidental's advances were only the most recent threat to their realization. In Terence's notebook from March 1998, he reflected, "The U'wa don't have a plan to fight Oxy. They just are. They are not dedicating resources to this, they are just trying to live. Fighting Oxy is part of trying to live."[3] He was starting to articulate a nuance in the relationship between protest and the underlying work of protection and defense.

At the direction of U'wa leadership, the working group ran a pressure campaign against Occidental. In the late 1990s this campaign became especially heated when Occidental prepared to expand operations onto the sacred site that, it claimed, *just so happened* to sit a few hundred meters outside the freshly contested boundary of the U'wa reserve.

To focus on the anti-oil campaign made sense. And the more time Terence spent visiting communities inside the U'wa territory, the clearer his analysis became that the anti-oil campaign alone was only part of a broader strategy. Foraging in the backcountry with his U'wa companions, or squatting next to the fire whittling a bow, he listened. Terence began to hear more and different U'wa leaders putting forth a vision for what they were calling, as translated in English, "people-centered development," an approach we today call community-driven planning for community ownership solutions.[4]

With the community asking him to shift gears into a longer-term agenda of community-driven planning rooted in self-determination, Terence sought from the working group a shift in stance from reaction to proactivity. He advocated for his colleagues to locate the oil campaign within this larger and more holistic approach.[5] Without this shift, the campaign risked being out of step with the U'wa. With this shift, the international solidarity had a chance to contribute more meaningfully to the deep and lasting fundamental changes for which the U'wa leadership called.

Strategic transitions like this take time. But developments on the ground were moving fast. I watched Terence try to hold the tension. By the winter of 1999, from Terence's perspective, the esprit de corps in the working group was weak. Seasoned colleagues in the group were trying their best to read the situation on the ground from afar. Terence, as the liaison, hadn't succeeded yet in persuading them to shift to a more holistic community-driven approach. And people were invested at different levels. Some working group members were salaried employees of moderate-sized NGOs for whom the U'wa anti-oil campaign was one of many. Others were unpaid volunteers with documentary film, journalism, or direct action collectives. Others were academics or lawyers. And then there was Terence, raising just enough money to get from project to project, prioritizing funds that could go directly to the U'wa, and living frugally to get by, as so many young people new to this work happily do.

These network characteristics are not atypical. But in the case of the working group, these dynamics led to Terence overseeing too many pieces. Because people were invested at different levels and with different organizational priorities, it was critical to institute systems of accountability and protocol. But Terence didn't have the bandwidth or skills under his belt to call for, create, and enforce robust systems of accountability or protocol within the network. The resultant lack of cohesion deteriorated trust. I watched Terence navigate the instability in areas ranging from campaign strategy and communications to budgeting and fundraising.

By winter, his view of what was needed to walk alongside the U'wa was evolving. He was no longer looking to the working group as his main source of collaboration. What had felt like a singular mission was no longer, and there was no form to the container to guide what would happen next.

To Change the Ways We Ourselves Walk

What I could see but not articulate then was that, at the turn of the twenty-first century, we were going too fast to create and maintain a strong container for the work. Terence was moving too fast. The U'wa faced an existential threat to their lives, lands, and waters. They called on us for help because the threat was coming from our culture. People like Terence and the working group members responded to the call with everything they had, working responsively and swiftly. Yet, at least for Terence, the work rarely reflected the value of balance that undergirded the vision of the world that the campaign aimed to defend. We lacked systems for balance.

In contrast, when the U'wa sent their representatives to engage with the riowá, or "the people from far away," the U'wa representatives stayed tethered to their home communities' cultural norms and systems, protocols that were rooted in the practices of balance.[6] This approach to engagement was essential: most of the U'wa history of contact with outsiders reflected the devastating effects of colonization, a legacy that led U'wa people to describe riowá as "the people who don't think well."[7] Whether interacting with Colombian state representatives, oil company executives, or solidarity NGO companions, the U'wa Werjayá, or wise ancients, insisted that the U'wa delegation follow community protocol to guard against being caught up in the temptation of moving in the fast ways of the riowá. The protocols protected the U'wa people's ability to work from their cultural roots in the slow ways of interdependence and non-harming. Their protocols were paramount and overriding. They were the container, without which there would be no principled way of engaging with the riowá.

Even today, for one of our younger U'wa colleagues to travel outside U'wa territory, it takes the approval not only of the elected officials in AsoU'wa but also of the Werjayá. For this colleague, her Werjayá live a two-day walk into the mountains, which she undertakes to consult them. Then, when she returns to U'wa territory after travel to the riowá world, she is required to undertake a ten-day ayuno, or spiritual cleanse, which entails no contact with any members of her family or community for the first four days, fasting, and walking the mountains to various touchstone sites of prayer. The actions are meant to reconnect her to place and home. It's how her elders ensure that she can traverse the two worlds and do this vital bridge work without getting hooked on the lures of the "inherited story of separation and supremacy" that she encounters when in the US.[8] When working with U'wa colleagues, we build their ayuno practices into our workplans to ensure that no critical actions requiring consultation are planned for those transition times.

Back in 1999, though, many of us were still learning how to move in relation to the slow work.[9] The cultural norms and protocols that informed mainstream international environmental campaigns and how we moved in relation to frontline rural communities did not match the depth called for by the U'wa. We said yes without comprehending that the U'wa communities asked more of us than reactivity. Yes, there was an urgent threat. But there was more. They were asking us to join them in maintaining the balance between the world above and the world below. We heard that call and lifted it up. Our own communiques started to tap into this rich language and context. But we did not yet comprehend that to walk alongside Pueblo U'wa as they requested could mean changing the ways we ourselves walked.

Terence foresaw all of this and sought more than a shift from the anti-oil campaign to a community-driven development agenda; he sought more than a shift in our ways of seeing. He sought a shift in our ways of being. The shift would entail comprehending and embodying what some call the still point. The still point is both the essential state of being and the container that enables us to sustain the dance of life. As T. S. Eliot described: "Except for the point, the still point / There would be no dance, and there is only the dance."[10] If we are to transform society in a manner that restores the equilibrium, we need to figure out how to sustain the still point.

Terence understood the still point. His study of hapkido watered the seed of this understanding. In Korean, *hap* means "join" or "coordination," *ki* means "energy" or "power," and *do* means "definition of an art, method, or 'of the way.'" Through hapkido, Terence learned "the way of coordinated energy." His familiarity with the way of coordinated energy provided a basis for mutual understanding, recognition, and more often than not, mirth, with U'wa spiritual leaders. In October 1998 they invited Terence into a house during a ceremony to take the cocara leaf off an adolescent Bocota U'wa girl, signifying that she was ready to be married. In a letter home, he wrote:

> When I arrived, the house was full of people and the same amount of people were sitting outside, listening. Three different groups were singing inside. Different songs at different tempo. Sometimes one would end and begin the song that the other was finishing (songs that last hours). Every once in a while, there would be silence, when the medicine people had all stopped their songs. Silence of voices, but not of sound. The reverberation of hours and hours of singing stays in the house, in the wood, in the earthen floor. Then the singing starts again. That is the reason we are doing this work: so that people can listen to singing.[11]

Defending the space for people to listen to singing defends people's access to remembering who they are.

The still point needs to be the organizing principle behind our actions. Terence knew, as I knew from working with the fishing and farming communities in the Philippines, that we do this work not just in defense of a rural community's dignity in the face of big oil, but in defense of ways of being that are vital blueprints for the future. Terence, Ingrid, and Lahe' shared an understanding of the still point approach.

They Went to Plan a School

In February 1999, Terence, Ingrid, and Lahe' went to Colombia under the auspices of the Pacific Cultural Conservancy International to visit with U'wa women and elders. They wanted to learn the conditions and needs of the U'wa people and how they could support U'wa plans for a more fully decolonized and self-determined system of education. Their mission focused on health, education, and territory. Berito and AsoU'wa arranged the visit, and the whole community played the role of accompaniment.[12]

First they stayed in the home of Berito, and later the homes of Daris and Ebaristo. Ebaristo was the first U'wa person trained as a lawyer, and Daris worked in U'wa education. Daris was raising four U'wa daughters including Aura, who was nine years old at the time of the visit. Daris didn't hold political office then—no U'wa women did as a matter of custom—but she presided over community affairs in other ways.

Daris introduced Terence, Ingrid, and Lahe' to elders, teachers, mothers, and spiritual leaders. She pointed their way into the hills and then into the mountains. She took them to drill sites and sacred sites. She accompanied their steps and framed their thinking. She lit the kindling, boiled the water, stirred the pot, and called the people together, keeping the door open as voices throughout those hills added their own thinking to the ideas just beginning to simmer for the new school.

At that time, state resources and social services in the territory were limited or nonexistent. Most of the remaining schools were funded by the Catholic Church, schools that still operated in the shadow of the legacy of the church's brutal "civilization" tactics. By this point, the church schools only provided instruction up to fifth grade. Those who wanted to continue their education had to leave the community. The oil company took advantage of this structural barrier to education and, starting in 1988, offered money to young people to study outside the community.[13] At the time of the oil company's offer, U'wa families were unaware of the company's expanded interests in the territory and, through a community assembly process, agreed to accept this offer for eight to ten selected U'wa young people each year. When Pueblo U'wa began to stand firm against oil extraction in their ancestral territory, they also began to reject this arrangement because it had come to feel like an attempt to pur-chase their dignity, which the U'wa refused to sell.

There has always been a system of U'wa education, of language, culture, cosmovision, and traditional ways. When colonialism, old and new, ravaged it, the U'wa harnessed the riowá education they were being forced to endure so that they could translate and advo-cate for U'wa needs and demands to the colonizers, the church, and state.[14] Certain U'wa leaders who were educated in both the riowá schools and U'wa traditional ways became seen as what my mentor Nadinne Cruz would call "knowledge brokers" between the worlds. These knowledge brokers were valued. But there had to be a way for the U'wa to foster these skills on their own terms. They were eager to reject the national and missionary educational systems in favor of building something new.[15] Ingrid and Lahe' understood this aspi-ration. Both had worked with Indigenous peoples across the globe to recover self-determination and decolonized systems of education that center Indigenous knowledge, ways of knowing, and ways of being practices.

When we say that "another world is possible," to me this is what we mean.[16] Educational programs like the one the U'wa Traditional Authorities, Ingrid, Lahe', and Terence were planning give us a taste of a world in which our labor reestablishes equilibrium. Among many transformative social movements today, this equilibrium work is sometimes characterized as transitioning the world from the "old" systems and cultures of domination, violence, and extraction to "new" systems and cultures of interdependence, resilience, and regeneration.

As in so many similarly situated communities around the world, U'wa leadership worked to build the new, which to them was really a return to the best of very old ways. The old, old ways before the men with guns; before the systems and cultures of domination, vio-lence, and extraction. The February 1999 visit focused on building this new. Even so, it took place in the epicenter and at the height of a battle against the old. A pitched battle in which the U'wa were the only side without guns.

We Called It an Inkling of a Chance

One Saturday morning in January 1999, in the Brooklyn studio shortly before he left for Colombia, Terence and I stood facing each other. We had just finished the hand dance. The hand dance was a simple game Terence and I would play, standing like a mirror in front of one another, hands together, palms and fingers flat against their counterparts on the other, barely touching. In the hand dance, one person gently leads with the suggestion of movement by one hand, which the other person's hand mirrors. In this way, one hand directs the movement of both bodies. Then a different hand takes the lead, sometimes reversing the flow, sometimes continuing the momentum. Eventually it becomes so that no one is leading, and no one is following. It is a game about sharing power. We played it often.

Terence picked up mid-sentence our ongoing conversation about whether I wanted this life together with him, to be pulled into the fray of his singular focus. I sat down. I had come back from the Philippines because I had wanted a break. Terence wasn't offering a break. He was in it. I pictured him riding a horse, already mid-stride. He wasn't asking whether I wanted to get on the back and ride with him. He was asking whether I wanted to get on my own horse and ride together.

In our brief time, Terence had demonstrated significant dedication to honing an inner compass through daily practice. From my training in yoga and meditation, I understood. But sometimes I wanted to relax instead. Sometimes I thought about having children and going to graduate school. Was having children compatible with having a partner who travels in a war zone working with a rural community that is fighting a US oil company? When I was centered in my own still point, the answer was yes, absolutely. When I was off-kilter or caught up in wistful thinking about what a "normal" adult life might entail, the answer was less clear. We both knew that I could hack it—that I had the qualities needed to stay in the fray. The open question between us was whether I *wanted* to stay in the fray. I hesitated. Thinking about it made me tired and scared. We prefaced any tentative statement that cast forward toward a future with a prayer for the "inkling of a chance" that it could work out. This conversation remains forever mid-sentence.

They Prepared to Enter a Country in War

That January, Terence and I tried to find a bigger Brooklyn apartment. Coming home from work in Manhattan, I would hop off the N/R train a few stations before or after our stop to go look at listings. We were dismal candidates given our nonexistent salary and rental histories. Sometimes he would meet me at the listings, and we would put on our best face. But most times, I would trudge back to the Grand Army Plaza studio alone to find him cooking dinner for us while still fully immersed in conference call after conference call to prepare for the upcoming trip.

One night as I sat on the futon balancing a steaming bowl of ramen on my knees, I listened to him talk on the phone with Ingrid and Lahe'. I had never met them; I had only been able to enjoy their boisterous laughter and auntie-like teasing about our newfound love when Terence would put the landline on speaker. On this night, the three of them were talking about security during the trip. They were preparing to enter a country in war, a conflict in which hundreds of thousands of people had been killed. And they were planning to travel to a rural community to learn from, work with, and support the U'wa, who were standing in the way of one of most powerful corporations in the world. Afterward, I asked Terence to describe their security plan.

The prior month, in the week before Christmas, Terence had been in the backcountry of U'wa territory. When he got back to the nearby municipality, and an internet shop with dial-up, he emailed me. In the email, he wrote his way through a dilemma he was facing about whether to accept an invitation from one of the more distant U'wa communities to visit their village, an invitation he was moved to receive. To travel there would, at that point, mean taking the public bus through rural territory, as availability on the one commercial flight back out had just filled minutes before. About his decision to take the bus, he wrote:

> Idiot, you say? True, I feel pretty certain of it, but all of this work is. Every day I spend in Cubará, every time I go to Arauca, every day I walk the borders of the territory. So taking the bus just fits into the rationalization I need to make to do all of this. I don't want to send this [email] because I don't want you to be worried. I am going to send it to be honest with myself and with you. Food for further discussion. The reality is that it is easy to rationalize times to be safe and the more you do it, the farther you get from Colombia, the more you stay in Bogotá, if that. . . . Maybe this is a message to be sent later, when we can talk about it, since it is not just about taking a bus trip. It is part of a larger conversation. So I guess I am sending it as part of that   If this letter fuels the fire to your arguments when I return, then good, more reason for me to listen. Believe me, I want to listen. Your cynical caveat might be that I can't if I am dead.[17]

Risk assessment and security were foremost on Terence's mind. So was honoring Pueblo U'wa's invitation to deepen the work. This balance was the conversation we were in.

If he needed help when traveling in rural areas, Terence did not think he could turn to the Colombian officials who interacted with the U'wa. On a prior visit, a state official had come by helicopter for a meeting, and although the U'wa leaders had asked him to provide Terence with a ride back to Bogotá to increase Terence's personal safety (and to enable Terence to continue pressing the advocacy point that the U'wa leaders were making), the state official had initially refused, then took him only partway back. Another time the local police had told him they would not be able to protect him outside the municipal area. I knew that he had felt unsafe on a recent trip, so much so that he got up in the middle of the night and moved locations. I knew that, in that part of Colombia, the oil pipe-line attracted armed violence, despite Pueblo U'wa's role in keep-ing peace through nonviolent means. I also knew that the FARC was one of the armed groups increasingly present in that region, along with the other guerrilla groups, paramilitary groups, and military forces. Even then, I questioned whether the armed groups and the oil company were working together. Much later, after the murders, we would find more of Terence's writing from the time, letters never sent, describing in more detail his belief that the FARC had gone full-bore in support of oil development and that he felt that he faced threats because of it.[18]

For the upcoming trip with Lahe' and Ingrid, he had not yet explained to me how the three of them were assessing risk or devel-oping security plans. That night in the Brooklyn studio, when I asked, Terence recounted the ways that the U'wa hosts would absorb them into the inner reaches of U'wa territory for most of their planned stay and, in that way, protect them. He explained that the times of great-est risk were during transit on exposed rural roads on the outskirts of U'wa towns, and that sometimes transit was necessary, as when coming to or from the regional airport. He explained that he had informed the US Department of State and US Embassy in Bogotá of the plan and, as usual, there would be no media or other communi-ques regarding the trip or the travelers before or during their stay.

In those days leading up to the trip, I asked Terence for the three of them to create a thorough plan for safety, security, and contin-gencies. I remember feeling stuck between the need for a thorough plan, the reality of the risks of rural travel amid armed conflict, and the steadfast focus that the three of them had generated with U'wa leaders on the importance and timeliness of their work. I saw that the three of them were cocooned in their focus on the opportunity. I was on the outside of that cocoon.

In our community of two, we didn't make sufficient time to revisit the issue. Did the three of them give these conversations the time they needed? Did they engage any broader community to make the time?

I do not know the answer. We were carried on the forward momentum toward departure day, and preparation was all-consuming.

Figuring out how we'd communicate during the trip was complicated. He didn't want to take a satellite phone this time because the last hadn't worked. We planned to check in at 8 p.m. Eastern time on whichever nights Terence would be near a landline. Because we were scheduled to move the same day that Terence was departing, we had already stopped our phone service. So I stocked up on international phone cards to use at the pay phone of the corner liquor store across the street. Otherwise, he agreed to call me at work during the day whenever he happened to be at the U'wa office in town. I was ready.

The morning of his departure, we took a taxi into Manhattan with his luggage and stopped at a photography store for some documentation supplies that he had promised to bring. After, we ate breakfast at the Starlight Cafe next door. Terence's hands fit my hands like every muscle in each had been shaped to meet that clasp. The last minute I spent with him was on Ninth Avenue at 34th Street, hailing a cab to take him to JFK. We didn't say anything, kissed. He put his hand on the window, bye.

The Last Time We Spoke

Terence's trip began on February 5. The month stretched out ahead of me, delicious with time for my own work at WEDO and the project of setting up our apartment. It was my first real apartment, with a lease in my name, shared with another. No parental co-signer, no sublet, no hippy commune, no squatting. It felt solid. I felt like an adult. At the same time, it also felt tentative. Terence was not there. Even when he returned, his stay could be brief. Lahe' had invited him to join her organization in Hawaii. He wanted to see how this trip went and then decide.

New York was a trial period for us, too—our attempt to be in the same place long enough to see who we were together. I unpacked a couple of Terence's boxes, shelving his books and finding places for his art and kitchen tools. I noticed how I was placing his things around the apartment. Things not of my style, not of my choosing or liking, placing them center stage with new eyes, loving these things because I knew how much Terence loved them. That's when I realized that *I* loved *him* and that I would rally for him, for us.

Soon enough, Ingrid and Lahe' joined Terence in rural Colombia. For much of their visit, they were in the backcountry, not near easy communications. Periodically they emerged back into an U'wa town along the roadside, and a flurry of calls would come. February 18 was one of those days. I was at WEDO going about my day. Unbeknownst to me, Terence had tried to get ahold of me several times. Our receptionist had not been putting his calls through because I had my office door closed and she assumed that I did not wish to be interrupted.

When we got on the line later that day, I thanked him for the two Manila mangoes that he had somehow arranged to be delivered to me at work for Valentine's Day. I asked him how he was feeling about us. He said he moved to New York because he had decided. I told him that I had decided, too. That I would be happy to move to Hawaii if that was where we needed to go next. That I was looking at it that way. "Good," he said. "Then it will all work out." There was a quiet calm. We played in the silence, allowing ourselves to be pulled both ways: into the desire to say everything and into the desire to preserve the sweetness by allowing everything to be left unsaid.

He told me about traveling with Ingrid and Lahe' and the community discussions they were taking in. He described the weaving of reverence and relationship with the U'wa, as well as the difficulties of traveling as three.

I told him that a working group member had issued a public communication with an update from the ground, including information about the visit. When Terence traveled within Colombia, the working group abided by an unwritten protocol that public communications should refrain from sharing facts that would reveal his whereabouts or planned activities. In this instance, I figured he must have okayed it. He had not. With news of the communique, he grew anxious and disheartened. It was a development that he had to address, so he hopped off the phone to attend to it.[19]

It was the last time I spoke to Terence.

On the morning of Thursday, February 25, 1999, on the way to the regional airport to come back home, they were kidnapped.

4

The Arauca River

Friday, February 26, 1999

On Friday morning, February 26, 1999, Terence's friend Leslie Wirpsa received a call from U'wa territory. "Terry was abducted. What should we do?"[1] The U'wa had waited at first before calling Leslie because they expected the three to be returned, as would be usual in this scenario in this context. The three of them had been taken by people who self-identified to the U'wa as the FARC. The captors told the U'wa that they wanted information from the three and that they would not hold them for long.[2] But by Friday evening, in the winter dusk, just before leaving the office for the weekend, I too received a call. A working group member called to tell me that our U'wa colleagues had also called them to say that the three had been taken and had not been returned.

Within minutes, I was swept into a whirlwind race against time that would continue uninterrupted for the next eight days. I didn't have a cell phone yet so I was tethered to my office line, balancing inquiries and offers of help from my officemates ("I know Vice President Al Gore—we could get him to intervene") with trying to reach Ingrid's husband and Lahe''s staff. I was also sorting out Terence's travel insurance situation with his mom, Julie, in this, my first direct interaction with her. He hadn't told his mom that he was traveling again to Colombia. I didn't know this. Apparently he had only told his grandmother, who had, until that point, been providing Terence direct financial support for things like insurance. The Department of State was also asking for a copy of Terence's passport. I didn't have it with me in Manhattan—it was in the apartment in Brooklyn.

At that same time, I was supposed to meet my own mother, Betsy, at the Crate & Barrel on East 59th Street, across Central Park from my office at WEDO. My parents had come up to New York for the weekend. My mom and I were going to meet once I got off work to shop for sundries to fill in the household gaps in the new apartment. She didn't have a cell phone, either. So I sent a co-worker to Crate & Barrel with a description of my mother. I asked her to find my mom, tell her that Terence had been taken, and that we needed a copy of his passport from the apartment back in Brooklyn. This was my mom's first trip navigating the New York subways by herself. She received the news, got herself back to Brooklyn, and told my dad what was happening. Together, they faxed the passport copy back to me from the video store up the street.

Later that night, I eventually put down the receiver of my office phone. I walked out into the hallway. I walked out onto 40th and Lexington and walked the length of the island to find my way back to my parents. I never once returned to that office or my beloved work there. I can't even account for what happened to my belongings.

When I finally met my parents back at the apartment, my mother looked at me and, for the first time ever, her eyes offered no reassurance. She was the oldest of five siblings in a family that prioritized education of the boys. To ensure her own education, she joined the convent and served as a Catholic nun for ten years. She was a resourceful survivor. She cooked dinner and cleared the plates. She started the laundry and swept the floor. She made the bed and she put me in it. She "stayed where staying was needed."[3] But her eyes couldn't tell me that it would be enough. She sat on the edge of my bed. I felt the beginning of an inevitable untethering.

Saturday, February 27, 1999

I remember people's feet streaming in and out of the apartment around an island of papers on the living room floor. We didn't have a table yet, so notes and press releases, clippings and faxes were cast across the slick of the hardwood. Evidence of our mobilization to end the kidnapping. The papers made a place for me to put my body when the rest of the world would not stop.

Only by the fact that people were there at all, descended upon our little corner of Brooklyn from all parts of my life, could I gauge the severity of what had happened. Caroline in the kitchen baking sweet potatoes. Kaki setting up the fax machine. Karin tending a make-shift altar. Alexa trimming a vase of purple flowers. There on the floor, I relied on the scrawled notes like stepping stones to the rest of the world. But the stepping stones were unstable; my feet faltered. I was searching for instructions where there were no instructions, a map where there was no map. Nowhere in those papers was a trace of Terence.

By the second day of the kidnapping, the families and communities of the three began working together for their release. As the press started contacting organizations from various social movements about the kidnapping, it became clear that we needed a coordinated media strategy agreeable to all three families. Trying to stem speculation and minimize harm, we organized an international conference call to air our views and agree upon a strategy. On that call, I helped represent Terence's family.

I know the sun rose that day, but I never saw it. The heat was cranked in the small apartment, but with so many people flowing in and out, the windows were also open. Outside the thin panes, the dark night arrived indifferently. From my refuge on the floor, tangled in the cord of the landline, I navigated the call. Three families, two Native North American communities, leaders of national and international Indigenous rights movements, environmentalists from three continents, human rights advocates from Colombia and across the Americas, and friendly but eager journalists. The families asserted an unpopular approach: we needed to confirm who had them and keep the kidnappings low-profile while we worked back channels for their release. The less of a public display, the easier the release would be. With insight from Ingrid's colleague Rigoberta Menchú Tum and many others, we had reason to think this strategy was necessary, and we knew not to communicate broadly about it. Some NGOs and others on the call were not receptive. Among even our allies, holding that line felt untenable.

During that call, I felt wholly unprepared for my role. Several elders and political veterans in the mix also seemed unprepared. My friend Katie's hands supported my back. At a certain point in the discussion, I had to step outside my body to continue functioning.

I could no longer take it in. As I lifted myself out in self-preservation, I let the part of my brain take over that knew how to listen, speak, synthesize, mirror back, and move forward. My heart had other places to be. For me, the truth of the matter was that there was no trace of our loved ones on that call, either. At the beginning and end of the hour, we invoked their presence to guide us, but they were not there. We were swimming in the dark.

When the call ended, I unraveled, spilling out over the papers strewn across the floor. My friends, who had been waiting in various quiet corners of our apartment, came rushing in. Gingerly, they scooped me up and placed me in the bed. I had nothing left. No reserves. No coherent spiritual framework. No reference point for moving forward.

My friends looked stricken. In their eyes, I began to comprehend the precariousness. We might advance the most sophisticated of strategies, we might call in every favor, we might work ourselves to the bone for their release. And it might not matter one lick. They could be killed in an instant while we were safe there in New York. In the acute emergency, the work in front of me was clear. The work was not a choice. I was beholden to a sacred duty that I did not choose and from which I could not turn away.

Sunday, February 28, 1999

On Sunday, the families released our first united family statement to the press, revealing all the information that we felt appropriate to share. We also sent gratitude to supporting organizations and implored them to consult the families before attempting any communications concerning the release of our loved ones. Arriving at consensus on a succinct joint statement had taken us all day. Afterward, I was standing in the apartment where the mini kitchen turned suddenly into the mini living room. Night outside was quickly rolling in. Nothing else was happening. Only my underlying and constant churn, the working and reworking of the edges of fear.

In that moment, I had a visitor in my mind. She might as well have been right there in the kitchen with me—a mother bear. With vivid clarity, I saw her come from the top of a wooded mountain, rushing down the slope in a fury of anguish and pure muscle. She came to envelop those of us standing at the bottom, to protect us, to shield us with her body and her roar. To repel what had arrived to do us harm. She moved with intelligence, with knowledge of a plan and fury that the plan had been interrupted. She barreled down the mountain as if to roar "No!" even knowing that it was too late.

I couldn't stay with the bear in the kitchen. It was too much. I moved my body instead into the community garden next to our apartment. There, I shielded myself from the street behind the compost stacks near the tool shed. I wanted to see if I could connect with Terence energetically. He was there. He came to do the hand dance with me in the garden. Erotic and light. We were light and laughing. We were barely touching. We were kissing lips like rose petals touching. Then he was gone.

Monday, March 1, 1999

On Monday, Ingrid's and Lahe''s husbands invited me to join them at the American Indian Community House in Manhattan to consolidate our response efforts. Since the late 1960s, the Community House has supported the well-being of Native Americans living in New York City and served as a place of intercultural exchange and advocacy. Ingrid was a member of their board of directors.[4]

Over the weekend, Native colleagues from all corners of the country had begun flocking to the Community House to mobilize for Ingrid, Lahe', and Terence's release. Coincidentally, the Community House was one floor above the yoga studio where I studied. The elevator ascended past the yoga studio. When the doors opened, we spilled out into the Community House's gathering circle. The ceiling and lighting were low.

Surrounding the open center area was a ring of offices and meeting rooms. Everyone quickly dispersed, seeming to know where to go. I followed to a large open room at the back. Lahe''s and Ingrid's husbands were sitting off to the left-hand side, tucked away in a library nook to be close to one of Ingrid's colleagues who was running point from an adjacent desk. They were mid-flow. I joined them, each of us getting the next action done, whatever it was.

About an hour in, a young gentleman took me aside. He put his hand on my shoulder and pointed at Rosemary Richmond, the beloved co-founder and executive director of the Community House. Over the years, she had led countless efforts to secure and assert the rights of Indigenous peoples in the Americas. Rosemary was presiding at an enormous wooden desk placed at the midpoint of the back wall, overseeing the activity of the room. The young gentleman said, "Remember that you are not the boss here. Rosemary's the boss."

I said, "Okay."

I asked him to make sure to keep telling me if I needed to be doing anything differently. From that moment, I adjusted my way of being there, in that space. I made myself smaller, observed more, and got into the flow of the leadership that was moving from Rosemary to the colleague running point. I felt relieved that the families were working together in this way. I felt relieved that someone was in charge and that my role was to get in line to help.

Getting in line meant getting behind the strategy that was emerging as fragments of intelligence surfaced.[5] Although incongruent, the fragments seemed to indicate that, indeed, extralegal armed actors had them—actors traditionally affiliated with populist causes. The families were consulting diplomatic experts quietly and deftly to understand how to come to a unified approach.

The chosen strategy was to continue to refrain from generating public attention. We had been advised that increased attention at that early stage could cause the captors to prolong captivity in hopes of wider international coverage. We were also at that point choosing to refrain from drawing upon US governmental actors for help. Instead, we were readying quiet negotiations through trusted diplomatic channels connected to the United Nations and Cuba.

Tuesday, March 2, 1999

At the American Indian Community House, time moved in an unfamiliar way. The hours passed instantaneously and stood still for millennia. The room was at once frozen in time and hurtling forward into the future. In this distortion, we found a rhythm. Each of us had a role. We moved forward in triangulation with each fragment of intelligence from the ground.

I was the families' communications representative. My role was to feed information back out to the multiple groups—information about how they could help or how they could refrain from this or that impulse they had to help. I sat with my laptop at whatever chair was available in the comings and goings of people, adding the fragments I knew about Terence's security situation to the mix.

Later that day, my friend Janice Rous, a craniosacral therapist, ordered a cab to bring me to her apartment on the Upper West Side.

She wanted me to take a break. Janice had walked into our lives a few months earlier when she offered to help at a fundraising event that Polly Howells and I hosted for Fran Peavey. At the event, she opened the doors and carried the heavy stuff. She saw that the room was filling and cued us up to make a pitch. She stayed late to clean up. Polly, Janice, and I had become fast friends. I was the same age as their children, so I benefited from their wisdom.

That first time I arrived at Janice's building, the elevator opened right into her vestibule. She greeted me at the door and invited me into her living room overlooking Riverside Park and the waterfront beyond. It was a sophisticated Manhattan penthouse that producers rented out periodically to shoot films. She led me away from the vista and into a small side office where she took me onto her bodywork table. Like a watchmaker delicately opening the back of a timepiece, she worked with my body to open the energetic channels, meridian by meridian. This was her craft by which she invited my body to stay tethered among the living.

Afterward, as I stood to leave, I told her that while she was working on my body, I saw Terence, that he came to meet me in the dream space on the table. I told her that Terence had his shoes off, that he was inviting me to take my shoes off, too. His feet didn't hurt. He just wanted to play. He was there, with relief, ready to play. He was free.

I walked into the hall to push the elevator button going down. Janice leaned her cheek on the back of her hand, gently bracing the doorframe at the threshold of her apartment. She told me, "Nothing now is too much to ask, Abby." I didn't understand what she meant. I left and took a cab back down to the Community House.

Wednesday, March 3, 1999

The situation was unfolding and changing every few hours. We had no way to know whether the captors would prolong the abduction for months, whether they had already killed them, or whether they were about to release them. Our lists overflowed with tasks we needed to tend immediately and with those needed to get systems in place for the long haul. At one point, we were comparing this kidnapping to other kidnappings in Colombia, projecting forward for the coming months. At another point, we learned information that led us to understand that release was just around the corner. On top of that, we still didn't know for sure who had them. We thought it was the FARC. We thought it was another guerrilla group. Earlier we had thought it could be paramilitaries, or the government itself, ours or theirs.

During the abduction, I made detailed accounts of what I thought Terence was experiencing. I made lists to compare notes with Terence against the reality of his experience when he returned. I had created fantastical scenarios of his return: the doctors, the shave, the press conferences, meeting his mother and father, the celebration with Lahe' and Ingrid, the somber discussions with the wider network about how to continue this work, but mostly this: Our bed in our new apartment, us silent together and safe. Terence on top of me, clean warm bodies, tender muscles, nourished. Terence, moving on top of me and beginning to weep. Weeping our love big. Kissing me like there was a tomorrow. Home.

Thursday, March 4, 1999

The week continued to move simultaneously in fast-forward and slow motion. Every decision demanded that each of us stay in the present moment, fiercely attentive both to intuition and massive coordination. By Thursday morning, we had confirmed on good authority that the perpetrators were most likely members of the FARC. We were working our contacts with the Catholic Church and the Red Cross internationally, in Bogotá, and in rural Colombia. Generally, in a situation like this, the Church, the Red Cross, the embassy, and other intermediaries would wait for the kidnappers to contact them. Any attempt to seek out the kidnappers could be interpreted to mean that money would be involved, which could complicate the process. So we waited. We worked with the Church, and we waited.

We had begun to establish systems to make decisions and communicate with the larger community of concerned friends and organizations. Our family phone conferences were streamlined into a series of update faxes and reminders about how family members should handle the media, the FBI, and the US consulate in Bogotá. By Thursday afternoon, we were sending an email directly to our best contact within the FARC, with strong counsel, telling him about how Ingrid, Lahe', and Terence were in solidarity with many of the FARC's stated populist principles.

If we had not established contact with the kidnappers by the following Sunday, the Church was prepared to pray for Ingrid, Lahe', and Terence during Mass throughout the entire region where the kidnapping took place. To pray that they be returned home soon to their families. It was our hope that in this manner local people would be able to provide information to the Church without inflaming the situation. We were readying ceremony and more public-facing engagement in the US, too, for when the time was right.

Late Thursday afternoon, an incongruous dread settled over the room. Everyone was suddenly tense and operating in slow motion. Some left to take a break. Ingrid's husband and I hugged each other and wept. At the same time in Los Angeles, Julie and Terence's little sister Jennifer found themselves weeping at the hairdressers.

We pushed through the remaining day. That night, the whole group at the Community House, together with Lahe''s husband on speakerphone from his house in Connecticut, evoked the energetic presence of the three loved ones at 8 p.m. Eastern, as Terence and I did every day when he was traveling. We asked them to be there with us in our thoughts. There was quiet. We parted in silence.[6]

Friday, March 5, 1999

Then Friday morning arrived. Communication with the federal investigators in Bogotá. Word from the International Red Cross. The instruction to prepare letters.

Then the call.

Three bodies across the Venezuelan border.

Ingrid's credit cards.

The Venezuelan police.

One woman with an eagle tattoo, the other with a triangle. And one young man, twenty-five to thirty, with dark curly hair. It was them.

5

The Rushes at
the Water's Edge

My Heart Reeled in Flight

Within minutes of the bodies being confirmed, men wheeled an enormous drum several times their size into the center of the Community House and surrounded it. They pulled up folding chairs on all sides, found their mallets, and started to pulse. The pulse filled the circle, drawing us out of the offices around the periphery where we were madly working against the raw news of their murders. The pulse climbed to an unbridled wail: an unrelenting, timeless, pregnant cry. To me, the drum made the sound of the earth wailing. Again and again and again and again. The sound seemed at once to both meet the anguish and announce it across the land and waters. It seemed to take me, in all my human smallness, and tether me to the lament of the collective. I was pretty sure that to surrender to the pulse would spell the physical breaking of my heart. I did what I could to stay standing.

I did not stay standing. When I collapsed on the floor, Polly and Janice—who had come at once upon hearing the news—flocked around and above me, their bodies encasing mine completely. The seal they created kept my splayed innards from pouring out across the floor. Within this seal, the drum continued to wail. To me, it seemed like the drum was beating down the rushes at the water's edge, making a place for my heart to sit as my heart at once also reeled in flight, escaping my body, circumnavigating Earth in chase.

My heart scanned the horizon for reassurance that this crime did not happen, scanned for the pathway back in time to before. Before the bodies dropped to the ground, before the bullets pierced flesh, before their final pleas and preparation, before the guns were loaded, before the young men who held the guns lost their innocence, before the river ran red with the blood of the armed conflict, before the river ran black with oil spilled in our names, before the first pipeline, before the first lights from the first camp housing the first pipeline workers, before the first road, before the first transmission of disease, before the first signing of the cross, before the first coins changed hands. My heart flew away, carried on the whisper of the wind: Where are you?

I Ate the Apple and Fed Him Big

Sometime later that day, two women pulled me aside, washed my hands with fresh sage, and took me to a table full of food.[1] One handed me a plate and told me to prepare a meal for Terence's spirit. I did. I fed him big because he was hungry. Then she told me to eat. That I had to become strong again. That Terence would want me to eat. I went and got two apples. One on Terence's plate. One in my hand. It took me six hours to eat that apple. But I did. I knew as she said it the challenge I had ahead and what that challenge would demand of me. I knew as she said it that the only way for me to go through this terror was to face it head-on and with love. To accept it through defiance. The words sounded good, but I did not know how to navigate the waters of such an enormous grief. There were not oceans large enough. I held my chin up high, not out of defiance, or to disguise my trembling lip, but rather because I was determined not to drown.[2]

Where Is the Land?

I had only Janice's instruction: *Nothing now is too much to ask, Abby.* On her table, in the dream space, Terence wanted to play because the bullets had already taken his body and he was free. Ten bullets, four in the face, five in the chest, and one in the back. His pain was gone. And now ours, the pain of those of us left here on Earth, began.

I called my mom from the phone in Rosemary's office. I told her that the bodies had been found. "Jesus," she said. "God damn it." It's the only time I have heard my mother take the Christian lord's name in vain. "I'll be there soon." I called my friend Caroline Laskow, who called everybody, and everybody came.

When it was time, my friend Nick Thompson helped me leave the Community House to go back to Brooklyn. The elevator going down paused to let on passengers from the yoga studio one floor below. The chatter and banter of everyday life flooded the elevator. I felt assaulted. I stayed standing as the floor dropped beneath me. I watched myself place a seal around myself, to insulate, so that I could continue to breathe.

Nick navigated our way to Brooklyn.

At my apartment building, he opened the door to the vestibule. Walking past the mailboxes, my eye caught the label scribbled in our landlord's handwriting, "Freitas/Reyes." It was another assault. My knees gave out again. It was like the air had turned into molasses and I could not move through it. Nick picked me up from under my arms and led me into the apartment, where more friends waited. I have no recollection of what happened next. I just remember that, from that moment on, my friends and my mom were on a round-the-clock rotation for months.

I Met My Fear

A few days later, my best friend from childhood, Karin, brought in the mail. Rifling through, she inhaled sharply. I looked up. She singled out an envelope and placed it on the makeshift altar we were maintaining in the hallway. She lit the candles. I walked over to Karin. It was a letter from Terence that he had sent from Colombia, postmarked February 7, but arriving in Brooklyn more than a month later.

"Fuck," I said. This was right after I'd gotten my period, which too had been late. There was no way at age twenty-five that I'd consciously wanted to be pregnant; I was glad that I got my period. But that didn't stop my emotional body from greeting the blood with grief. It meant that now, with finality, the last inkling of a chance that Terence Unity Freitas would live on, even if only through a child, was gone. It meant that he was really gone. But then again, now a letter had arrived. So maybe not? It said, "Happy Valentine's Day. Sorry I am not physically there to tell you everything I will want to say by the time the 14th rolls around. Things like, 'rin.'" Terence was practicing Tagalog, the Pilipino language I was teaching him. It was how we were, at this early stage, saying I love you. Mahal kita. I love you. Mahal rin kita. I love you, too. The letter continued:

> There are other [things to tell you] too, many, like the excitement that comes with the possibility of breaking old patterns in relationships and making something new. You asked if I was worried that you couldn't hack [it]. I'm not, at all. I know that you can hack. What I don't always know is if you have fully decided that hacking is what you want—it may not be. There are times when I feel it and others not, but recently completely—you have been very present. And for this, **mahal kita**. It makes me want as well. And I do, I want you. I want you just how you are now, changing at your own pace, and not for me. With this thought I will have a very happy Valentine's Day, with you, all day and all night. Mahal na mahal na mahal na mahal kita. —Terence[3]

Decades later, I can read this letter with self-compassion and know the truth of Terence's observation, that I was already in a process of change. I know that I was, even then, indeed, already inserted in what Paulo Freire would call a permanent process of searching and change, marveling, even, at my own uncompletedness. I was already then committed to the inner journey, the fruits of which would enable me to be available to my fullest capacity in service of the collective journey to "mend the long arc."[4]

But back then, in the hallway of the Brooklyn apartment, and for many years thereafter when I would come across the tattered envelope, I looked at the letter with ambivalence. It was an ambivalence that masked fear. I was afraid because I had lost my partner in the work of becoming.

Terence invited me into a shared pursuit of inner life. He extended the invitation from a place of stillness within himself, stillness seeking partnership in balance with me. I trusted the still point. But when he left for Colombia, I was not clear whether I wanted that with him. Though he invited me from the still point, nothing he was doing out in the world looked like balance to me. I couldn't answer bigger-picture questions when I felt like I was triaging daily life. When he was killed, our sangha, or community, of two instantly changed forms. He was on the other side and I was stuck here, still triaging. He could no longer animate our journey; he could no longer play his role. The script had been flipped and I was reeling.

At first I treated the kidnapping like a sprint. Breathless, shooting straight like an arrow, harnessing resources and focus toward one aim: bringing them home. After the murders, I kept on moving. People, lands, and waters remained under threat. I continued to move like an arrow, while at the same time, the murders had fundamentally altered the terrain below. I could not stop my flight. I could not alight for fear that the earth might not be able to receive me if I did. The ground had shifted to accommodate the chasm of grief and I could see nowhere to land.

But people around me were watching my flight with care. I picture them now as though with extra-long lassos in their hands, eyes trained toward the sky, vigilant and standing by. Healers, teachers, friends, elders. My mother.

I was watching, too. Everyone knew that our efforts to address the unresolved murders and continuing threats to U'wa self-determination were not sustainable. We couldn't produce quality work at this pace; at best we could react. Proactive and game-changing approaches were not available to us when we were reeling.

As the months passed, I began to see that the trauma, politics, and continued threat to people and places I loved were not going to cease any time soon. This was not a sprint. It was not even a marathon. I didn't need to be racing straight as an arrow—my attention in fact was being pulled in multiple directions at once. It wouldn't have mattered if I had dug in, preparing to go the distance. I wasn't being asked to go the distance. I was being asked to go to the depths. It wasn't just a chasm. This was the open water of grief. To survive, I needed to learn how to move through water in an entirely new way.

6

The Frozen Earth
at Gavilan Ranch

I Met My Sorrow

Days after the murders, my mother and I returned to California to meet the bodies. We left Polly's house in New York for Fran Peavey's house in Oakland. It was right before NATO began bombing in Kosovo, where Fran had been working extensively with women and child refugees.

When I was fifteen, my friend Karin and I saw an ad in a community newspaper for a summer camp in northern California. We wanted to go. It was a coup to get our parents to let us leave our northern Virginia summer routines of gymnastics camp and swim team. But, we pleaded, we would stick together and learn a lot. There were kids going from around the country. We would raise the money ourselves. Nothing was working. "We can write about it on our college applications!" And they let us go.

The ten-day camp took place along the Navarro River in Philo, a northern California forest town, and was called Creating Our Future. High school students designed the camp to teach other high school students about leading from the heart in environmental and social change organizing. Adult allies, including a former manager and members of the Grateful Dead, co-created the camp.[1] Fran Peavey was one of the teachers.

For half of a century, Fran articulated, practiced, and taught what she called heart politics in myriad social and environmental movements. Using the tools of listening, strategic questioning, reflection, and creative engagement, heart politics works on a human scale to effect sustained social transformation by valuing connection across difference, power with instead of power over, and accountability through community. In *Heart Politics Revisited*, Fran wrote, "Heart politics . . . is about making a deep connection with the life found in a specific place, culture, or area of land. Since the connection is with life, it is inconceivable to think in terms of organizing to kill, to punish, or destroy."[2]

Fran was larger than life. During nuclear proliferation, she was the atomic comic, touring the country with a standup comedy routine that brought people closer to each other and the absurdity and threat of nuclear annihilation. When she could see that the US media was not telling the whole story of our involvement in various international conflagrations, she sold all her belongings, gathered her savings from her high school science teaching job, and traveled around the world. She sat on urban street corners and rural plaza benches with a canvas cloth spread out before her that read, in English, "American Willing to Listen."[3] She listened, realized she wasn't any good at listening, regrouped, learned more about listening, and tried again. Over time, she distilled a listening practice that she later called strategic questioning.

Strategic questioning is rooted in the understanding that the solutions to any given challenge rest with the people experiencing the challenge. It relies upon deep listening as key to formulating relevant and open-ended questions that respect autonomy and honor the wisdom, knowledge, and experience already present in the people answering the questions. Fran called strategic questioning a tool of rebellion and brought this kind of listening to many significant efforts for social justice.[4]

In the 1970s she supported the Pilipino manongs, or elder men, as they, together with others, led the fight to save the International Hotel, a vital community home for San Franciscan immigrants too old to continue working in the fields of California's Central Valley. In the 1990s she mobilized Bay Area women to support women refugees in Kosovo with practical material aid, humor, opportunities for artistic expression, and policy intervention to stop harm. Spanning these decades, she worked alongside Dr. Veer Bhadra Mishra, Goldman Environmental Prize winner, engineering professor, and the mahant of the Hanuman Temple in Varanasi, India, to improve sewage treatment and clean the Ganges River. In this work she also brought together women in their roles as water keepers and researchers from across South Asia.

About once a year, beginning with the summer high school camp and continuing through college, I would bring a stone to the doorstep of Fran's writing shed, a wooden and windowed structure tucked behind the Oakland house she shared with her partner Tova Green. For years, Fran held daily 4:00 p.m. consultations there for the cost of one stone. It was like office hours in reverse, for those seeking a university of unlearning. The stones piled deep along the threshold and surrounding deck. I added my stone to the pile to receive periodic tune-ups for my projects.

Terence had picked me up once from a planning meeting at Fran's. We were working with women water protectors in Kathmandu to organize for improved water quality and access. Terence sat on Fran's couch and chatted with women from Fran's heart politics circle, including one who has, from that day forward, together with Polly, remained a steady supporter and financial sponsor of the U'wa people's work for community defense.

My mother and I stayed at Fran's house for a few days in the weeks following the murders. Fran's house had one landline. I was using the landline to talk with a journalist who was writing a feature about Terence and the murders for the *LA Weekly*. Fran needed the line open because Representative Barbara Lee was trying to get through to her for advice about Kosovo. Fran was frustrated that I was tying up the sole phone line. She weighed the difference between the outrageous loss of three lives already taken in Colombia and the outrageous loss of an untold number of lives about to be taken in Kosovo—a number Fran was committed to minimizing. When asking to use the landline, Fran remarked, "Abby, go hold dying babies in India. Do that, and your gratitude will overwhelm your grief." Fran, who had seen plenty of death and dying from war and other atrocity, pointed to the way I maneuvered through grief as a marker of my various forms of privilege. She seemed to be saying, "Move on because there is plenty more work to do." I took this in. It was not the gentlest advice, but it was quintessential Fran. I needed a beacon. She offered this one. In many ways, I did what she said. I just kept going.

I Met Julie's Wails

After we left Fran's house, my mother and I made our way down to Los Angeles. Two of the three bodies had arrived at LAX from Caracas. United Cargo had encased their caskets in huge wooden crates.[5] As we walked into the hangar, someone slid open the side panel of Terence's. The plain box sat without ceremony in the middle. It was marked "head" at one end and "feet" at the other.[6] Someone draped an Earth flag over the casket, a gesture in response to the Department of State's insistence on welcoming him home with an American flag. I felt my mind lift out of my body, to stand apart from what was in front of me: my partner's bullet-riddled body in that box. The part I remember most clearly about meeting the bodies was the way Terence's mother, Julie, wailed. She shrieked, in fact. High-pitched shudders, loud and without end. It was piercing and total.

After the undertaker put the caskets in the hearses, we left the airport in a string of solemn cars. The United Cargo hangar was my introduction to the City of Angels. And to Julie.

We spent the next month together in North Hollywood, traversing between Julie and Melinda, who was Terence's godmother and one of Julie's best friends. My mother sat with Julie on her living room couch, listening to story after story about Terence growing up. She worked with Julie in the front garden, weeding and talking. She fielded the well-wishers who arrived at the house in a constant stream of words and tears. When the words ran out, she walked with Julie in the back garden, picking citrus, not talking. It became clear that my mother was a base of stability not only for me but also for Terence's mom. My mom kept doing what was in front of her to do. And often that was the work of simply being present and bearing witness. She was *doing* the work of *being*. Of being there for a lot of hurt and wounded people, helping us remember how to come back to ourselves even amid the grief.

During the month in Los Angeles after the murders, every day was fraught. The mortician had moved the box that held Terence's body to the Westwood Village Mortuary, where Julie had made arrangements. One day, the mortician invited us to come look at the body. I remember that the people around us at Julie's house had strong opinions about whether we should go look or not. Some thought it would be too much. Others thought we would never have closure unless we looked. Julie and I were ambivalent. Looking at the body would make the situation more real. For myself, I didn't necessarily want it to be more real. At that point, I was floating above reality. Hovering over the scene was so much safer than touching down into the fray. Because when I did, no matter where I stood, I was on the losing side of the tug-of-war between the unending barrage of requests for me to respond to the political, legal, financial, and logistical matters that follow murder and my undeniable—but repeatedly violated—need to lay my own body down. I had decision fatigue. I had every kind of fatigue. I don't remember deciding whether to go to the mortuary or to stay at the house. My body got in the car.

Along the way, Melinda told us that the mortuary was notable for having interred celebrities like Marilyn Monroe and Dean Martin. Rounding the corner upon arrival, she also told us that the mortuary was home to the family tomb of Armand Hammer, who had directed Occidental for much of the last half century from its corporate headquarters, which we were then just passing. I looked back over my shoulder through the car window. We were in the shadow of the canyon made by the towering corporate buildings in Westwood, monotonous and bland. I tried to picture Terence meeting Berito on the doorstep of that building during the late 1990s street protests against Occidental, when people who cared about Indigenous rights and the earth repeatedly flooded that intersection with one message for Armand Hammer and his shareholders: Oxy out of U'wa land.

The next minute we were at the mortuary. In my memory, there was no one to greet us. There were no staff members. We let ourselves in a side door and the casket was sitting in what appeared to be an entryway—propped opened halfway. Julie keened again. I looked at Terence's doctored and gray face and tried to see where the bullet holes had been. His neck was bloated, and his mouth was puffed larger on one side. I cleared the skin of powder near his right temple. It was black. I looked under the plastic to see his chest. I wanted to touch the muscles of his arms. His feet. I did not.

This was the body I had invited to make a home in my body. This body had been violated and pasted back together. Twenty-three years later, on another visit back to Julie's house to help her with Terence's boxes, I read for the first time the coroner's autopsy report. The bullets fractured Terence's skull in five places. Standing there at the mortuary, looking at his face, I had imagined bullet holes in an intact skull. I had never contemplated that his skull was destroyed. But the coroner reported that the skull was so destroyed he could not fit the pieces back together. No brain matter returned to

Los Angeles with the body. His brain must have emptied out onto the field where his body was dumped.

I did not recognize Terence in this body. Nothing at the mortuary or in our ragtag caravan of familial grievers provided any emotional or spiritual container for our experience of looking at the body. I, one who can usually make ritual out of anything, had nothing. Instead, the only thing available to me was in my own head. I picked up my private conversation with Terence to say, "Well, look at that. You really are dead. Where does that leave you and me?" I went back out the side door and sat in the car.

I Could Not Meet My Mother in the Yurt

Patty and Michael Gold, stewards of Gavilan Ranch, were like second parents to Terence. Terence spent summers scampering the foothills of the Jemez Mountains in New Mexico where the Gold family ran Cedar Mountain Camp, an overnight summer camp for kids. In his teen years, he'd worked there as a counselor. Terence had told the Golds about us. The day before Terence's memorial service in Los Angeles, Patty walked up to Julie's porch. She looked at me. She cupped her hands around my face, and I said, "I'm Abby." She said, "You're Abby. Yep. You're Abby."

In a morbid logistical conversation while he was still alive, Terence had told me that if he were to die, to bury him at Gavilan Ranch. So, together with Patty and Michael, we made the preparations. The problem was that when Terence was killed, it was still winter in the high desert; the ground at Gavilan Ranch wouldn't thaw for weeks. With the ground frozen, we decided to keep Terence's body frozen, too, while we waited. His body stayed at the Westwood Village Mortuary. His grandmother was mortified. We were all mortified. We couldn't quite look squarely at the decision without feeling unease. It was as though we were all frozen in time.

On the endless road from Albuquerque to Gavilan Ranch, jack-rabbits and roadrunners darted across the route. The Jemez beckoned in the distance. Peeling off the road to the west was a gate that looked like something straight out of an old Western movie. The gate announced our arrival at the ranch. From the gate, the land sloped slightly uphill, soon opening to an expanse of alternating mesa and ravine. On the far side, the ranch nestled up against the horizonal ridgeline of a higher plateau beyond. At its base sat a great house where the Golds stayed when they were on the land. Dotting the mesa were the bunkhouses, canteen, pool, and other camp facilities from the summer program.

For the month leading up to the burial, I stayed there with the Golds. Patty put me to work cleaning the camp. I beat the rugs against tree trunks. I swept and cleaned every surface. I clothed the beds in fresh linens. I opened the windows and filled the flower vases. I closed the windows against the desert silt and cleaned again. I prepared Gavilan Ranch for Terence's homecoming. For the day we would finally place his body in the ground.

I was grateful for the work. I tended every detail, as though preparing for a big party. When Julie inquired about fitting Terence's casket into her Volvo wagon, the owner of the mortuary instead personally drove it from Los Angeles to Gavilan Ranch, never charging for the service. When the hearse arrived, we put the casket in the garage. My bedroom shared a wall with it, and I was uncomfortable being so close. I asked to move to a different bedroom. My heart was tethered to the casket, but I couldn't bear to be near it. It hurt too much.

Once I cleaned out the yurt, we moved the casket there. It was just an empty yurt with a casket in the center.

In the days after my mother arrived from Virginia, as the others were trickling in, I barely saw her. I was playing host, playing any role so as not to sit still. My mother, I later learned, was sitting in the yurt. She was sitting in the yurt because it was the right thing to do. She was "staying where staying was needed." She sat for hours. Eventually others realized what she was doing and sat, too.

I did not enter the yurt.

At some point, some of the men of Terence's life removed the body from the casket and took it from the yurt to the porch of a nearby building to prepare him for burial. Red Star, a Chumash friend from Los Angeles, knew what to do and how to do it. Together with that knowledge, he had brought enormous sacks of fresh-cut white sage. The men washed the body, then wrapped it in strips of red cloth, tied in with the sage. I watched from the steps of the yurt. Some of the women of Terence's life gathered around me. Julie, too, eventually. We sang. We sang him safely home. We sang the wounds healed. We sang with a prayer that he might be released, that we might be.

On May 27, 1999, on Terence's twenty-fifth birthday, we buried him. When his brother Kian and father Peter, together with the other men, lowered his wrapped body into the earth, my anguish, too, was released. I collapsed onto my knees toward the grave. I felt my own brother Jason on one side and my father Nelson on the other swoop down in a singular, attentive motion. My hands loosely held the many trinkets of Terence's that I had been carrying with me since the day of the kidnapping. A baby owl's wing that Terence had col lected from the woods. A piece of obsidian he had worked into an arrowhead, which my thumb had continued to work in worry this whole time. A silver turtle pendant that my mom had given me, that I had given to Terence, that the Department of State had sent back to us with his belongings. A turtle I had given him as a reminder to slow things down.

The trinkets had been like companions. One by one, I dropped them into the grave. This part of the accompaniment was over.

I Could Not Take God as My Lover

I met Ram Dass in the late 1980s at the same summer camp where I met Fran Peavey. In spring of 1999, I went to talk with him about how to navigate the loss of Terence.

Born Richard Alpert, he and academic colleague Timothy Leary helped introduce a willing US public to psychedelics. Later, after devoted study with his teacher Neem Karoli Baba in Kainchi, India, he took the spiritual name Ram Dass, came back to the States, and helped introduce a generation here to the practices of yoga asana and meditation.

At the youth summer camp, Ram Dass's wry stories lured in us high school students, giving us vocabulary borrowed from Sanskrit to describe the kind of seva, or selfless service, to which many of us were devoted. He helped us see the long arc in which we were working for environmental and social change. And he made us feel like we were part of a lineage stretching backward and forward in time. He did this with few words. Much of it was through sharing silence together. In sitting with us, he invited us into a place where we were enough and so was the world. With Ram Dass, we could tap into the knowledge that the peace we longed for in the world was already present inside of us. We called him "RD."

I would visit RD for periodic tune-ups over the ensuing years until his death, just as with Fran. He taught me how to bridge my inner knowing and my work in the world. When we talked about my projects, our banter would tug me gently until startling me into focus on the true purpose of the work. The true purpose of the work, Ram Dass helped me articulate, was to create conditions for people to remember their true selves as their universal selves, not separate from the rest of existence. It was to help people "turn on" and "light up," as he would say, not referring anymore to the drugs.

When a catastrophic stroke left him virtually wordless, our increasingly rare conversations began to take place almost wholly at the level of purpose, unbound by space or time. When I went to visit him after the murders, he was still living in San Anselmo in a craftsman bungalow in the damp redwood forest north of San Francisco. We sat in his wood-paneled living room, RD in his wheelchair, me on the sagging couch, the dim windows framing a back yard shaded by towering trees.

Artificial lights brought by a film crew brightened the room. The film crew was there that day filming *Fierce Grace,* a 2001 documentary with Ram Dass about death and dying. Director Mickey Lemle recorded my conversation with RD and included it as the final scene in the film.

The filming had its awkward moments. For example, the crew wanted footage of me approaching RD's house by car. I had not driven a car since before the murders. My mom had been driving me everywhere, including there, to San Anselmo that morning. As with so many other elements of practical daily life during the first few months of grief, the thought of driving overwhelmed me. In the exhaustion of grief, the space in my brain was too crowded. Making space for a task like driving felt again like trying to make my body move through molasses. I got behind the wheel with the cameraman in the passenger seat. He had me drive onto the highway. I started laughing. I was concentrating so hard on driving while also trying to answer the interviewer's preliminary questions. We had to do the take more than once, back and forth on the highway, before the footage conveyed the feeling of a convincing conversation. The crew was mercifully patient.

Back in San Anselmo, settling into the couch, I told RD about the first time Terence came to me in a dream after the murders. In the dream, Terence stood at the threshold of a doorframe, just outside the room in which I stood. I was standing in a yellow-painted room, near a kitchen table backed by windows. I rushed toward him. He retreated. I was unable in the dream to cross the threshold of the door. We stood suspended. Even so, his arms were also somehow wrapped all the way around my waist in embrace. I flooded him with words, so relieved that he was finally there, remarking, "Whoa, this time has been such a trip. Where the fuck are you? Where have you been? I've been looking everywhere for you." Terence didn't answer. He just looked at me with kindness. I kept talking. Eventually I said, "What am I gonna do?" Meaning, "What am I going to do *without you?*" Finally, he spoke: "Oh Abby, this was small peanuts. You will have this love again, big love, and when you find that love, I will be there."

When I finished relaying the dream, Ram Dass exclaimed and wept. To Ram Dass, of course, the dream was about universal love: when I tapped into universal love, I would be free. I would be free of the illusion of separation, of the illusion of birth and death, coming and going. And it would be exquisite.

That sounded dreadful to me. To me, this dream forecasted the love I would find again. Here, on this earthly plane. With a person. A person who was not dead. But RD was in a reverie, the cameras were rolling, and I accommodated the gap between us without fanfare. Without the tantrum that I wanted to have about it being unfair to be still here when Terence was gone.

Ram Dass said, "Take god as your lover."

Back home, I tried to integrate the teaching into how I understood the world. But I was in what Rilke called "the startled space which a youth as lovely as a god has suddenly left forever."[8] During the long hot Brooklyn summer, sitting alone at the table for two in our tiny, empty apartment, I would burst into tears. In the startled space, it was too lonely to eat artichokes by myself. I ate standing up. I learned that if I cried in the shower, I didn't need a sleeve. I kept my t-shirts stacked in one half of the dresser. Sometimes when writing I would look up with a halt, expecting him to walk through the door. One morning before waking, he planted a huge, long kiss firmly on my lips, eyes brilliant and skin clear, radiating. Then gone.

In contrast to RD's teaching, I did not want to take god as my lover. I was still looking for Terence.

I didn't want Terence as a butterfly, visiting me there at our kitchen window. I didn't want him as the rising sun or as the pigeons flying in unison over Lafayette. I didn't want him as a metaphor. I wanted him there. I wanted him brushing his teeth beside me. I wanted him holding my head in the crux of his arm on the couch. I wanted him washing the pot as I chopped the veggies. I wanted him there, to take my shoulders down, hands on my shoulders guiding me down, saying, "Rest now, Abby, rest. Tomorrow is another, tomorrow we will do the rest. Tomorrow. Rest now, Abby, rest."[9]

Of course, I understood intellectually that it could never work out with me and Terence, him being dead. But at the time, it all seemed negotiable. I guess one could say I was back in the bargaining phase of grief.

As I negotiated, I was in a holding pattern with fear, and my imagination ran wild. Why did they shoot him in the back? Did the force of the first bullets turn his body to allow the shot to enter his back? Had he turned to run, despite the tie on his hands and the bag over his head? Did they dislodge a final shot once his body had already slumped to the ground? When my mind was not busy reconstructing the past, it was often breathlessly scanning the future. I couldn't find any solid ground. At times, it seemed like it would be easier to go where he was.

It turned out that murder was just the beginning. Murders, unresolved, produce a ton of work. Extrajudicial killings committed abroad in Indigenous lands where US oil pipelines attract armed violence produce a ton of work, for years to come. After the murders, there was much to triage. Tending to it tethered me to the earth.

I experienced a narrow margin between the horror of the past and my terror of the future. Mercifully, that narrow margin revealed itself to me as the present moment. I remember clearly kneeling back on my heels on the living room floor of the Brooklyn apartment, smushed between past and future. I remember finding the breath, latching onto its rhythm, in and out, in and out. In the breath, in exactly that moment, which was the only moment that was actually happening, I found refuge. Terence was not being shot in that moment. I was not struggling to build a life without him in that moment. I found myself doing a scan of body and heart, mine this time, learning again and again with each breath: hey, I am not dying in this moment. The breath is going in and coming back out. I remember clearly experiencing myself in my body, peering out on the world from inside my body. From this nest, I could attend to my daily life without the clutter and clamor of what had already happened and what was yet to come.

I learned how to walk the narrow margin of the present as refuge. Some people called it the state of shock. But I knew there was something real and irrevocable about that liminal place. I felt relief and, at times, ease. I began to befriend impermanence: to curse it less and to walk in its cadence. I had heard poet Aya de Leon speak of the "loving death face of God," an evocation that came close to describing the internal accompaniment I felt when dwelling in this place.[10] Walking with this loving death face of god let me shed the cloak of the fear of death. Without that fear, my reason to be here, alive, toiling on this planet, came into sharper focus: to give and receive love, which included creating conditions for other beings to do so, too, and fiercely defending that space.

Frustratingly, I could only access this clarity fleetingly. Much of the time, I was hanging out on the banks courting Charon, ferryman of the dead, to evoke Joan Didion's description of the vulnerability of the bereaved.[11] If I was going to remain stuck, I needed to figure out how to sustain my capacity to *stay* in the present moment. There had to be strategies beyond coping. I needed to learn how to invite myself to dwell in my inner life. I knew that the first step was to learn how to welcome my heart back into myself. I knew that there were teachers for that.

I left New York to set out to find them. Terence's boxes in our brand-new apartment in Brooklyn had for the most part never been unpacked. Later that summer, my dad wheeled them with care to the corner post office and shipped them to Julie's house in Los Angeles, where some of them still sit in the garage. By fall, I was back in the west for good.

Part 2

I want to be with those
who know secret things
or else alone.

—RAINER MARIA RILKE

7

Two Ponds in the Tusas Mountains

I Moved toward My Anger

On my way back west that first summer after Terence died, I went to Vallecitos. Vallecitos is a mountain retreat center for social change workers to learn and practice contemplation along with other forms of slowing down. Deep within the Tusas Mountains in northern New Mexico, on lands ancestral to the Ute and Jicarilla Apache Nations, Vallecitos is nestled at the opening of a little valley where the waters of the surrounding mountains pool into two interlocked ponds. The ponds mark the Vallecitos entrance.

The first day there, teachers wrangled around thirty of us into what is called noble silence. After a few days, they shepherded us into a deeper silence through the stillness of walking meditation. In the dark wood of the main hall, they told us to let the soles of our feet kiss the earth with each step. They then suggested we pattern the in-breath and the out-breath to match the shift of weight from one foot to the next.

We walked single file around the periphery of the room. It took me awhile to follow the instructions. Quickly my mind wandered. I would forget what I was doing. Other times, the act of shifting weight felt like a perilous leap of faith. Without fail, the earth would rise to meet me. I marveled at this, the consistency. When I finally dropped in enough to let go of the instructions and trust that there was nowhere else that I needed to be, I looked up. Outside the window to the left of the fireplace stood the elongated trunks of a pair of birch trees. In that moment, I comprehended that I was not separate from the birch trees. With a sense of belonging, I let my shoulders down and warmth arose along the length of my spine.

The moment was fleeting. Taking the very next step demanded my attention. I was absorbed in wonder at the mechanics of getting my foot to move forward. As I paused in reverie, I noticed the line of fellow meditating activists back up comically behind me. I kept walking. I had tasted the nectar of the practice and felt allured by it. I felt grateful to the teachers and to the group.

Later that week, I stole away to go yell in the woods. After that, I jumped in the first pond. It was snowmelt and freezing. When I backstroked across it, sunlight caught in the drops of water that cascaded off the arc of my moving hands. In those sparkling drops, I caught a first glimpse of joy, and of the possibility that joy can coexist with grief. It was a private victory.

This first glimpse of joy pierced something in me that allowed me to notice and begin to work with my anger. Little did I realize then how much anger had lodged inside me, and in how many different realms of my being. Entering each new realm of anger startled me and left me aghast. Mercifully, right away after the murders, my psyche had known how to titrate my exposure to the anger, to bring it to the fore bit by bit. Somehow I knew to save the most viscerally threating realms of anger for last—once I had some skills.

I Titrated the Anger Internally

Day-to-day support to the U'wa required direct confrontation with the geopolitical, economic, and industrial forces that drove the international conflict. I took public-facing action in concert with several concentric circles of colleagues.

Most closely, I began working with Terence's friend Leslie Wirpsa, the political scientist who had been his hapkido partner. Fairly quickly after the murders, Leslie and I took up the U'wa Defense Project, the initiative Terence had started with Berito, the U'wa leader. Through the U'wa Defense Project, we mobilized a very small staff of women lawyers and scholars based in California and Bogotá, including those who most closely maintained guidance from AsoU'wa. With fiscal sponsorship from the Rainforest Foundation in New York, the U'wa Defense Project remained an organizational member of the broader working group, playing a couple of roles distinct from the more public-facing anti-oil campaign. The U'wa Defense Project focused mostly internally on building U'wa institutional capacity and infrastructure to support Pueblo U'wa's legal cases and aspirations for community-driven development—the nascent body of work that the murders had critically curtailed.[1]

In parallel, the public-facing work also took enormous coordination and energy to stay focused collectively on Pueblo U'wa's core demands. Rallying for the public-facing work was difficult, but it was not the hardest thing. The hardest thing for me, in those early days, was meeting and managing the anger I felt toward the wider circle of colleagues in the anti-oil working group.

The last time I talked to Terence—me on the landline in the WEDO office in New York, him at the U'wa office in the town at the edge of U'wa territory—I had informed him of the public statement by his colleagues about his travels and he quickly ended the call. To him, the news stung of group misalignment. The wobble in alignment threw into relief how precarious it was to conduct work on the ground, in a war zone outside the United States, without a strong container for it back home. I did not draw a causal or even correlational line between the communication and the kidnapping. I did not. But it did not feel clean to me. It made me angry. In my human smallness, in the immediate aftermath of the murders when I could control so little, I just wanted our colleagues to see and acknowledge this one piece of the awfulness and to clean it up impeccably.

The problem was that I didn't know how to ask for what I needed. I didn't yet know how to make requests while staying on my side of the fence, refraining from judgment and blame. I didn't know how to make requests without being attached to the outcome. Marshall Rosenberg's guide to nonviolent communication had just been published, and I lacked familiarity with the types of tools for navigating conflict that are by now so readily available in progressive social movement training settings. Instead, I added to the mess. I cast daggers during working group meetings and used sarcasm to express dissatisfaction. Participating in the working group felt like a place of harm and of little personal agency. I didn't have the skill, endurance, or discernment necessary to invite our colleagues into the real work of accountability and repair. And the outside world was not stopping to wait for us anyway; there were bigger fish to fry. Eventually I withdrew myself energetically from the working group. I shielded myself so that I could stay in the fray on other fronts.

But my difficulty with the working group colleagues kept coming back to me, like a gnat in my ear. Constantly in my ear. My worry over the situation adversely affected my concentration and well-being. I didn't like that there was an agitation that I didn't have the presence of mind to modulate.

From Vallecitos, I kept going west. I landed at Mount Madonna, an ashtanga yoga practice center in the Santa Cruz Mountains of California. My college friends had grown up in Mount Madonna's residential community. When they told their parents about the murders, the community readily and generously took me in.

At Mount Madonna, we studied the yoga sutras, or proverbs, of an Indian sage named Patanjali. Patanjali's second yoga sutra directly addresses the kind of mental agitation I was experiencing with respect to my working group colleagues. The sutra refers to the gnats in the ear as the chittavrittis, or the thought waves of the mind.[2] According to the sutra, the practice of yoga, or union, is to achieve the cessation of thought waves of the mind. Some people call the chittavrittis the "monkey mind" so that we can picture the trickster monkeys of our mind, and thereby take ourselves less seriously. When my friend Shelagh saw me struggling with nagging thoughts about the working group colleagues, she taught me a practice:

> See yourself as if standing by the side of a stream. Place a lotus flower into your cupped hands. Bring to mind the image of the person who is looping through your brain on an infinite track (the chittavrittis). Shrink the image down to the size of the lotus and neutrally (or, when available, lovingly) place this person into the lotus flower. Bend down and place the lotus flower to float atop the water. Watch as the current takes the lotus downstream. Follow the water until you can see the lotus no longer. Breathe.

When I do this practice, sometimes there is a moment once the water curves out of sight when my mind is clear, when the chittavrittis have stopped. It is a small mercy. There is a pathway back to what the Buddhists call the island of oneself. Like when I've harnessed the gentle energy of the woman-who-tames in the strength card in tarot. I know myself again and compassion arises. Other times, the monkey mind begins right away again and I need another lotus. Often the streambed is full of lotus flower offerings from my monkey mind, and I must laugh at it.

Once when I did this practice, as I tried to place the subject of my agitation into the lotus, I realized that I needed a pair of scissors. Sticky strings were preventing me from getting the unwieldy agitation to stay put in the flower. I used the scissors to cut the strings. Once the lotus was off downstream, the scissors got their own lotus, too. I laughed out loud and turned to walk away from the banks, freer.

For the more formidable sources of my anger, such as thoughts of what the FARC soldiers did to Terence's body, I called upon more potent imagery. While still living in Asia, I once saw a display in a Buddhist museum in Ulaanbaatar: room after room crowded with the monsters that traditionally guard monastery entrances. They were larger than life, papier-mâché sculptures of muscular, blue-faced, fanged, bulging-eyed, merciless guards. I had no context to understand their role in Buddhism. Then I walked into a white-walled room with one single installation. It was a white, square, knee-high platform that expanded almost to the four corners of the room. In the middle of the platform stood one small rendition of a temple. Across the wide expanse of open space in four directions, at the midpoint of each side of the platform, one monster guard stood at attention. Then I realized. They are not there to scare people away from the monastery. They are there to protect what is already inside, to allow those inside the monastery or the mind to find and trace the breath without inviting in the insidious chatter of replay, relive, revise, forecast.

After the murders, kneeling on my living room floor in Brooklyn, navigating the narrow margin of the present moment, I remembered these monastery guards. When scenarios of Terence's murder, or rage about the unknowability of the future, crowded me out, I could evoke the monastery monsters. I could evoke the part of me that was learning how to use fierce benevolence to sweep out the courtyard of my mind and guard the space for inner stillness to have a chance of taking root.

I Titrated the Anger in Community

In Washington, DC, members of the House used the murders as a rallying cry to increase US funding to the Colombian military—despite that military's abysmal human rights record spanning four decades of escalating internal armed conflict, when guns held by any side had never proven a viable means toward peaceful resolution. Washington sought, among other things, to link US provision of guns, money, and training with Colombia's agreement to open more territory to oil extraction. It made sense to fight Washington; we needed all hands on deck to answer Pueblo U'wa's call for international solidarity to protect their territory from further militarization and oil extraction. As we geared up, however, I found myself instead detouring to clean up a fundraising issue much closer to home, a detour that tested my ability to modulate my anger and showed me the importance of having a skillful community to call upon for help.

Within days after the murders, a handful of working group member organizations were at a philanthropic funders' network meeting. The donors included people close to the U'wa cause and Terence. Without consulting Terence's family or the U'wa leadership, participating working group members took the opportunity to begin raising funds in Terence's name.

My friend André Carothers was one of the donors in the room. André and I had met in Washington, DC, when I was still in high school and he was the editor of *Greenpeace* magazine. We spent time backstage at Grateful Dead shows together. Over the decades, he was always looking out for me. During the meeting, he stepped outside to call me to let me know about the fundraising. The news sent me reeling. Perhaps it wouldn't have if there had been harmony and deep, trusting relationships with Terence among working group members. Perhaps I would have seen it the way others must have: this was a heightened moment, surely an emergency fund would come in handy, the donors in the room want to do something about the injustice, let's ask.

But there wasn't harmony. There hadn't been deep and trusting relationships, especially around fundraised money. And because the activists hadn't called Terence's family to discuss it with them before they took advantage of the opportunity, it smarted. One of the first matters I remember handling immediately after the murders was to tell Julie about the fundraising being done in Terence's name. She wanted it to stop.

I had to write a letter to the colleagues who were raising the funds. It took me three days to write with support from Polly and Julie's friends who brought their wide-ranging skills to bear—therapists and editors, philanthropists, even a comedian, Terence's godfather. The first draft I wrote was flaming, over-inclusive, blaming rage. The next few drafts were simmering and smoldering reasonableness. The penultimate draft was icy understated resignation. Finally, my angel editors squeezed out of me some drops of understanding and compassion. In the version I finally sent, I stayed on my side of the fence, blamed no one, and made the request on Julie's behalf. The letter was well received and the request readily, readily honored. The activists agreed to have the funders designate the resources for charitable use under direction of AsoU'wa with Julie's oversight as facilitated by U'wa Defense Project.

Shortly thereafter, my friend Kaira Jewel Lingo treated me, Taj James, and other college friends to dinner in Brooklyn. She was spending down her last material possessions before leaving the United States for the Plum Village Practice Center in Bordeaux, France, where she would live for the next fifteen years as a Buddhist monastic. There, she would study with Sister Chan Khong, the first fully ordained monastic disciple of Vietnamese Zen Master Thich Nhat Hanh, and Nhat Hanh himself.[3] Nhat Hanh was affectionately known by fellow practitioners as "Thây," which means teacher in Vietnamese. Now a venerable elder herself, Sister Chan Khong had accompanied Thây for decades, having directed their humanitarian projects since the 1960s. When they were in their twenties and still in Vietnam, Sister Chan Khong and Thây together ran the School of Youth for Social Service. Their work for peace led Martin Luther King Jr. to nominate Thây for the Nobel Peace Prize. When exiled because of their work, Sister Chan Khong and Thây created Plum Village in France. In so doing, they made a place for their hearts to sit, even as their lands and peoples were ravaged half a world away. After dinner, Kaira Jewel gave me Sister Chan Khong's book *Learning True Love: How I Learned and Practiced Social Change in Vietnam.*[4]

Learning True Love became my field guide to working deeply to transform anger so that it does not cloud one's advocacy for peace.

In it, Sister Chan Khong describes how, during the Vietnam War, the youth school covertly ran medical supplies and rice to villagers who were trapped behind the lines of battle on both sides of the conflict. They did so on bicycle. Frequently during these excursions, combatants killed the young monks and nuns. Some in the crossfire, and some on purpose.

Later, after Thây and Sister Chan Khong went into exile, their calls for an end to the war built to a crescendo. Some monastics from their community who had stayed in Vietnam protested the war by self-immolating. Governments from across the world began turning to Thây for consultation. In her book, Sister Chan Khong recalls the extreme pressure they felt to respond swiftly, knowing what was at stake. The war was killing their friends and obliterating their homelands. Moreover, the rhetoric and cadence of the war seemed to demand a matching reaction. It felt primal. But they also knew from their lifelong practice and vows that responding in anger would not deliver peace, which was their aim.

Even in this context, both while still in Vietnam and later abroad, she, Thây, and their community took every seventh day as a day of mindfulness. Every seventh day, they refrained from responding to the war. Instead, they made tea, walked, sat contemplatively, walked some more, rested, and sat again. They did this practice all day long. They did this practice to have a prayer of a chance at calming their anger. So that they could respond to the world from a deeper understanding of what was happening and what was needed.

This story fascinated me. The practice sounded 100 percent impossible. My circumstances were nowhere near as grave, and yet even in the small response needed to stop people from fundraising in Terence's name, it took at least six adults from our community to slow me down enough to ensure that I would not create more harm. What on earth was I going to turn to when it was time to face the real adversaries, the ones perpetuating oil extraction and war in U'wa territory? For years thereafter, I carried my dog-eared copy of Sister Chan Khong's handbook with me everywhere.

8

The Cubujón River

We Practiced Ways to Work with the Anger

Right after the murders, walking alongside the U'wa offered me plenty of opportunities to practice working with anger in the political realm. I did not bring deep experience or expertise in politics, but I valued learning from those who did. After all, to shift from dominant power to community power in the political realm was essential to community-driven development, the work Leslie and I most closely supported. In the wake of the murders, Pueblo U'wa continued to assert their right to self-determination and sacred governance. They took that assertion to the halls of power. Dominant power in Washington, DC, and Bogotá, however, proved time and time again to be unsurprisingly tightly bound and beholden to big oil.

Thankfully, many of the US-based U'wa allies were seasoned Latin Americanists on Capitol Hill who advocated for human rights in the context of the emergent policy realignment to globalization.

They took the lead, with mainstream environmental campaign organizations deftly bolstering their efforts. I, in turn, took my lead
from Leslie. To inform strategy that bridged between Washington
and the U'wa Nation, Leslie drew upon her long-standing professional relationships with the Capitol Hill–based Latin American
human rights cadre, which included many Colombians. In the political realm, I turned out to be utilized as somewhat of a jane of all
trades, good at fixing things with a good level of broad knowledge.
Often my role seemed to come down to facilitating Terence's
family's deployment of the moral authority bestowed upon them by
the wretched fact of his murder.[1]

When members of Congress moved quickly to use the murders
to justify more war, we knew that if we hesitated in response, we
risked irrelevance in the news cycle, which I came to understand
could spell irrelevance on the House floor. Our response capacity was
stretched thin because, at the same time on the ground in Colombia,
Oxy took advantage of the political moment to settle deeper into U'wa
ancestral territory at Gibraltar. These maneuvers introduced me to yet
another realm of my anger. I couldn't afford to be thrown off-kilter. I
observed that our U'wa companions seemed to modulate the anger.
The source of their steadfastness seemed to be collective and rooted
deeper than the anger pooling on the surface. I tried to take their cue
to harness a power deeper and truer than the anger itself.

We Defended against the Political Vultures

In March 2000, I walked into the Capitol Hill office of Representative
Sam Farr along with Roberto Pérez, the then-president of AsoU'wa.
President Pérez hailed from the U'wa communities that lived closest
to Gibraltar. Representative Farr represented Santa Cruz, California, where Terence went to college. It was the third congressional
office we visited that day to solicit support from US policy makers to
pressure Colombian president Andrés Pastrana to halt Occidental's
impending oil extraction in U'wa territory.

As we sat in the waiting room, we learned that Representative Farr had pushed our midday appointment to an hour later because coincidentally, right at that moment, the House of Representatives was voting on "Plan Colombia." Couched as part of the war on drugs, the two-year, $1.3 billion military aid package for Colombia would do nothing to reduce drug abuse here at home, but it would instead drag the US deeper into another terrible internal conflict. The plan was expensive, ineffective, and inhumane, serving to throw fuel on the fire already consuming Colombia. Over the course of the next hour, we sat in Representative Farr's vestibule and watched the TV monitor of the House floor as the votes in favor of approving Plan Colombia climbed. It was no surprise to anyone that the House, and later the Senate, eventually passed the plan.

Leading up to the House vote, over fifty representatives from peoples' organizations in Colombia came to congressional offices to advocate against Plan Colombia. These farmers, clergy members, human rights advocates, journalists, trade unionists, and Indigenous peoples sought to bring to the table their perspectives about what was happening to marginalized communities throughout Colombia as the result of war, agrarian reform, and alignment of Colombia's development strategies with those of the World Trade Organization. In the Colombian countryside, they called the policy realignment a social genocide.[2]

This social genocide was being carried out under the banner of globalization, from economic policies marginalizing poor farmers to the hoarding of land by Colombian elites speculating on the promise of mega-project developments. The legal and extralegal armed conflict greatly aided this social genocide, producing, at the time, more than two million internally displaced Colombians and 400 massacres in 1999 alone. In the 1990s, Colombia earned the dubious distinction of being home to over 60 percent of the world's kidnappings and over half the murders of trade unionists. In the years since, these numbers only worsened, with land and Indigenous rights defenders also topping the ranks of the slain.

With this war purportedly to eradicate drugs, the US fed another one of our most costly addictions: oil. At the time, 60 percent of Colombia's exported oil came straight to our refineries. Shortly after the House vote, Senator Paul Coverdell from Georgia asserted to the *Washington Post* that this war was important to the US to secure our oil interests.[3] The mother lode of that oil was thought to lie in the Samoré block, underneath Pueblo U'wa's ancestral territory. Plan Colombia tied extensive military aid to Colombia's willingness to open further its petroleum resources to foreign corporations. Members of the Senate had laid the groundwork through prior bills urging Colombia to undertake measures intended to open its economy fully to foreign investment and commerce, particularly in the petroleum industry, as a path toward economic recovery and self-sufficiency. The International Monetary Fund made similar demands.[4]

When it passed, Plan Colombia amplified displacement and swiftly changed the face of the agrarian landscape, providing perfect circumstances for an oil company, once again, to use the chaos of war to settle in—a process that threatened Indigenous communities with being wiped off the map. Because of their adamant commitment to nonviolence and neutrality from armed actors on all sides, the U'wa had become a popular symbol of resistance to this social genocide.

Throughout the House debate, Occidental, with its history of Colombian operations spanning nearly the duration of the internal armed conflict, ferried the oil-as-economic-panacea message through Congress. When we got to the Hill, every member of Congress with whom we met said that Oxy had been there seeking meetings two weeks before. Oxy's message was that Plan Colombia's success would rest in that country's ability to revive the economy, with "oil development [as] the foundation for this recovery."[5]

In testifying before a House subcommittee in support of Plan Colombia, Occidental vice president Lawrence Meriage implored that without increased military protection for US oil companies in Colombia, the US would risk losing the ability to operate in this country's increasingly violent countryside. In the same breath, he added the suggestion that, in addition to fighting drugs in southern Colombia, the US should also consider sending some of that military aid to the northeast to "help augment security for oil development operations," where, to no one's surprise, his corporation was in the process of establishing the new well on U'wa ancestral territory.[6] Six months earlier, Oxy's path had been cleared when Colombia issued Oxy the next license to proceed with exploration at Gibraltar, in the disputed area just outside the state-recognized U'wa resguardo. To justify this action, despite findings to the contrary by other Colombian governmental agencies before and after, the minister who issued the license claimed that no U'wa people lived on the disputed land and therefore no consultation was needed. He declared complete the constitutionally required community consent process and environmental review, even though Pueblo U'wa continued to voice its vehement opposition and had been privy to no such process of environmental review.[7]

The U'wa Made a Nimble Pivot, and Devastation Ensued

In a move the U'wa had often contemplated with respect to other parts of their fragmented ancestral territory, during the fall of 1999, the U'wa proceeded to buy the key parcels of disputed ancestral land at Gibraltar.[8] As a legal matter, Indigenous peoples should not have to buy private property to guarantee their territorial rights, but Pueblo U'wa chose this strategy in response to the times. At Gibraltar, the parcels were in the hands of neighboring non-Indigenous campesinos. These particular farmers agreed with the U'wa regarding the dangers of fossil fuel extraction and did not want the drill site there, either. They knew the land would be better protected if retitled to the U'wa than it would if the land remained unaffiliated.

U'wa leadership communicated this strategy to us while I was in Colorado participating in the pilot cohort of the weeklong Art of Leadership training in what would later become the Rockwood Leadership Institute, named after the neighborhood in Washington, DC, where co-founder André Carothers grew up. The cohort included a few environmental organizers like me but was mostly comprised of environmental grant makers—including many of the very same donors who had responded to the contested call for emergency funding in Terence's name right after the murders. With the blessing of AsoU'wa and in coordination with Polly in New York, André and I raised most of the remaining needed land funds that same day.

Soon thereafter, on behalf of the entire U'wa people, U'wa leadership contracted to purchase the Bella Vista and Santa Rita farms. The many hectares of the two farms encompassed the land within which the Gibraltar well was slated.[9] The strategy was rapid, led from the ground, and effective. Immediately after the parcel purchases, hundreds more U'wa people began living on the farms. While a strategy born from a long legacy of Indigenous organizing, this experience was my first with a variation of what we now call landback.[10]

The monies raised, however, were only part of the price paid. A few months later, the notary who performed the registration of the land sale contracts was killed.[11] And by late January 2000, heavy machinery arrived, attempting to open a road to the drill site. At least several hundred Colombian police and military troops invaded the farms and surrounded the U'wa people who were living there.[12] They cut the U'wa off from supplies, lured U'wa leaders out with false promises to meet with Occidental or military leadership and then blocked their reentry, threatened that their water supply would be poisoned if they did not leave, and worse, that they would be killed. By January 25, 2000, the U'wa had been squeezed.[13] Backed by an eviction order issued by a judge pertaining to four hectares within the farms, government troops, accompanied by government officials and others, forcibly removed the remaining twenty-six U'wa people from the full acreage of the Bella Vista and Santa Rita farms by helicopter.[14] Two days later, a group of U'wa people including elders, women, and children, returned to the farms, only to be driven away by force and tear gas.

Meanwhile, hundreds of U'wa people had taken to blocking the main road through the town of Cubará in a civilian strike "in defense of the social rights of the U'wa and the people of the Sarare area."[15] The roadblock aimed to prevent Oxy's further access to move their heavy machinery. At times, the U'wa were joined by caravans of non-U'wa students, local campesinos, members of the Catholic Church, farmers' unions, national legislators, local Occidental workers, and other Native peoples of Colombia and Ecuador, in numbers that swelled into the thousands within a month. By spring, the blockade had morphed into an open-ended occupation that continued through the fall of 2000. Throughout this time, troops continued to block U'wa access to food and medicines, restrict their movement, and disperse people through violence.[16]

They Were Pushed to the Edge

Early on in the conflict, local combatants from the National Liberation Army, the other major guerrilla group in Colombia, unhelpfully destroyed a load of Oxy's road-clearing equipment. Reiterating their commitment to continuing peaceful defense of their territory, the U'wa urgently denounced the equipment destruction as aggravating the conflict.[17] They also strongly rejected what they described as the collusion and close coordination between the Colombian military, the FARC, Occidental, and the Occidental subcontractor to protect and safeguard Oxy's vehicles, equipment, and machinery through physical and psychological mistreatment of the civilians.[18] Nonetheless, at least one deadly exchange ensued. On February 11, 2000, the troops descended by helicopter on 450 U'wa people who were peacefully protesting near the Cubujón River. The troops used heavy machinery and tear gas against the men, women, and children gathered, forcing them to throw themselves into the river.[19] Another

200 protesters were also removed from additional blockade sites in Las Canoas and La China that same day.

U'wa leadership, together with legal assistance from Martin Wagner at Earthjustice, filed a petition for precautionary measures to the Inter-American Commission on Human Rights. The petition alleged that police and army actions included forced evictions, arbitrary detentions, unlawful seizure of property, physical and verbal violence, intimidation, the blockage of food and medicine, the drowning death of at least one child, and the temporary disappearance of eleven people. The petition asked the commission to urge the Colombian government to stop all activity that violated Pueblo U'wa's rights.[20] Twenty years later, in addressing a petition that included many of these same allegations, the commission cited the militarization of U'wa territory and existential risk it posed for the U'wa as an important factor in holding Colombia responsible for human rights violations under the American Convention on Human Rights.[21]

All this violence in response to U'wa mobilization was happening as we accompanied the U'wa leaders to Capitol Hill. In Washington, we worked with Representatives Farr, Barbara Lee, and Cynthia McKinney to organize twenty-five congressional colleagues to co-sign a letter to President Pastrana of Colombia calling for him "to halt construction of the well site until [his] administration can guarantee that this project will violate neither the U'wa people's fundamental human rights nor the environment upon which their lives depend."[22] Soon thereafter, a delegation of European parliamentarians went to the drill site itself to monitor the situation.

Meanwhile, Occidental continued to make its rounds. Representative McKinney, then in her first period in Congress, said she had never taken a meeting with an oil lobbyist before, but she wanted to take this one. She knew that U'wa President Roberto Pérez was also on Capitol Hill that week. As with U'wa presidents before him, Roberto's core aim continued to be face-to-face engagement with Oxy. When Occidental's Meriage entered Representative

McKinney's office for his scheduled meeting, she was seated at her desk surrounded by ten of us, including Roberto. I sat on the couch, packed in with working group colleagues. The Oxy lobbyist was flustered. He tried to shame Representative McKinney, but she shut him down. She asked him about the impacts of the Oxy project on the U'wa. She asked him to describe what, if any, actions the company had taken to comply with requirements for community consultation and consent.[23] Finally, Meriage admitted that Pueblo U'wa had not been properly consulted about the plans for the drill site or the road leading up to it. This admission underscored a key factual element that we needed to establish in the various legal actions that Pueblo U'wa was taking.

We Found the Royal Land Deeds

None of these actions, however, succeeded in preventing the escalation of armed violence and attempted manipulation of the community. While a Colombian court had temporarily suspended the exploratory activities at Gibraltar—citing the potential for the project to violate Pueblo U'wa's fundamental rights, including the right to life—a higher court had once again allowed Occidental to resume construction.[24]

Within months, U'wa leaders announced to the government the existence of colonial titles for that land from 1661. These fourteen "Royal Land Deeds," issued by the King of Spain, formally recognize the vast expanse of U'wa territory as belonging to the U'wa, not the Spanish Crown, from time before Colombia was created as a nation-state.[25] With the formation of the Colombian republic, the state took ownership of the subsoil of all the lands it owns, but with the colonial titles, it was clear that the U'wa lands don't belong and have never belonged to the state because they've always belonged to the U'wa.

The U'wa had always known that the colonial titles existed, but contemporary U'wa leaders had not known their whereabouts. It is said that, over the centuries, the individual custodians of the colonial titles would invariably die, seemingly in relation to their possession of them. In response, U'wa leadership eventually hid the physical titles. Over time, through the generations, they could no longer find them. Then, in the months after the murders, during the repression of the U'wa resistance at Gibraltar, a historian who had worked in the national archive for fifty years called U'wa leaders to inform them of the continued existence of these titles, just as the leaders were preparing additional legal filings to halt the pursuit of expanded oil exploration. The U'wa presented the colonial titles as yet another argument for not being evicted from their ancestral territory again.

The Colombian government ignored the existence of the colonial titles. Their response came implicitly two weeks later, when Colombia poured massive military resources into the region to protect Occidental's equipment as the company moved its final pieces into place for drilling at Gibraltar.[26]

9

The Gulf of Siam

We Ventured into the Belly of the Beast

During this same period in 2000, in his push for increased military protection for his pipeline and drill site, Occidental's Meriage testified before the US Congress that the guerrillas also extorted a war tax from Oxy contractors and protection money from Oxy's local workers.[1] A US corporation openly admitting that its contractors and workers were paying the very extralegal armed forces that Congress purportedly aimed to counter raised a host of questions regarding the real role played by that corporation in Colombia's development debate. Occidental paraded around Washington with avid enthusiasm for President Clinton's military aid package, extolling the oil industry's virtuous assistance to Plan Colombia's goal of economic recovery as a step toward civil society. As the U'wa case attested, however, Occidental's presence in Colombia smothered that aspiration at every turn for many rural Colombians living in areas where Oxy operated.[2]

The short-lived injunction against Oxy's exploratory activities at Gibraltar would have more likely been upheld over time and implemented in a politically stable environment. But political stability in the region was not actually in an oil company's self-interest; oil extraction on disputed lands enabled by violent repression is easier under cover of the chaos of war.[3]

Meriage's doublespeak on Capitol Hill was nothing compared to the condolences he had the audacity to offer to Terence's mother shortly after the murders. On April 30, 1999, while I was in New Mexico preparing Gavilan Ranch to receive Terence's body, back in Los Angeles Meriage invited Julie to attend Occidental's annual shareholders meeting. For the previous several years, outside Oxy headquarters, the working group had mobilized massive street protests to amplify U'wa demands of the company. Julie had been planning to participate in this year's street mobilization together with Terence's little sister, Jennifer. In consultation with U'wa leadership and members of the working group, Julie decided to accept Meriage's invitation to go inside. She wanted to experience what it would feel like to be in the belly of the beast and to see whether the presence of her moral authority and her words of steadfast commitment to getting Oxy out of U'wa territory could help ferry the message from the streets into the meeting hall. When she called me that evening, she said that during the meeting, Meriage tried to hold her hand as he called the guerrilla murderers atrocious. She couldn't reconcile Meriage's gesture with the actions of his company's incipient expansion of oil operations on U'wa ancestral territory. He betrayed no acknowledgment of how his actions were implicated in the intensification of violent conflict in the previously peaceful region. She couldn't reconcile it because it was unreconcilable.

We Transmuted the Anger with the Colombian Government

On the Colombian side, there was more doublespeak. Juan Mayr, the Colombian minister of environment, was responsible for executing Colombian domestic environmental legal protections. He was reputedly good at it. In 1993 the Goldman Foundation even awarded Mayr with their coveted annual prize, which is often referred to as the Nobel Prize for environmental advocacy. Mayr was no stranger to Pueblo U'wa. In 1998, Berito also became a Goldman Environmental Prize winner, and Terence had both brokered meetings between Mayr and U'wa leadership in Bogotá and met Mayr during community meetings out in rural Colombia. But Mayr was not an uncompromising environmental champion. He also used his ministerial platform to open up ancestral lands to increased oil extraction, even when the communities had said no. Mayr issued Oxy the license to drill.

On October 7, 1999, seven months after the murders, Mayr was in Washington, DC, and requested to meet with US-based environmental advocates for the U'wa. No U'wa leadership was present in the United States at the time. In consultation with them, the U'wa advocates agreed to take the meeting and prepared an advocacy agenda. The meeting would take place at the Washington Hilton.

It would be the first time since the murders that U'wa advocates would meet with Mayr. It would also be the first time that a representative from Terence's family would meet a representative from the Colombian government. I knew that I had the potential to direct my anger about the murders at Mayr; his doublespeak made him an easy target. I also knew that, for my own survival and to be of any use as an advocate, I needed to keep my soul from flying in anger, as Thây would say. While my colleagues prepared us substantively for the advocacy aims of the meeting, I prepared by turning to Sister Chan Khong's book.

Before the meeting, we met up in the hotel lobby. One colleague directly started in to help get us all on the same page. But he interspersed his focused review of the advocacy aims with caustic remarks about Mayr. When it was my turn, I let him know that I understood the advocacy aims. I wanted to shift the energy.

I relayed a story from Thây. While in exile during the Vietnam War, Thây received reports of the brutal treatment of the boat people, less than half of whom reputedly ever made it to a friendly shore. Many refugees perished at sea, often through violent attack by profiteers

along the Gulf of Siam, who themselves hailed from desperate circumstances. In one instance, Thây read a letter about a twelve-year-
old girl who jumped overboard to kill herself after being raped by a
sea pirate. Thây later reflected:

> When you first learn of something like that, you get angry at the
> pirate. You naturally take the side of the girl. As you look more
> deeply you will see it differently. If you take the side of the little girl,
> then it is easy. You only have to take a gun and shoot the pirate. But
> we can't do that . . . If you or I were born today in those fishing vil-
> lages, we might become sea pirates in twenty-five years. If you take
> a gun and shoot the pirate, you shoot all of us, because all of us are
> to some extent responsible for this state of affairs.[4]

Thây wrote a poem to tease out and claim his true names as including that of the girl who has been raped, that of the pirate who has
committed the act, and that of the politician who created the circumstances. To me, the poem was like a set of instructions and an
invitation. I didn't want to walk into the meeting having made a
monster of Mayr. I didn't think it would be productive or strategic.
I was curious about what could become possible, if anything, if we,
through our own wholeness, appealed to that of Mayr.

My colleagues thumbed the edges of their briefing papers. One
of them jumped in, attempting to verbalize some intellectual connection between the poem and the advocacy aims of the meeting.
Another looked at his watch, and then looked at me sideways. In the
ginger voice of accommodation, he said, "Oookay, Abby. Shall we go
inside?" It felt like I was from another planet.

But as we walked in, I realized that I was okay with that. I was
doing what I needed to do to be able to enter the meeting with my
humanity intact, and I was grateful that my colleagues were holding
the purportedly more substantive pieces of the agenda. I could see
their humanity, too, and the gulf between us. I was fascinated with
the challenge: What would it take to bridge this gulf? What would

need to change in our approach to mainstream environmental advocacy for us to reconnect with source as a starting point for developing our advocacy strategies? What could become possible when we prioritize staying whole and seeing the humanity in our adversaries? What shifts in our strategies become apparent when we incorporate the inner work as integral to the advocacy work?

During the meeting, I participated vociferously in making our advocacy aims. I also propped up a photo of Terence on the conference table. I asked Mayr to remember that his own heart beats to the rhythm of something older than the city, to remember a security more whole than that which comes from always watching your back, to remember a quality of caring for each other and the earth that the dollar could never buy. Tears welled in his eyes, but he still did not revoke Oxy's license to drill.[5]

We Transmuted the Anger with the US Government

Seven months after the murders, in the lead-up to the 2000 US presidential race, I read a *Wall Street Journal* editorial account of Vice President Al Gore's family's significant inheritance of Occidental Petroleum and Occidental subsidiary stock and his family's long-standing personal relationship with Occidental directors.[6] At the time, Gore was America's leading mainstream environmental champion. On the bookshelf of the Brooklyn apartment that I would have shared with Terence, there were two copies of Gore's book *Earth in the Balance*: my own, and, sitting next to it, Terence's.

I sat down and reread the poignant message Gore had asserted in 1993. He insisted that policy makers and the general citizenry alike must take into account the environmental and social cost of our coveted Northern affluence. I thought back to Terence's description of the time he met with Gore briefly in Washington, DC, at a gathering for the 1998 Goldman Environmental Prize recipients. Terence accompanied Berito to the meeting with Gore. How strong a statement of solidarity for the vice president of the United States to meet with an Indigenous leader from the cloud forest of Colombia, recognizing his people's adamant resistance to a US multinational oil company. Gore, Terence, the U'wa leader, and the principles of an earth in balance, standing there together in the garden for photos.

I was irked to see Gore continuing to profit personally from Occidental's exploits. I wanted him to think how much brighter his family's prospects would be if he removed the shadow cast by his family's complicity in the horrors faced by our family and those of the U'wa. I wanted him to divest his family from Occidental and answer the requests from the U'wa advocates to explain his position on that company's actions in U'wa territory. I also wanted him to engage his peers in Washington, at the development banks, in Bogotá, and the private sector in the sincere pursuit of alternatives to military escalation and fossil fuel extraction as the means to address Colombia's economic woes. I didn't want his silence on the U'wa-Occidental conflict—an emblem of the wider sustainable development debate he championed—to continue to corrode the standards he set for the American public with *Earth in the Balance*.

My colleagues in the anti-oil campaign created and executed a narrow approach to elicit comment and action from candidate Gore.[7] In support, I wrote an open letter to Gore as vice president, echoing these demands.[8] Representatives Barbara Lee and Cynthia McKinney sent Gore similar letters at the same time, additionally imploring Gore to meet with U'wa leaders. While Gore responded publicly that he could not interfere in a domestic Colombian matter, he told the representatives that, at his request, Secretary of State Madeleine Albright had spoken to Colombian president Pastrana about the precarity of the U'wa situation. This deflective action was a start. In my letter to Gore, I experimented with a parallel approach. I wanted to see what it would be like to try to bridge to our common humanity the way Thây practiced. I wrote:

> Look again at what stirred you to work for the earth in the first place. Take a minute from your campaign, go to the forest, any

forest. Take a walk alone. Feel the pulse of your heart beating in time with that of the rivers running. Feel the soil underfoot, like your muscles stretching, resilient and alive. Breathe in the blessing of being alive. Think of Terence and the U'wa working to defend that basic human right, of life. Think of the Colombian military last week forcibly removing U'wa families from their ancestral and legally owned land to provide armed and protected access to Occidental's equipment and staff houses. Think of the newly granted US budget for this very Colombian military, the largest sum given in history, making Colombia the third largest recipient of US military aid. Think twice about where you have chosen to put not only your family's money, but that of the taxpayer as well.

Gore responded privately to me that both he and Tipper read my letter, that my words touched their hearts, and that he was personally watching the U'wa situation "every step of the way." He remembered meeting Terence and Berito in 1998. He lauded Terence's calling and expressed sorrow for his death.[9] But he disposed of our demand that he divest his family from Occidental by saying that he was not the responsible trustee to take such action.[10]

Gore, together with Democratic party centrists, was eager to skirt the issue, hoping his back-channel engagement was enough to insulate the presidential campaign from the activists' threat. It was curious to me. I hadn't viewed our work as a threat. I had viewed it as an invitation to step up into leadership for the earth. I thought that's what we were talking about. Our superficial interaction with Al Gore tugged at a deeper hunch: to find the kind of leadership for the earth we needed, we would have to foster it elsewhere.

Our Grief Is Not a War Cry

All the while, the US-led criminal investigation of the murders ran in the background. By 2002, a grand jury in US District Court in Washington, DC, handed down an indictment that charged the

FARC and six FARC operators with homicide, conspiracy to commit homicide, using a firearm during a crime of violence, and aiding and abetting.[11] President Bush's attorney general John Ashcroft described the killings as terrorist murders and heralded the indictment as a significant step in the war on terror, concurrent with his administration's proposed $98 million in *additional* military aid to protect Occidental's operations in Colombia.[12]

By then I was in law school. The day the Department of Justice announced the indictment, I skipped class and stole away to the law school courtyard, where I sat on a cement bench tucked in at the foot of towering gingko trees, the trees of memory. I remember sitting with my laptop balanced on my knees, ear cocked, working by phone with Julie and Terence's friend Leslie to craft our response. In it, we objected to the administration's twinning of the pursuit of justice for Terence's murder with the pursuit of the war on terrorism in which more US dollars would go to train Colombian troops to defend the beleaguered Occidental oil operations there.[13] To amplify our voices, for the next several days we endured briefings and interviews, achieving sound bites at best.[14] For one television interview, the shirt I wore read "Our grief is not a war cry." The next year, when Colombia agreed to extradite one of the named defendants, we responded again to the press with this statement:

> While we appreciate the US prosecutors for moving forward on these criminal proceedings, we greet Colombia's extradition announcement with heavy hearts and lingering questions. We adamantly condemn FARC's actions, which the Colombian Supreme Court calls "extortive kidnapping and homicide," sometimes also known as kidnapping for ransom. In reality, though, no ransom was ever sought. For an extralegal armed actor such as the FARC whose modus operandi traditionally includes asking for ransom, we have to wonder why this case was an exception. Was no ransom asked because FARC had already been paid? We support the US criminal proceedings to the extent that the prosecutors are vigorously pursuing such inquiry.

Further, when we read that the US Congress has newly given millions of dollars for military protection of Occidental Petroleum's pipelines in rural Colombia, we cannot help but question whether the US oil company's continued presence in the region may be serving as a magnet for exactly the kind of armed violence that took the lives of Terence and his colleagues in 1999. What kind of thing does this US corporation do that requires 98 million dollars in guns and soldiers to protect? In evaluating this case, we support and encourage the federal prosecutors to ensure these questions are also on the table. Without answers regarding this wider context, the story doesn't square.[15]

The indictment and extradition regarded the men with the guns. I wasn't that interested in them. I wanted to know who paid for the guns and who gave the instructions to kill.

10

Tomales Bay

We Met Leadership in Defense of Mother Earth

When I started studying at Berkeley Law in the fall of 2001, I left the U'wa Defense Project in hands far more qualified than mine. With good people coaching me, I let go enough to watch the Project's new staff take the work under the umbrella of one of the larger organizations that had been part of the working group, where the Project has thrived through ups and downs all these years since.

After law school, I joined the board of EarthRights International and eventually served as co-chair. A much larger organization, EarthRights litigates on behalf of communities around the world against extractive industry companies and their financial backers. Serving EarthRights provided a platform where I could learn from and collaborate with a global set of peers and earth rights defenders whose life experiences, like mine, heightened our shared understanding of what is at stake when protocol is weak. Together with

EarthRights staff and global experts in the field, we ensured the strength of protocols for staff who engage in high-risk activities.

From a base near the Thailand-Burma border, EarthRights also runs advocacy and community leadership schools that attract young earth rights defenders. In one school that we learned about, Earth-Rights brought together young people from the headwaters to the delta of the Mekong River. Students from six countries learning about the rules of human and environmental rights—and how to organize and lead their communities to assert these rights. They learned how to stay safe as organizers in places where big companies have big guns. But they also learned and shared skills about how to talk with each other across the barriers of language, history, ethnicity, and culture. Where their elders may have been divided over generations, these young people, unified in the fight of their lives for the river they love, were learning how to hold both the pain and the beauty at the same time.[1]

At EarthRights I saw the kind of leadership in defense of Mother Earth that I believed in. How could we weave together this approach with that of U'wa leadership on the ground in Colombia?

We Fostered Leadership in Defense of Mother Earth

In the years immediately following the murders, U'wa elders instituted a temporary moratorium on international travel to the U'wa territory. They said that if they couldn't keep people safe when they were visiting, they didn't want them to come at all.[2] With Terence gone, and the moratorium in place, there were fewer opportunities to collaborate in person. Nonetheless, the international solidarity campaign ramped up, commensurate with the oil company's increasingly aggressive maneuvers and Pueblo U'wa's increasingly dire need for international witness of the violence being waged against the U'wa bodies that were blocking Oxy's way. By 2002 the campaign had prevailed: Occidental pulled out of U'wa territory, citing their failure to strike a viable well at Gibraltar. U'wa leadership and international supporters exhaled, celebrating the moment. They claimed the win as the result of the multifaceted international effort that spanned a decade of hard work—as well as the spiritual work of the Werjayá who had been diligent in their prayerful communications with the earth this whole time, requesting, as they would later tell it, the oil to move.

The sense of victory, however, was short-lived. The Colombian state oil concern Ecopetrol soon took over the drill site to pursue gas extraction. And with the US-based target of the anti-oil campaign gone, many of the US-based anti-oil campaigning organizations soon enough shifted their focus and resources away from the U'wa struggle. This shift happened even as U'wa leaders were vigilant to point out that their struggle for recognition of their territorial rights and self-determination was far from over.[3] At this point, with the U'wa Defense Project that Terence had begun already subsumed within one of the larger campaign-based organizations, prioritization of U'wa education and community-driven planning had taken a back seat. In February 2009, marking the tenth anniversary of the murders, a group of U'wa women wrote from their sacred lands to the families of the slain:

> What we had with our three friends was a new survival plan, one with socio-cultural, territorial, environmental, economic and political components, all in defense of the principles that characterize our people in this fight. Today, our just and noble fight is in serious crisis. With the loss of these three lives, we were robbed of an opportunity and the right to say what we think, to make our dreams a reality, to defend what is ours, to build a different world, to be free . . . We feel alone and orphaned when we think of the loss of all we had.[4]

The U'wa women, together with Ingrid, Lahe', and Terence, had sparked a flame. The murders extinguished it. But some of us still living wanted to find other ways to tend the underlying embers.

During those years, in our individual and collective capacities, U'wa allies channeled support so that U'wa youth could attend school without the "help" of Oxy. Selected by their community to receive these new scholarships, many U'wa youth set off to high school this way, with a commitment to come back home afterward to serve the community. These community scholars included U'wa boys and girls. U'wa girls, in receiving permission to go to school, had overcome the U'wa tradition of protecting girls from leaving the territory for education.[5] Indeed, by boarding in town and attending town schools, U'wa girls faced a pernicious and misogynist threat. U'wa girls' education included learning to navigate patriarchy in the many ways it shows up, from cultural prejudice to devastating and impairing psychological, physical, and sexual violence.

Aura, Daris's daughter who was nine at the time of the murders, made her way through high school supported by her family, and as a young adult she began working with the U'wa governing body. She wanted to go to law school. Her elders wanted her to go as well. With the help of many hands, at twenty-six years old, Aura became the first female, and second ever, U'wa lawyer. After law school, Aura secured an internship with the EarthRights office in Lima under the tutelage of seasoned Latin American human rights lawyers. There, Aura taught the non-Indigenous staff as much about community lawyering as she learned.

In her role as a legal advisor to the U'wa governing body, she became one of the leaders of two of the largest stands against state use of U'wa ancestral territory since she was a child. The first was a 2014 protest action against a natural gas exploration platform called Magallanes—a follow-on to Oxy's failed oil wells at Gibraltar—that included a twenty-day occupation of the station by the U'wa Indigenous guard, a three-month roadblock by the community, and direct negotiation with the Colombian government. In a historic, if limited, victory for the U'wa, the state oil and gas company Ecopetrol responded to the action by dismantling the Magallanes gas exploration platform.[6] The second demonstration was a multi-season action that began shortly thereafter to demand that the government close public access to, and thereby restore the dignity of, Zizuma, an ecologically fragile and sacred mountain top and headwaters in U'wa territory. Over Pueblo U'wa's objection, riowá continued to treat the area as a Colombian national park.

In the meantime, courts still had not answered Pueblo U'wa's earlier calls for accountability for the violence that public forces had rained down on the U'wa encampment that blocked Oxy's access to begin drilling at Gibraltar in 2000. Aura and U'wa leadership sought to bring justice to the U'wa in defense of self-determination, including at the sites of Gibraltar, Magallanes, and Zizuma. In December 2016, Aura and U'wa leadership, in collaboration with EarthRights lawyers Juliana Bravo Valencia, Marissa Vahlsing, Wyatt Gjullin, and Colombian counterparts, submitted legal briefing on the merits, thus reviving the community's long-standing petition at the Inter-American Commission on Human Rights.[7]

On September 28, 2019, the Commission found Colombia responsible for human rights violations under the American Convention on Human Rights. In their report, the Commission detailed recommendations the Colombian government would need to act upon right away to comply with the Commission's decisions and to avoid the case being sent to the Inter-American Court of Human Rights. For the government to comply, they would have to adopt legislative measures to guarantee the right to free, prior, and informed consent and the recognition of ancestral territory in Colombia; guarantee Pueblo U'wa's right to its ancestral territory; provide reparations for the damages from the last two decades; provide the U'wa with other assurances to judicial and administrative remedies; and adopt all necessary measures to ensure that extractive projects directly affecting the U'wa that do not comply with consultation and consent requirements under international law do not continue, and that new ones are not initiated. Pueblo U'wa's demands of the government of Colombia went beyond what the Commission recommended, in focusing on the full realization of the right to self-determination, but even so, the government of Colombia did not comply with the Commission's lesser demands.

In October 2020, the Commission decided to refer the U'wa case on the merits to the Inter-American Court of Human Rights. That decision meant that the U'wa Nation's claims against the government of Colombia would finally be heard in an international tribunal, a forum with the power to issue an injunction against the Colombian government and order it to pay damages.

Aura had cultivated the capacity to broker knowledge in the highest courts of the land while staying rooted in the values and practices of her traditional culture. By age twenty-nine, in 2020, she won election as mayor of her hometown and served with impact. From the rivers of southeast Asia to the cloud forests of northeastern Colombia, it is this kind of leadership in defense of Mother Earth that I respect, nurture, and follow.

You Are Holding the Key—It Is Time to Unlock the Door

Three years before the U'wa case would be referred to the human rights court, Aura came to the US to participate in the World Indigenous Law Conference. The conference would allow her to update an international Indigenous audience about the most recent developments in the U'wa campaign for community defense. My colleague Dr. Sandra Álvarez and I hosted Aura. Sandra taught political science at Chapman University and had been walking alongside U'wa women leaders as both a scholar and an ally since shortly after the murders.[8] She worked through a volunteer organization called Mujer U'wa that she co-founded with other Indigenous and US Colombian, Latina, and Indigenous North American women, an initiative of women defenders of the culture.

In the days before the conference, Aura, Sandra, and I took time to sit with the whole story of community resistance from Aura's perspective as she came of age into community leadership. We sat as a trio on my bedroom floor, the diffuse winter sun scattering across the room. Aura reminded me of some pieces of the story that U'wa elders were left holding after the murders. The fragments were familiar to me but buried. They were about the circumstances of the kidnapping—circumstances that, if substantiated, would expand the scope of our query. Years before, U'wa elders had shared with me the fragments, but to protect living people, we recognized a lonely truth: we could do nothing to try to piece together the fragments without increasing the threat to more people's lives. In response, I had stowed the stories deeply away in the pockets of my memory. As Aura reminded me of some of the U'wa elders' experiences, I reeled. With her words, Aura stirred my memory and gingerly invited me anew to share the burden of grappling with the stories we had tucked away.

Later that day, as dusk fell, we were looking through my files for some U'wa documents—copies of the colonial titles. With Aura at the helm as a community lawyer, the legal team was ready to use the colonial titles again as part of the argument before the Inter-American Commission of Human Rights. But the copy of the colonial titles held for safekeeping in the U'wa office in Colombia was off-limits to Aura directly, because she was a woman. It was believed that the colonial titles contained a powerful energy with which U'wa elders did not want a young U'wa woman to come into contact. So to help the stateside legal team working with Aura, we needed to secure a copy, and my files were one possible source. Later that evening, once we finally located the colonial titles in the basement files of another colleague, our conversation shifted to Aura's final agenda item, that of the potent dream life that she and her mom, Daris, were experiencing.

Aura and Daris had been dreaming in tandem scenes of territorial defense. Daris wanted me to know that Terence had been coming to her in her dreams repeatedly with the same message again and again. In her recurrent dream, Terence said, "You are holding the key. It is time to unlock the door." When Aura relayed this message, Sandra, Aura, and I sat in silence. I turned to their eyes for any instruction about what I should do now.

In the months following Aura's 2016 visit, I told Julie about Daris's dream. *You are holding the key. It is time to unlock the door.* With a heavy sigh, Julie, too, sat in thoughtful silence. Her silence was an active tempering, an internal negotiation with overwhelm—the overwhelm that seeps in through the edges for either of us when that door is even marginally opened.

"Do what you want with that information, but don't let it take over your life again." She said it not in defeat, but in defiance. The wry defiance of a mother who has lost her child. She was saying it's not worth it if it stretches you too far. If you're going to act on this, do it in a way that doesn't tip the balance. *Everything now must be done in a sacred way.*[9]

What Does It Take to Unlock the Door?

I worked with Julie's instruction. How do we act on this imperative in a manner that does not tip the balance? In a manner that does not repeat the violence? How do we ready ourselves for taking that leap? I have come to believe that we have been readying ourselves all along.

In one way, the murders halted our momentum. In rural northeastern Colombia at the close of the twentieth century, an oil pipeline, together with the machinery and allure of new extraction, drew armed violence to the region, creating the conditions for the 1999 kidnappings and murders in U'wa territory. The violation stole more than their lives. The violation also encompassed the forceful and wrongful imposition of a hubristic worldview, which is only possible when the people doing the imposing have been cut off from their connection to their root cultures and the earth. The oil company and the imminent permits to drill at Gibraltar violated Pueblo U'wa's right to self-determination. The U'wa responded by reaching out to us to aid in their defense. When we answered the call, we did so in ways that revealed our own disconnection from root cultures and the earth. But these were the ways available to us in that time. Terence, Ingrid, and Lahe' knew different ways. The U'wa communities knew different ways.

The murders stole from us the agility to pursue deeper strategies, ideas, and plans that draw from a much deeper well than reactivity allows. The oil company may not have even known this weakness. Their violence—the violence of imposing oil projects that bring ecological and cultural death—defined the terms of the game. And they beat us on those terms. They beat us in that, in the region where they were operating, the voices were extinguished of three of the people who were going in deep with the U'wa to define and assert a different set of terms, indeed, an entirely different game. The game of maintaining the equilibrium and reweaving the web of life.

That violation enrages me still. At the ten-year anniversary of the murders in 2009, U'wa leadership still characterized the murders as having halted progress toward their vision for people-centered development. To be sure, there have been important victories and mobilizations during this time, but the murders undeniably set us back.

Terence might say that our biggest victory is that we did not succumb to their violence in return. While the murders halted momentum, we responded by sending a lot of the work underground. I would like to think that the time underground was critical for regrouping, reconfiguring, retooling ourselves into the people we needed to be to answer the community's call with the depth and rigor demanded. To discover who we needed to be to maintain the equilibrium and reweave the web of life. To defend the sanctity of the earth temple so that all hearts may come back home.

These very metamorphoses currently capture the imagination of people who shape many of today's progressive social movements that aim for transformation. If Terence was right that we are holding the key, what does it take to unlock the door?

To Learn to Live with the Flux

After Aura's 2016 visit to our southern California home, I went north to turn myself squarely to these tugging questions. I went to Mesa Refuge, a house on the San Andreas fault north of San Francisco.

Mesa Refuge is a place for writing at the edge of the restored wetlands of Tomales Bay. Looking below from atop the mesa, I could not tell whether to call it water or land. Like grief, the terrain was in constant flux.

Historically in Tomales Bay, this ambiguity had led some humans to levy and barricade the valley to control the flow of the water, confinement that endured for a century. It was a place that reminded me of the commercial fishponds in the Palawan of my youth, constructed on top of the drowning mangrove forest. As with the fishponds half a world away, there in Tomales Bay, it turned out that control of the waters was killing us; the ecosystem was dying. The humans of this coastal town engaged a deliberative and lengthy community reckoning to figure out what to do. They chose to unlock the door.

While writing, I walked down below the mesa, traversing the remnants of the floodgates they opened. They let the water flow in and out again, giving the wetlands a chance to equilibrate. The habitat restored itself. Within two years, the number of migrating bird species doubled. The resilience of this place was instructive. To unlock the door is to set the intention to get ourselves back into right relationship and do what it takes to invite the whole to come along with us. It is messy and uncertain. It requires us to learn to live with the flux.

11

The Mahwāēw River

I Let the Current Take Me

The Colombian peace process began spelling out the rules for the FARC's demobilization and transition to civilian participation in 2016. At the same time, it prepared to invite families like Terence's to enter the formal process of the Truth and Recognition Chamber. During this transition, the FARC advanced a parallel process called a peace delegation. In a set of activities guaranteed by Norway, hosted by Cuba, and facilitated by Spain, the FARC sought to arrange opportunities to reconcile and apologize for specific past wrongs in hopes of inching FARC ex-combatants further from future prosecution in Colombian criminal courts. In so doing, the FARC identified three particularly heinous and high-profile acts for which they sought to orchestrate private apologies followed by high-profile public expressions of reparation. Our case, the case of "los tres indigenistas," or "the three Indigenous rights activists," as it had anomalously become known in Colombia, was one of them.

While the FARC's original invitation was to convene in Cuba, Ingrid's husband and family instead invited representatives from all three families to meet with the FARC legal advisor on the Menominee reservation, Ingrid's ancestral land in northeastern Wisconsin. Terence's friend Leslie and I, representing Terence's family, had arrived the night before and stayed at the casino hotel on the outer edge of the reservation. The next morning, we drove to the meeting place.

Settling in, we shared greetings with those in attendance. I hadn't entered the gathering alert for hostility. But as I made the rounds, I came to understand that anger was present. And it was directed not entirely at the FARC, but also, in part, at me.

I had heard that some people blamed Terence for acting recklessly, a blame that was at times tucked into a generalized critique of non-Indigenous environmental organizing and solidarity campaigning. I could understand that blame; it is a common reaction after shared tragedy, and I had felt angry at Terence, too. But I didn't know that, over time and by extension, some people had also been blaming me. Maybe others shielded me from it. I had sensed its contour in the lonely distance that existed between the families and myself during the intervening decades, but I didn't understand it until that day.

When Terence, Ingrid, and Lahe' went to Colombia, the three of them traveled together. They envisioned their next big work in the world, together. During the kidnapping, the three families agonized through the hard work of the release efforts, together. The three families sat stunned together in the hours and days following the murders, listening to the wailing song of the drum. Each in our own way, we watched as the murders ripped apart the lives of our families and stripped us of agency. For myself, I moved through this time thinking we were having a shared experience—again, a common reaction to atrocity. Right away, Indigenous organizations and tribal governments associated with Ingrid or with Terence's own work had written heartfelt condolences to Julie, noting her son's courage and thanking him for his work.[1] But after we went our separate ways to bury our dead, we did not reconvene. For the most part, Terence's family was not involved in activities that various Indigenous nations together engaged after the burials. I had attributed that dispersion to the need for Indigenous-to-Indigenous space and to the fragmentation of grief. For both, I had much compassion and respect. Every time the world celebrated Ingrid's decorated life and grieved in a public way for the loss of her, I stayed away out of that respect. I had also stayed away because it was too painful for me, in the absence of a shared understanding about why our families were moving through that time separately, to watch Terence be set aside as stories of loss got told on the global stage. I didn't understand the full picture, and I stayed away.

Until that day, seventeen years later, I didn't understand that there was a specific grievance directed at me. The grievance was that I could have and should have done more to prevent this tragedy from happening. That I should have amplified further the severity of the security risk involved in traveling to rural Colombia, to a disputed oil drilling site, in the middle of the armed conflict, to prevent them from going to Colombia at all. That I should have amplified further the risk that Terence, specifically, faced in the zone and more effectively discouraged Terence from working with Ingrid and Lahe' to travel to U'wa territory. That during the kidnapping, if I had been more vocal about the risk Terence faced, it could have led us to respond to the kidnappers with a different strategy.

I learned that this assessment was present—that I had not done enough to save them—within the first five minutes of my arrival at the 2016 gathering, as we attempted to make our greetings. A few minutes later, we sat at the meeting table for the morning session. With care, I set aside the bundle of hurt so that I could focus on the FARC lawyer's proposal.

He came prepared to broker a reconciliation. He presented an outline for a public event we could host in Cuba or in Colombia itself, in which the FARC would apologize and the families would forgive. But Leslie and I had come prepared with a series of questions for the FARC lawyer about the relationship between the FARC and Occidental during that period of the Colombian conflict. From comparative cases and political science literature, we knew that, in Colombia and elsewhere, multinational corporations have paid guerrilla organizations, paramilitaries, and even some military leaders for protection of their facilities.[2] This includes oil companies. From Oxy's own congressional testimony, we knew that Oxy's contractors and workers had been paying the FARC a war tax and protection money for operating in the region during the time of the murders.[3]

The FARC lawyer did not know how to factor in the questions that remained unanswered about the relationship between the FARC and Occidental. Answering those questions was not part of the formula that the FARC had sent him to lay out. It appeared that the FARC lawyer came to us with the assumption that the facts of this case had been established and settled long ago. Flustered, he asked us rhetorically in return, "Why didn't you examine that question years ago? Why raise it now?"

While my body stayed in my seat, his questions sent my heart flying. It felt impossible to respond even though the answers were basic. In the aftermath of the murders, people in the zone had questioned whether FARC members were helping Occidental move its oil drilling equipment into place. But even with the best legal and community organizing team in the world, conditions were not in place to ensure that an investigation wouldn't be met with more killing.

The other factor was that the murders ripped us apart. While I kept waiting for a time when we together, the three families, could turn squarely to the investigation of the facts, the reality was we couldn't do that work together. For Terence's family, we prioritized staying in the background as many skillful hands worked to create conditions to allow for the possibility of reweaving some of the fabric of connection between Pueblo U'wa and Ingrid's and Lahe''s families. The U'wa did not refer to Ingrid and Lahe' as "indigenistas." To the U'wa, Ingrid and Lahe' were "hermanas U'was de otros pueblos," or U'wa sisters from other nations; the ripped fabric was unbearable. To make space for the possibility of reweaving was paramount. The process unfolded in a manner that preserved autonomy and moved in its own time. Any robust and coordinated investigation of the facts had had to wait.

That morning, Leslie and I did not respond to the FARC lawyer's rhetorical questions. The meeting that day was not being facilitated very skillfully, and I was not in a position to fix it. There was no safety in that room. I watched myself retreat.

During the lunch break, I walked outside, crossed the parking lot, and traversed the knee-high grasses of an adjacent open field. When I came to the edge of the woods, I stopped. I waited, standing there in the humidity of the sticky autumn grasses, breathing. I waited and called my heart home.

That afternoon, the FARC's public relations proposal did not result in an agreement. And soon enough Colombia's formal peace process would supersede this early attempt by the FARC. There, too, detailed truths about the facts of each case would take a back seat. As in many transitional justice processes, Colombia's Truth and Recognition Chamber would be tasked with investigating broad truths regarding the patterns and practices of violence during the war rather than specifics of each instance of devastation. And although the accompanying truth commission would elicit survivors' stories as a technology of memory, it would not be invested with a strong investigative function.[4] Unbeknownst to us at the time, the meeting with the FARC lawyer foreshadowed the need for us to continue to hold our questions with forbearance.

Nevertheless, after the meeting concluded, a few life-changing things happened for me. First, although officially we were there to consider the FARC's proposal for apology, during the in-between times, the ground was softened among the families in a way that created conditions in which I could attempt to repair what I had not realized was torn. To the extent that I could, I apologized on Terence's behalf. I apologized for Terence's shortcomings, and I apologized that they were killed. On behalf of myself, I apologized for my shortcomings, and I apologized that they were killed. My heart beat steadily within the temple of my awareness.

Second, conditions were created for us to visit the bank of the Mahwāēw River, a main tributary that runs through the Menominee Nation. It was August hot. The sky refused to open, even with the close of the day. The day itself had ached, swaying under the weight of our visit. Something had to give.

When we got to the river's edge, the moving water provided a feeling of mercy. Within the Menominee Nation, with permission, I swam briefly in the Mahwāēw River. I let the current take me. It was a soft way to greet this place in the language of surrender. I floated on my back down the river and let the water pull me toward the bend. The trees along the banks crowded in, fecund with summer's end. The current was moderate, and the water eddied out often; I could have exited the river from an eddy with ease. But there was no safe harbor on land for me that day.

I Turned Back to Butterfly Upstream

Instead, I turned back to butterfly upstream.

When I rejoined the others atop the rocky bank, I knew that I had reached my own limit. I wanted to crawl into a hole, mortified as I was to have realized that day the expanse of the space between us. At the very same time, it was a kindness to have been invited to join the others for dinner that night. A kindness I readily accepted. Instead of crawling into a hole, I went to dinner, where the ground was mercifully further softened.

Later I learned that *Mahwāēw* means the one who howls, the one who cries. It refers to a wolf. The Mahwāēw River then is also known as the Wolf River. You can go to the river with your howl and your cry and let the water take it.

At the Mahwāēw, I began to understand what it means to let the water take it. And to still meet up back on the shore. The message I got was: Everybody's working with the hand they have been dealt. And everybody's trying their best. It is your job to figure out how to stay when staying is needed. It's your job to figure out what work is yours to do, and what is not. When you figure it out, do that work, and don't delay. The day is hot, and it's only getting hotter. Surrender to the current, and at the very same time, when there is work still left to do, turn and move yourself back upstream. The reprieve is in the discernment. There may not be redemption. But when you learn how to read the water, discernment brings reprieve.

12

A Tangle of Frozen
Bramble, Glistening

We Did Our Best in the Time We Were Given

One morning a few months later, during the 2016 World Indigenous Law Conference, I had a sidebar conversation with Chief Oren
Lyons. Chief Lyons is a Faithkeeper of the Turtle Clan of the Onondaga Nation, whose shared ancestral territory encompasses much
of the northeastern United States. Together with Ingrid and many
others, Chief Lyons advocated for decades to shape and assert the
rights ultimately adopted in the 2007 United Nations Declaration on the Rights of Indigenous Peoples. At the 2016 conference,
reflecting with Chief Lyons, I questioned whether I could have and
should have done more to gain and share a fuller understanding of
the level of threat that Terence faced in Colombia. And if the threat
level had been more widely understood, whether we would have han-
dled the kidnapping differently. Recognizing the weight with which

I was carrying it, Chief Lyons recalled his own actions during the kidnapping and the massive amount of coordination and work that we all did. He said to make sure people know that we all did the best we could. That we did everything we could have done in the time we were given. And that the kidnapping and murders were not our fault. That fault rests with the FARC.

I was grateful for Chief Lyons's clarity. It has still taken me years to internalize the clarity myself. *The kidnapping and murders were not our fault.* Right. *And,* if I could turn back the clock, would I do anything differently? Absolutely. I am sorry that, as the person closest to Terence at that time, I did not intervene more assertively and effectively during their planning discussions before the trip. I am sorry that I did not insist upon them sharing a written version of their safety, security, and contingency plan. I am sorry that I did not insist that any such plan be vetted by chosen loved ones before embarking. I am sorry that I trusted the momentum and urgency that the three generated before the trip. I am sorry that I made myself small inside the American Indian Community House during the kidnapping. I am sorry that I lacked experience and prescience, that I didn't know enough to shout from the rafters that we needed to scour the intelligence from a different angle to get underneath the FARC's motive. I am sorry that I did not understand for all these years that there was a silence I needed to answer. I am sorry *and* the kidnapping and murders were not our fault.

Two Women Reweave

During that same conference, Aura met for the first time Dr. Henrietta Mann. Dr. Mann, a member of the Cheyenne and Arapaho Tribes of Oklahoma, is a renowned Native American scholar and activist credited as a key designer of several Native American Studies programs at universities across the United States. She presided over some of the activities at the 2016 conference.

After Aura gave a keynote address alongside Chase Iron Eyes of the Standing Rock Sioux, Dr. Mann approached Aura to tell her what

Ingrid had meant to her. In reply, Aura showed Dr. Mann a photograph of an U'wa girl who was named after Ingrid. The girl's mother, when she herself was a child, had been around the periphery during the 1999 meetings with Ingrid, Terence, and Lahe' in U'wa territory. When pregnant years later, the young mother asked Daris to ask Ingrid's husband for his blessing to name the new baby girl after Ingrid. Ingrid's husband gave Daris the blessing to use the Menominee name for Flying Eagle Woman, as Ingrid had been known. Aura shared this story with Dr. Mann.

Watching them talk briefly, Dr. Mann and Aura, I felt a sense of heaviness. The weight, or gravity, of these two Indigenous women leaders talking. One an elder and one very young. From very different communities and yet connected by this painful shared history. Then I realized that I, myself, observing them, had imported the sense of heaviness. Watching them, I realized they were just having an interaction. The past was present. The hurt of the past was present. But it wasn't heavy. It just *was*. In fact, it was quite lovely, this way of remembering and honoring Ingrid. I glimpsed the possibility that someday perhaps it wouldn't feel so heavy to me. Perhaps it would just *be*. The possibility brought relief.

Get Our Hearts up off the Ground

Some years ago, I participated in facilitating a subgroup during a national training hosted by, among others, Tom Goldtooth and Casey Camp Horinek. Tom is from the Diné and Dakota tribal communities and is the director of the Indigenous Environmental Network. Grandmother Casey is an elder from the Southern Ponca Tribe in what we now call Oklahoma. She played a lead role in the fight to stop the Keystone XL tar sands pipeline expansion and is the founding chairwoman of the Movement Rights board. Over the course of the training's few days, those of us who had known and worked with Terence, Ingrid, and Lahe' years back found each other and exchanged stories.

At the training's closing circle, Tom said, "We take care of our wounded warriors. And this is how we do it. We have a wounded war-rior here and we want to welcome her back into our circle. I am from the Bear Clan and we take care when we see one of us whose heart is on the ground. We help lift that heart back up. Terry came and taught our communities about the mining laws. He came as an ally into this work, and he sacrificed his life for it."

With that, four women joined Tom in the center of the circle and pulled me there. Grandmother Casey said, "Sometimes you need to be scolded by an elder. I am giving you that scolding. It's too long. You are done. You are done grieving them. Let them go into the spirit world. Don't hold on to them any longer. You have work to do in the world and they have work to do in the spirit world and you all need to be getting to it."

She turned her gaze to Tom and said, "You, too, Tom." Tom started to tear up, remembering. In that moment, a burden lifted; I understood that I was not the only one carrying this story of Ter-ence's goodness. I could carry the story in my heart, and still let it go. Tom then told a story that an elder had told him. Four men had come to the territory. They waited on the edge of the territory for a whole day, waited because they knew they could not just walk in without being invited. Finally, toward dusk, a member of the community walked to the periphery of the territory and said hello, welcoming them in.

Grandmother Casey said, "In our culture, we'd be stroking and combing your hair, to comb the grief out of your hair. We are here coming to tell you it is time now." The woman from Hawaii sang a song. The woman from California offered words. Grandmother Casey said, "I am giving you this medicine with all the love that comes with it."

She hugged me. Her shoulders cascaded in movement as she too wept. In my mind's eye, I saw a fluttering of wings, large and rapid and dark, arcing from the southwest toward the southeast. Unstop-pable, the birds moved swiftly, with work to be done, with a known target, with a known set of challenges, with dexterity and agility, flying together, as though having been unleashed. As though they knew the time was now. And they were moving forward with the work. Almost regardless. Almost regardless of who was ready, and who was not ready. Grandmother Casey said, "It's time."

Movement Strategy Lessons from the Jemez

Tom remembered that Terence had come and taught them mining law. He was their ally. He was welcomed in. He is missed. In describing Terence this way, Tom helped ease my own guarded inquiry about the extent to which Terence had been a welcome ally or a fool.

The summer after we buried Terence, I returned to the Vallecitos Mountain Retreat Center in the Tusas Mountains near Taos. It had been five months since the murders. Walking one morning, I saw as if for the first time the expanse of the land, down by the river to the east. The jutting cliff face, large, cut sharply into the valley. I saw Terence big in that expanse and felt for the first time a mourning for our species that we lost him. I was mourning Terence the earth rights defender, mourning the loss for the earth. I felt for the first time the grief in the loss of our potential to manifest as a pair of earth rights defenders. I mourned finally how sad it was that he was torn from this life that he loved, *loved*. The relationships with people here on earth that he relished. Corralling kittens with his younger brother Kian. Kayaking with his little sister Jennifer. All the things here on earth that he savored, that he saw in the essence and loved at the elemental level.

Terence is buried in the foothills of the Jemez Mountains in New Mexico. In the Jemez, a few years prior, folks from various parts of the environmental justice movement had come together to draft principles of democratic organizing. It was during that time that Tom and Terence were working on education in Indigenous North American communities about mining law. The Jemez principles are: to be inclusive, to emphasize bottom-up organizing, to let people speak for themselves, to work together in solidarity and mutuality, to build just relationships among ourselves, and to commit to self-transformation.[1] Terence lived guided by these principles.

Underneath these principles lives the concept of protocol: on any given land where you are operating your life, take care to learn the protocols of the peoples who are of that land, and then organize your operations in alignment with those protocols. An Acjachemen auntie once reminded me that sometimes protocol means taking time. You may wait at the edge of the territory. It takes as long as it takes. Do what's yours to do, and don't leave it halfway done. But let it have the time it needs. The parts that are not yours, don't try to fix them. There's nothing to fix. Learn to move with the broken pieces.

We Stand on the Shoulders of Giants

In the late fall of 2018, I returned to the Mahwāēw River as part of an encuentro, or exchange, among social change workers who called themselves "community rebuilders" from both the Menominee Nation and a mix of community organizations from Santa Ana with whom I collaborated in my work at the University of California.[2] The snow had already arrived. For some southern Californians in our delegation, it was a first.

We piled into vans to see more of the Menominee territory while our hosts described key moments and landmarks in the tribe's history. At one of our first stops, the delegation stood at the junction above the rocky slope where I swam during the late summer two years earlier. The junction is one of the places where the Menominee Nation stood to negotiate with the government of the United States during the treaty era. Those same rocky slopes also became a symbol of resistance and vigilance more recently when, in defense of the river, communities mobilized and defeated a proposed metallic sulfide ore mine that would have wreaked havoc on the waters. Around the time of our visit, this protective action continued in a parallel campaign to stop permitting of another proposed sulfide ore mine. This time the effort was to protect the Menominee River to the northeast and, in turn, the entire Great Lakes watershed into which both rivers eventually run.

Later that day, a young Menominee woman took me aside. Although she was just a child when it happened, she knew the story of Ingrid, Terence, and Lahe'. We were standing in the new snow next to the front grill of a pickup truck outside the community rebuilders' office. Behind her, a tangle of frozen bramble glistened as it caught the setting sun. Beyond the bramble, fields lay fallow, nestled in for the winter.

She took me aside, in part, to let me know that, through her spiritual gift, she could see that Terence was there with us and that he was happy we were connecting. He was also worried that I was still holding so many pieces of this story. She described an image of me trying to gather and hold many pieces of paper. I took that information in, thanking her, familiar as I had become with Terence showing up like this from time to time. As we continued talking, two new realities became available to me that had not been available before.

First, our conversation helped me place Terence back into temporal context. She reflected, "Terence was young. He may have done stupid things." I agreed. Terence agreed, too. His notebook from March 1998 reflects, "My life is this: brave, stupid, lucky. Brave, stupid, lucky. Stupid, brave, brave, lucky."[3]

Terence was young and may have done stupid things. Letting that be so created the counterweight I needed to reinstate the agency that Ingrid and Lahe' also each had as community leaders almost twice his age in choosing to travel to U'wa territory that fateful winter. Could it be that, in choosing to go, Ingrid, Terence, and Lahe' had sized each other up—two experienced organizers and one youth organizer—and assessed that, on balance, the strengths they each brought mitigated their weaknesses? As a trio, the pull to go was strong. Could it be that, on some fundamental level, going was what the truth demanded of them?

We will never know the answers to these questions. But we do know that we live in a world in which some people live in constant danger and other people choose to accompany them in the struggle. Terence, Ingrid, and Lahe' each made the choice to go and stand with a community in which they knew people were facing tremendous risk to their lives and in so doing put their own lives at risk. Speaking only for himself, Terence's notebook from March 1998 reflected his perspective on this dynamic: "After talking with [U'wa leader] Roberto Pérez, I again couldn't see why I shouldn't risk my life if he and so many other U'wa were risking theirs."[4] I could comprehend their individual and collective choices to go, *and* as someone who lost a lot, I had to acknowledge that I was often furious at them for making it.

Second, my young Menominee colleague pointed out that one lasting societal effect of their choices, perhaps the most important one, was to help make a way for us to be where we are now. From her perspective, social movement mobilizations like Standing Rock and so many others around the world were seeded and fertilized in part by the vision, work, bravery, and sacrifice of people like Ingrid, Lahe', and Terence, together with the communities they walked alongside—communities at the heart of the rise of climate justice. Like we always said, we stand on the shoulders of giants. Despite his youth, Terence was one of those giants.

During our conversation, I stopped acquiescing to versions of the story in which Terence was a one-dimensional character—either lionized or demonized. I stopped taking the brunt of defending him. I stopped identifying myself so closely with him. Finally, I could look at him, from my perch here among the living, and say, "Yeah. Terence was young. He may have done stupid things. I'm allowed to be angry at him for that. *And* we stand on the shoulders of giants." As if a door in my mind had opened, letting the cold wind rush in, I was free to see Terence clearly as someone with faults *and* as the fierce, bold, visionary, strategic, humble servant of social justice that he also was. At the twenty-year mark, I went ahead and acknowledged him that way. Both. And.

Redirection

In reflecting on these various interactions, I also had to acknowledge that it was a distraction to think we could have controlled the outcome. Getting killed may have been unpreventable had they or we made no mistakes. The notion that their deaths were preventable rested on the idea that the responsibility lodged with someone other than the people who killed them. On top of that, accountability often escapes the people who are responsible for *initiating* cycles of violence. Instead, we live in a culture that blames victims for the violence they experience. That cultural norm has had an enormous impact on my life.[5] Once I could see the distraction, I stopped careening. I redirected my focus. First on myself. Then on my U'wa companions. And then on the perpetrators and sponsors of the violence.

Part 3

I don't want to stay folded anywhere,
because where I am folded,
there I am a lie.

13

Shell Beach

I Tasted Freedom Like I Tasted Salt

From the corners of my mouth, I tasted freedom like I tasted salt. It was the spring of 2018 at Mesa Refuge and I was taking a break from writing. I was floating on my back in the brackish waters off Shell Beach, carried by the wind and tide deeper into Tomales Bay. The sky was brilliant and open blue. Every so often the treetops lining the peninsula peeked in. I let the tide take me. After a spell, I turned and butterflied back to shore. Paddleboarding and then biking back to the writing refuge through the town of Inverness, I felt the earth stretch out before me and I was at home, alone in the choices before me. Unencumbered. Without brackets. Without shifting tone or voice. Just me and the world. At home.

When I got back to the house, I took a nap, which I never do. After I awoke, Julie called. We'd been playing phone tag for a year. As we caught up, I told her I'd spent the last two weeks writing myself into a better understanding of what it means to be beholden to her son, absent for the last twenty years. I told her that I'd done this writing from a porch overlooking the restored wetlands of the Tomales back bay, looking across into the hills of Inverness, and beyond that the sea. I told her about swimming at Shell Beach, where the bay current pulled me out gently and I was free.

"Abby. Do you remember?" She reminded me that Terence was born in Inverness. He was born in these hills I'd been staring at for the past two weeks. She told me about his birth.

Julie had come north from San Francisco to a doctor here in Inverness because he was willing to accompany her through a home birth when others were not. This was a time when midwives were being arrested for practicing. Dilated to two centimeters, she walked those hills with the doctor and his two daughters. After the walk, her body was open, and the doctor welcomed her to give birth in his own home. Terence's head crowned in brow presentation, which meant that the circumference of his head would require the largest possible opening of the birth canal. The baby needed to turn to prevent injury. The doctor didn't have those skills in his hands, so he asked a midwife to come over. When the midwife entered the door, the energy in the house changed, and so did Julie's body. The baby turned, adjusting his head, slipping out into the world with his mother intact.

I hadn't remembered this story. Julie and I sat silently on the phone. It was always like that with us.

The first year after the murders, Julie and I talked on the phone every day, sharing the private hell of grief. When nothing felt normal, at least we could share the company of Terence's absence. As time passed, we came to treat each other as extended family, sharing a holiday here, a vacation there. I found myself turning to Julie for more ordinary matters, like tips on which vendors to frequent at the Hollywood farmers' market, or how to really leave the next few relationships I attempted. As I pined for a child of my own, Julie insisted that motherhood would come my way if and when I was ready for it, perhaps when I least expected it.

Which is what happened.

I met Sunil Gandhi at a sushi restaurant in Alameda, California. I had just finished taking the bar exam and had braided my long, thick, unruly hair in two plaits down my back. We went bowling and he told me he admired my form. Sunil is an expert in developmental neuro-biology. His passion is discovery of the mechanisms of the mind. He has the ambition and capacity to change medicine. I recognized his commitment to have an impact on the world and was drawn to it. Earlier that year, his mother had given him an ultimatum to settle in with a partner and start the householder phase of his life. By the time I learned of her ultimatum, I was already onboard. Undaunted by my dramatic past, Sunil knew how to step forward again and again to meet me in the bigness of my life and my need. He did not shrink away or seek safe harbor. Soon enough, he, in fact, became my safe harbor.

Sunil and I were very lucky; we tumbled right into parenthood. As we prepared for each homebirth, Julie was our sounding board for childbirth decisions. When our boys were little, she was the one I called for reassurance that it was okay if our toddler refused to eat dinner one night or if we let our newborn fall asleep on his side. I liked what she taught me about letting go enough to allow the kids to find their own way. I found it to be easier said than done.

From my vantage with very young children at the time, I could barely feel the contours of what it would take for me to let go when the time was right. To trust not only my children but also the world that would receive them. I found it difficult to fathom. I thought of Julie. How do you trust as your child moves out into the world? Is it a matter of holding your breath and hoping for the best? How do you ever trust again when your oldest child comes home in a casket? When Julie keened at the sight of the casket at the United Cargo hangar, someone reflected that her cries that night were of the kind uttered universally and only by mothers who have lost their children. I have not been privy to the sounds of many, if any, other mothers grieving. When my boys were babies, thinking about Julie's loss would make my milk let down.

Yeshi Neumann, one of San Francisco's beloved homebirth mid-wives, prescribed the Buddhist practice of tonglen to cope with this strong desire for our children to be alright. People often use tonglen to get a handle on otherwise unmanageable anger or jealousy—or any strong desire that has the practitioner in its grip. Tonglen teaches that it is not about holding your breath and just hoping for the best. Tonglen cultivates compassion toward one's own suffering through awareness of the universality of that suffering. It helps the practitioner understand which aspects of the desire they can control (the suffering) and which they cannot (the pain inherent in the strength of the desire for a certain outcome).

In this case, the midwife invited me to use tonglen to work with the suffering that comes with the universal desire of mothers for their children to thrive. She invited me to breathe in the desperate desire of mothers everywhere for their children to be okay and the suffering that mothers everywhere experience because of it. Then hold these mothers in the mind's eye as the breath pauses at the cusp. Then breathe out relief to the mothers. I was to include myself among those receiving relief. Tonglen, like prayer, does not promise resolution of the strong desire. It promises, with practice, only relief. Relief from the wanting and the misperception of control over the outcome. Compassion for being in the rough and tumble of it. I thought of Julie. I breathed in and out.

In the summer of 2009, our family stayed at Julie's house during a visit back to Los Angeles from San Francisco. My pregnancy with Julian was just starting to show. At Grandma Julie's house, our older son, Kiran, was in toddler heaven. Vintage Fisher-Price farmhouse toys and an actual farmhouse out back with real hens, bunnies, and turtles to feed. Kiran trailed Julie around the yard and neighborhood, returning home barefoot with muddy knees and a huge smile—a testament of true little-boy delight.

On our last afternoon, Julie went out to the garage. She came back in with Terence's baby blanket. She wanted us to have it for our boys. It seemed right. We accepted the tremendous gift with an easy love.

The next year, I put a picture of Terence up in our house. It was the first time I had done so in the decade since the murders. It hung in Kiran and Julian's room, so that they could learn Terence's story over time. It was a photo of Terence backpacking in the Olympic mountains in Washington. He was halfway up a tree on the banks of the Hoh River, sleeves pushed up and grip strong. He was at home in the woods, where his mom, palm extended and heart wide open, allowed him to grow into his own.

At age three, Kiran studied the picture. He asked why my friend was climbing that tree, and how his hands were holding on. I looked at Terence through Kiran's eyes. I told him that Terence just really loved to climb trees, and that he climbed so many trees that his hands got strong and could hold on tight. This was an easy story to tell. Kiran was perfecting this skill, too, in the cherry trees lining Golden Gate Park, where he would wedge himself up as high as he could on his own power and, gripping a bough, swing himself down when his tiny hands would give, which was almost immediately.

Harder to explain to three-year-old Kiran was the story behind my tears when he would round the corner and find me weeping. It was 2010 and British Petroleum's Deepwater Horizon had exploded in the Gulf of Mexico, causing the largest marine oil spill in history. During the monthslong spill, I experienced a familiar foreboding and agitation, my mind edgy and occupied, my heart tethered to the faraway sea being smothered, much in the same way I used to orient south after Terence was killed, my inner gaze arcing over the southern horizon to the land that took him. As then, my furtive search for an answer bumped up against the stunningly immutable truth that nothing could change what had already happened. Nothing I said could put the blood back into the earth. No court of law or congressional hearing could put the blood back into Terence's broken body, or the thousands of beings like Terence whose lives had been taken in these oil wars.[1]

My prayer, as a young mother, was that my sons' hands would grow strong with the experience of knowing and loving the forest, or the seas, that they would climb as many trees and waves as it would take for them to develop an abiding allegiance to their defense. But as proud as I would be to have sons who act in the world with as much integrity as did Terence, my deeper prayer was, of course, that they would never know the face of death he was shown. Murdered resisting a pipeline's advance into sacred lands? They didn't need to hear this story as babes. The unmitigated flow from a broken pipeline sounding the death knell of entire ecosystems? Probably not. Recognizing the agitated ache in my voice, Sunil skillfully redirected the boys, who, by then, had begun sending life rafts down from the living room couch to the rug, busily hoisting up into safety all remaining stuffed animals floating out there in the poisoned sea. Kiran was satisfied for the moment. Sunil had spared him the anxiety that surely would have flowed from any greater comprehension of loss.

Our children were born into this context. They knew Grandma Julie. And they knew Auntie Daris. It was Daris who taught us how to tie Kiran onto my back so that I could carry him as a toddler while Julian grew in my belly. They were born into a family story that included people who were missing because of unresolved political murder. A family story that connects them to the daughters of Daris who were adolescents when Terence was kidnapped within hours after leaving their community's territory. When our children looked to the daughters of Daris, they saw girls born into a country ravaged by internal armed conflict who grew up to help lead the U'wa people as they continue to assert their right to self-determination and sacred governance. When our kids entered adolescence through the gates of the COVID-19 pandemic, they could indeed trot out a root-cause analysis of contemporary social and environmental ills. But the way they each grappled with the ambiguity and the unknowability of the future was not as rote. As their mother, I felt the territory was uncharted.

During the first spring of the pandemic, Julian made a collage for his virtual sixth-grade yearbook page. The image featured a selfie in which only his eyes were visible between his shaggy, wild, stay-at-home-order curls and his dominating face mask. Surrounding him were photos of two larger-than-life murals. One paid tribute to Kobe Bryant, whose untimely death earlier that year seemed to foretell Julian's own unraveling as the pandemic killed basketball, his one true constant companion. The other mural honored George Floyd, whose murder by police that spring unleashed racial justice uprising that at once mobilized and terrified Julian. He couldn't reconcile people demanding justice out on the streets with the health directive that staying home was how to stay alive. Through his eleven-year-old eyes, these conditions created no way to win. On the bottom edge of the collage, he wrote, "I can't breathe," and "Mamba out."

By the first pandemic summer, Julian had shut down. He isolated himself within the isolation, defiant and sullen, responding only to video games and social media about video games. One night, I drew his bedroom curtain closed and sat on the foot of his maple bed frame, busying my hands by laying smooth the tangled quilts. I lingered to tuck him in, a tenderness I could no longer expect he would grant. On this night, he pulled me close onto the pillow next to him and said, "Mom, you have never felt the way I feel. You have no idea what it is like to have no hope." I listened. I told him that I heard what he was saying. After a few minutes passed, to contest his notion that I had no idea how it felt, almost in a fret, I started in on my own stories. He said nothing. I quickly realized it was not what he needed. He couldn't hear right then when he was working so hard just to be seen. I held him, kissed him goodnight, and sat vigil outside his bedroom door.

In desperation for Julian to know belonging, in the closest I could get to a version of prayer, I returned to the practice of tonglen. I marshalled in my mind's eye a global community of mothers similarly yearning for a world in which it might be possible for their children to thrive. In my mind's eye, I marshalled compassion for all mothers with this strong yearning, and relief to all the mothers, including myself. I recalled Julie's story of Terence's birth in Inverness, the way her baby responded to the hands of the midwife and turned just in time for his birth. I recalled my own body floating in the salty cold waters at the base of those very same hills so many years later. The day I had slipped away from the shore, held by the current and free, held by the hands of all these mothers and midwives guiding me for all these years through the waters back home to the island within myself. I recalled opening my eyes briefly against the bright blue sky to glimpse a bald eagle soaring above. The eagle played with two other birds in flight. I watched as they passed quickly out of sight, over the hill toward the sea.

We Unlocked the Door

The day after I spoke with Julie about Inverness, I wrote a letter to Daris and Aura. My US-based colleague, Lorena, was going to Colombia and she offered to take it.

> *Dear Daris and Aura,*
>
> *I send you greetings from the Mesa Refuge in Point Reyes Station, a town in California just north of San Francisco . . . Yesterday, Terence's mom Julie reminded me that Terence was born this month 45 years ago [across the water from here] in a town called Inverness.*
>
> *I came here to write about what happened twenty years ago, there on your land. I came to sort out my own understanding of what it means to me to be beholden . . . I feel beholden to the U'wa people for the gift you have offered the world, your world view, and your understanding of the role human beings have in protecting and restoring the equilibrium. I feel beholden to the sacrifices of Terence, Ingrid, and Lahe'. I feel beholden to the land and waters themselves for the gift of life and all the teachings and sustenance and example of persistence they offer. I came here to the Mesa Refuge to write myself into a new understanding of how I move through the world both beholden and free. How to move into action in a different way than I usually do. How I can move into action now in fulfillment of my sense of gratitude and duty in ways that also express my conscious choice and joy in the choosing. You know, for so long, a heaviness has accompanied the work I've done to walk alongside you. And I wanted to get free of that heaviness. I came here to write. I wrote, and I am free.*

So today I write to you from that joy. I am ready to understand more from you, Daris and Aura, about how you are currently holding the dream that Daris has been having, the one in which Terence comes and says, you are holding the key. It is time to unlock the door. I want to walk alongside you in a good way, in a clear and joyful way, drawing upon the power that we all know and relish, channeling from the earth/Sira [U'wa creator], to understand more what it means to unlock the door. Maybe it's related to the murders, maybe it's beyond that. Maybe it's both . . . My first inclination here in this letter is simply to let you know that I am listening and that I would like to walk alongside you as you are holding this question: what does it mean to unlock the door?

I also wanted to tell you that I read now, finally, the message from the U'wa women . . . that you wrote in February 2009 . . . As part of your message, you said that you still hope to be able to share with the US families [of the slain] certain sacred spaces and teachings that your ancestors have passed on to you. Aura brought me the same message in person when she visited California. And it echoes the message Berito first brought to the families in April 1999. I wanted you to know that I have received that message now . . . I am ready for the learning. I am open and clear. I am here. . .

In deep prayer, in deep gratitude, in joy, listening,

Abby

About a month later, Daris and Aura replied with a small bundle of tobacco. Their letter instructed me to mix the tobacco with water and to sprinkle the mixture around the periphery of my home. I did. I did as though in greeting. As though in acknowledgment, delineation, fortification, and commencement. We had begun.[2]

14

Bloodletting

I Felt the Allure of Early Exits

Before I can recount what came next, I need to share how I became ready to receive it. In the fractured years after Terence's murder, my body often felt like it was breaking, as though functioning without all its vital organs. My heart was in flight and my lower back was frozen under the strain. My hips, the source of power as a woman, were off-kilter and my pelvic bowl felt robbed of all security.

Shortly after the murders I said to Ram Dass, "Here's all this work I'm doing out in the world. And here's all this work I'm doing on the inside. I can see that the inside work could take lifetimes to realize. Why don't I put down all this work in the world, go to the mountaintop, and just do the inner work."

Ram Dass said, "No." This conversation was shortly after his stroke. He wasn't saying much. Through gestures, his hands said, "It's not one," shaking his hand to the left, "or the other," shaking his hand to the right. Instead, drawing a column with his hand down the center of his body from head to heart, he made a gesture of continuity and said, "It's this." It was as though he was saying, "Do both. Do both at the same time. You don't have a free pass. Go to the mountain *and* keep working." It reminded me of Fran Peavey's instruction to just keep going.

I was an overly earnest student. Shortly after that conversation, I left New York for Mount Madonna in California. On one level, I went to the woods thinking that there, finally, I could find the stillness and rest I craved. I would let the earth hold me and recycle all that pain back into the earth. On another level, I was still keeping very busy dealing with the Sisyphean political aftermath of the murders. Within months, I enlisted the teachers at Mount Madonna to give me a second cabin in the woods so that I could run a makeshift office of the U'wa Defense Project. I learned yogic practice. I ran the U'wa Defense Project. In trying to do both, I did neither well. One day, in the middle of the busyness, out of our office fax machine tumbled a note from Julie with a calligraphed reminder from Catholic monk Thomas Merton that

> there is a pervasive form of contemporary violence to which the idealist fighting for peace by nonviolent methods most easily succumbs: activism and overwork. . . . To allow oneself to be carried away by a multitude of conflicting concerns, to surrender to too many demands, to commit oneself to too many projects, to want to help everyone in everything is to succumb to violence. The frenzy of the activist neutralizes work for peace. It destroys the fruitfulness of our work because it kills the root of inner wisdom, which makes work fruitful.[1]

I could see the incongruity, but for two years I went on like this.

At Mount Madonna, an Ayurvedic doctor visiting from India took my pulse and said, "What are you doing with all that anger?" I didn't have an answer for her. I was there looking for the answer, but I didn't know how to find it. I didn't know how to find rest, or what it felt like in my body. My body may have been yearning for it, but my mind didn't want to cede control.

To cope I would steal away into the redwoods behind the office cabin. I would go deep enough into the woods that no one could see me, lay my body down, and unzip my spine with my mind's eye. I would let my life force energy drain out into the earth. In that emptiness I felt a stillness. I felt my body sink down as my mind's eye traveled up, tracing the arc from California to that cow field in Venezuela where Terence's blood had long ago soaked the soil. In that stillness, I felt relief.

I arranged my life to accommodate this need. When I left Mount Madonna for law school the following year, I worked for the human rights law clinic where the director, recognizing my fragmentation, assigned me nominal editing tasks to complete at a corner desk behind which I could lay my body down between classes.

The one time in all these years that I went back to Gavilan Ranch, New Mexico, I opened the gate and beelined it for the small hill where Terence's body is buried. Without thinking, with sin-gularity of purpose, like a barn horse coming home, I lay my body down on the grave, cheek turned to the grasses, palms spread open cupping the sandy soil. The high desert, accepting of so much human sorrow, took his body, ruined by ten bullets, as an offer-ing. It transformed the body's brokenness once again into the basic elements.

I, too, wanted to return my warped, broken parts to the earth. Perhaps I was "practicing for death" as Maggie Nelson called it when she laid her body down next to the train tracks in the middle of the night during the trial for her aunt's murder.[2] Perhaps I was holding vigil, as Erica Garner did weekly for years by laying her body down on the Staten Island street corner where police had murdered her father with an illegal and lethal chokehold. Lying on the grave, my body could relax. There, or in the community garden in Brooklyn, or the redwood forest in the Santa Cruz hills, my body on the earth could rest. I longed for it.

I did this bloodletting in private. In public, I was busy ringing the mindfulness bell, teaching others the practice of coming back to the breath. I played this role in organizations, coalition meetings, at policy briefings, trainings. When I became a mother, wherever we moved, I organized mindful mama circles. I had figured out how to harness inner awareness to turbocharge my running around in the world. But in the quiet of the night, I found solace in emptying myself out. I wasn't stilling my mind. I was avoiding pain. It was a fundamentally disembodied time.[3]

How to Stay with the Pain

When our kids were little, someone gave us *The Goblin and the Empty Chair*, a children's book about grief by Mem Fox.[4] In it, a family is bereft by the death of a loved one. The book shows how each family member manages to get through daily life. In each vignette, a goblin shows up, moving invisibly to help take some of the load. In one story, the sister is awake in the night. She cannot sleep. The reader wonders, How could a goblin, this thing of which we are supposed to be afraid, help this little girl? The answer is simple and profound. The goblin sits by her bed. He "stays when staying is needed" so that the child can let go enough to rest. Everybody else in the family is in their own process of loss. The little girl can finally rest when someone has stayed when staying is needed. Reading this story to my kids, I could never read past this page without my voice giving way. Attuned, my children would crane their necks up from the book to see if my eyes were watering. I was overcome by this suggestion that the thing we fear is often the thing we need. To stay.

My own mother wasn't afraid to stay with the pain. She had mastered the practice of staying when staying is needed. I watched her model *how* to stay. But as my children grew into adolescence, the related question that they were holding was slightly different. In their ambivalence about inheriting a seemingly irreparably broken world, their question was, *Why* does one stay? In all this grief, what can make it worth it to stay? This existential question is shared by many: When the hurt is too much to bear, and checking out seems more available than sitting with the hurt, why on earth would one stay? For myself, the answer is a paradox. It is only through learning *how* to stay, and staying, that I have come to remember *why* to stay.

What does it take to stay in the body, or to come back to the body, after trauma? To come back to the community after the circle has been broken? When it seems easier to spin out in busyness in the thousand virtuous and not virtuous ways we do, what does it take to choose to home in on the still point?

How to Stay Still/Here

In choreographer Bill T. Jones's 1994 piece *Still/Here*, the dancers describe the act of being still here, of surviving when the ones you love have been taken, in this case by AIDS. A few years after the murders, in a shoebox of college mementos, I found a postcard from the performance. The postcard featured Jones, eyes cast down, gazing at his hands covering his heart. I identified with the photo's expression of being one who is left.

In *Still/Here*, Jones shows us survival in two inseparable parts: being *still*, despite not knowing what is to come, and being *here*, in the body. Being here means staying in the body, keeping all the parts, moving around the still point as an act of integration, iterative, and cyclical. Presence as an act of resistance. As an act of beauty. Bloodletting and staying anyway. Heart opening even as it breaks.

Not the heartbreak of love lost, but the one we endure by being awake in this moment of unprecedented global change and seemingly intractable inequity. The heartbreak of explaining to our children the brilliance of what healthy coral reef used to look like, or how the moist morning air used to feel when spring broke. The heartbreak of explaining how to stay safe around the police, or that sometimes a money-making purpose may not be compatible with protecting life. Of talking about Flint, or Black Mesa, and what families back in the Philippines and India do every morning to make their water clean enough to drink. The heart breaking open when we watch our kids pour the kitchen sink wastewater into the garden, an offering disguised as economy, a mother's small prayer that they will learn reverence.

To be awake in this time is to hold both the heartbreak and the beauty. Cultivating the capacity to hold it all requires us both to make supple *and* to strengthen our container. As individuals, our containers are our own bodies. As groups of people, our containers are our communities. To make supple *and* strengthen our own bodies and our communities requires the same action of us. It is the action of staying, of being here. It is the action of rest. The definition of rest, in fact, is to cease work or movement in order to relax and recover strength. The kind of rest that comes when we refuse to check out. When we allow the pull toward staying to be stronger than the relief that we gain by draining our energy away. When we coax ourselves back into connection.

Staying allows the contradictory pulls to resolve themselves. Staying allows us our experiences of sorrow, anger, fear, despair, and emptiness—and gives them the breathing room and witness needed for deep and lasting change. This kind of presence enables us to remember, as Joanna Macy teaches us, that sorrow is born from love. That anger springs from our passion for justice. That expressing fear takes trust and courage. That emptiness means there is space for emergence, and for me, the cultivation of equanimity. That these energies—the foundations of right action out in the world in many traditions—are already available to us and our communities when we allow ourselves to look.[5]

We are living in a moment when everything tells us we are out of time. So we do a lot of fast work. But the success of our fast work hinges on the slow. This is what Ram Dass meant. His gesture of a column from head to heart wasn't a gesture of continuing to *do it all*. It was a gesture of integration.

15

Ma Ganga

You, My Dear

Integrating head and heart only became available to me once I began
to pay attention to what was happening in my pelvic bowl.

For a long time, it could look as though I were going about daily
life while still tugging at the thread of the "inkling of a chance" Terence and I had shared. Certainly, toiling away like Penelope, that
mythic widow in limbo, perpetually weaving and unweaving, could
explain my exhaustion. But that was not what was going on. It wasn't
allegiance to Terence; it was unresolved trauma. Typical of people
with murder in their family, I was still reeling. My heart still could not
alight. My wisest self, the self who saw the world through the wolf's
eyes, was still too busy scanning the horizon to rest.

The lyrical poetry of mindfulness practice taught me to prepare
the temple of my inner awareness for my heart to return home. That
practice, in my imagination, centered around the heart energy center
of my chest, or fourth chakra, in Sanskrit. In contrast, the practice of

tending the pelvic bowl takes place physically below the heart center, down in the first and second chakras of the root and sacrum, in the base of the hips. This area, energetically, is associated with issues related to security, like sex and money, physical safety. During an art project at Mount Madonna, I made a hanging mobile out of found objects to represent all seven chakra energy centers of my body. I chose a chaos of knotted and splayed dried kelp to represent the state of my second chakra. I knew even then that I had issues to resolve in the pelvic bowl, but figuring out how took me twenty years.

The pelvic bowl is comprised of the sacrum, the ilia, the low-ermost part of the spine, and intersecting bands of muscles that together form part of the hip joint and the pelvic floor. It is the base of my body and the source of my stability. Anatomically, the pelvis looks like an actual bowl. As with a bowl, the pelvis can get off-balance. When the bowl is tipped, not only am I physically out of alignment, but I also feel out of balance energetically. I feel as though the bowl's edges have become frayed and tattered, its shine dulled. To restore balance in the pelvic bowl requires active practice.

One practice I learned is a guided meditation by Jumana Sophia.[1] I found it on the internet. The purpose is twofold. First, to clear the past out of the pelvic bowl. And second, to identify the needs that the practitioner is trying to meet by holding elements of the past inside the bowl. The desired outcome is for the practitioner to be able to see the past, especially past lovers, as woven into the web of life that surrounds and sustains them and to assign the task of meeting the unmet needs to one's present self. In so doing, the bowl empties and becomes hallowed. In the mind's eye, one might light a consecrating candle or place some water as benediction of the renewed spacious-ness. The practitioner thus begins to take care not to tip the sacred bowl, with increased awareness of what actions move things out of balance and what actions maintain the balance, physically and ener-getically. Indeed, physical therapists, too, liken the strengthening of pelvic floor muscles to lifting the waters that support the pelvic bowl to remain buoyed and stable.

Though it didn't start out this way, inside myself, clearing the pelvic bowl is the work of the mistress and the matron. The mistress is what I call the one who hustles. When my wisest self was still reeling in flight, the mistress was minding the keep. She did not rest. She worked hard, full of movement and activity, spinning many plates. She navigated scarcity, gathered the resources, and got the job done. She was a fighter, and she often won. No stranger to the corruption and compromises of the world, the mistress moved with more savvy than the archetype of the maiden, making deals and compromises of her own as needed to stay safe. She noticed the pelvic bowl was overcrowded with elements of the past, cluttered with remnants of her own dealmaking. She knew something had to change, but thinking about clearing the pelvic bowl made her tired. The most she could do was hit play on the internet recording of the guided meditation.

Sitting still in this practice, listening to the recording, allowed me to notice that I also inhabit the energy of the matron. The matron is what I call the one who presides "like a mountain, solid and free."[2] The matron sees the long arc and, like a discipline, chooses spaciousness and abundance. She discerns which people and resources to invite in. She tends to the work that only she can tend and lets the rest go. That discernment allows her to turn squarely to the work that the mistress may never wish to complete. At first, it was the matron who cleared the pelvic bowl, while the mistress watched reluctantly from the corner.

Once I learned how to keep my pelvis clear, I finally understood that I did not tend this interior temple of my awareness so that Terence could alight. I tended this temple so that my own heart could come home. I got it. I really did. I got it that I was alone here, exquisitely alone. I could welcome Terence back not as some spirit that alights, but as part of me, part of the web of life that supports me, together with the ancestors, the waters, and the earth. I wasn't looking for him anymore. I wasn't sending my heart on missions in flight, scanning the horizon for a place to land in the ocean of grief. I wasn't unzipping my spine to drain my life force out in an attempt at replicating the refuge of the stillness of the grave. I no longer minded that he was a metaphor. Ram Dass's instruction to take god as my lover no longer smarted.

I spent years sweeping the steps and beating the rugs, tending the day-to-day ugliness of political violence. I could finally see that I did not spend these years merely in flight, but also preparation. I could finally see the fragmentation of my life as an effect of trauma, not personal failing. Aware of the fragmentation's provenance, I found the tenderness and generosity to forgive myself for the incongruities borne of it. I stopped the hypervigilant over-functioning. I stopped looking for someone to save me from the exhaustion. I stopped trying to fix or eliminate the part of me that was exhausted.

I finally understood that the job of the matron is to tend the mistress with compassion and patience so that the mistress is not confused about who is in charge. The matron is in charge. No longer minding the keep, the mistress is finally free to catch her breath. She can more readily offer her hard-earned wisdom, wisdom that quietly insists that I go beneath the anger and move in the world from spirit, not logistics. The mistress and matron now live as sisters inside me through this compact of compassion forged in my pelvic bowl. Together, they protect the root of my stability. This self-administration of tenderness and generosity is what it looked like to take god as my lover. I said to myself with regard, "It's you, my dear." What I needed was already present on the inside and had always been. I was at home in the home that was waiting, in the "temple of my adult aloneness."[3] I let the exquisiteness of the paradox be enough.

How to Come Home

This inner sanctum of solitude is maintained through community. I bumped into this second paradox in the summer of 2017, when my mother and I took my children to the Plum Village Practice Center in Bordeaux, France. Plum Village is the community in exile that Thây and Sister Chan Khong co-created when they couldn't return to

Vietnam during the war, where my friend Kaira Jewel had gone to become a nun. At Plum Village, this project of coming back home *is* the whole project. The intentional community, modeled after millennia of monastic communities before it, organizes itself around the project of bringing the heart back home into the body. They call it coming back to "the island within oneself." Our family spent the summer listening to dharma talks, or teachings, and practicing the skills of mindfulness through the chores of daily life. The purpose of the practice is to bring one's awareness back to the present moment, which is where the island of the self is located.

We camped on the edge of a plum orchard in the Lower Hamlet, one of five farms that house the lay and monastic sangha, or community. One morning, I listened as nuns and monks filed into the Lower Hamlet Hall. As they entered, the power of their silence hushed the murmur of the practitioners gathered inside. Hundreds of us sat on cushions on the floor, stood in the rafters, and balanced on the open windowsills. The crowd adjusted itself to enable the nuns and monks to stream forward in two steady lines to the front of the hall, where they formed an ensemble facing us. Sister Chan Khong stood as an elder among the youthful nuns in the front row. Thây was not present. He was already in Thailand, finally making his way back home to his root temple in Vietnam, as was his wish for the end of his life. In his stead, a younger monk sat like a mountain next to the enormous bowl-like bell in the middle of the ensemble.

Accompanied by the bell and sometimes a guitar, for the next twenty minutes, the mostly a cappella group chanted the name of the bodhisattva Avalokiteśvara. Twenty minutes of just the name. A bodhisattva is any person who is on a path toward enlightenment and who labors to end the suffering of all beings. Avalokiteśvara was a bodhisattva warrior of compassion and is portrayed throughout history at times as male, at other times as female. Statues and stories depict such warriors with a thousand arms and hands, helping everyone. They represent the human capacity to keep engaging even when a good outcome does not feel possible, even when the cards are stacked against the continuation of life. Their purpose is to prevent harm and to defend a space in which love can thrive; this is what Buddhists call *right action*. They cultivate love with an understanding that we humans are neither separate from the rest of life nor from one another. They teach that love plus this understanding equals compassion, and, when there is true understanding, then compassion compels action. Avalokiteśvara looks deeply at the suffering in the world caused by the misperception that we are separate and works tirelessly to unseat that misperception and its ill effects.

As the nuns and monks were chanting, I felt included in a long lineage of dedicated humans. I felt their conviction and clarity of purpose. I also felt discouraged. The example they set just seemed like a lot more work. It didn't seem like stopping, when all I really wanted to do was to stop. The dialogue in my head circled around the refrain *yes/but*:

Yes, I too see that right and compassionate action is to stay engaged. But look at the price we paid.

Yes, I get it that there is no other work really worth doing than that which opens and defends the space for love and understanding. But I'm exhausted.

Yes, I am aware that Avalokiteśvara was exhausted, too. So exhausted that their heads exploded—to even comprehend the suffering in the world required eleven heads. They had to grow eleven heads. But I only have one head.

Yes, I get it that Avalokiteśvara saw the suffering in the world, wanted to relieve it, and never rested. But I don't think that's right. I think you must rest.

And what I heard in return, as the monks and nuns came back into silence themselves, was that everyone gets tired and discouraged, which is why we have what they call "daily practice." Daily practice, like their singing practice, trains us to move from yes/but to yes/and. They practice in community to co-generate the energy needed to keep going, mirroring for each other the discipline of sticking with the still point. They are creating the container, both in the body and in the community, the body politic, for this dance. And the dance includes rest. Our efficacy can increase and sustain when we slow down to go fast. Slowing down can look like inner work but it is not solo work; it is a community practice by necessity. Daily practice helps us acknowledge what *is*, and work with the paradoxes of multiple coexisting, seemingly contradictory truths, including this one: the work of changing the world is infinite and will never be finished. *And*, it is still worth doing.

In 2021, while visiting in her Berkeley living room, Joanna Macy handed me a weathered scrap of paper scribbled with a note from Camus's *Resistance, Rebellion, and Death* essays: "We have nothing to lose but everything. So let's go ahead." Joanna's invitation into forward momentum reminded me of the stance of our mutual friend Fran Peavey. In the 1980s when people would tell Fran that cleaning the Ganges River in India was impossible, she would respond, "Well, then we better get started." People consider the river holy and speak of it with an honorific transliterated as "Ma Ganga." Even so, raw sewage flow and weak river governance mean deadly fecal coliform bacteria counts there. Fran met the impossibility of a clean Ganges River with the question, "How are we preparing our children to clean up the river?"[4] It was a long-arc question that invited forward movement despite the impossibility. She devoted the final third of her life to the challenge. I perceived Fran as someone who never stopped.

In 2010, sitting next to Fran's deathbed in San Francisco, I asked her about stopping, about rest. She reflected that she didn't experience her daily life as busy. That she took a nap almost every day. This blew my mind. I questioned how it could possibly be true. Fran was always on the move—it was the model I was following. I had a hard time imagining a daily nap for myself. My mother keeps a photo of me as a toddler, asleep sitting up with a corn cob in my fist. She said that strapped into the high chair was the only time I napped. As then, the conditions of relaxation that would have to be in place for me to *be still* enough to nap would require a sea change in how I organized my daily life, and in the daily life of the people around me. It would require daily practice, in community.

~~~

Back in the Lower Hamlet Hall at Plum Village, the nuns and monks sustained an active silence. Reverberations of the chant remained, building an energy that permeated everything. We were absolutely still. And absolutely active. Collective energy coursed through us. We were holding both stillness and action. It felt like a collective experience of what happens inside an individual body during the second virabhadrasana, or warrior, lunge in yoga asana. With the lower body sustaining active engagement, the torso from the pelvic bowl to the heart center can sustain quiet stability and spaciousness. For integration, both parts are necessary, stillness and action. It felt like a prerequisite for collective, aligned movement.

To Insist on Our Entire Bandwidth

To practice holding both the stillness and action is indeed akin to exercising a muscle; it strengthens with use. By the time the U'wa women and I were ready to reconvene, I had strengthened this muscle inside myself.

In preparing this book, Daris, Aura, and I searched for a way to meet again in person. We thought the easiest way would be to tack days onto the tail end of their then-yet-to-be-scheduled hearing at the Inter-American Court of Human Rights, which would likely take place in San José, Costa Rica. When COVID upended the court's hearing schedule, we thought instead to meet up in Lima, Peru, at the home base of EarthRights' Amazon office. When political instability in Lima made travel there impractical for the U'wa, we needed a new solution. During this flux, as though right on cue, Terence came to me in a dream. I was surprised to see him because, for the last decade or so, he had pretty much kept radio silence in my dream life. In the new dream, we stood together in the middle of an empty classroom wedged between a jumble of student desks. He put his hand on my shoulder, looked into my eyes matter-of-factly, and said, "You know you are going to Bogotá, right?" I said, "Yes, I know," and the dream ended. Within days, Juliana Bravo Valencia, the lead EarthRights attorney on the U'wa case, invited me to meet with Daris and Aura in Bogotá. I said yes.

I prepared for the trip. I marshalled my friends, who swooped in to arrange the travel completely, elegantly. I marshalled the US Embassy's senior regional security officer and our assigned FBI special agent, who swiftly put a plan in place for my personal security. I marshalled my NGO and Colombian colleagues, who found an interpreter and helped assemble gifts to bring to the community. I marshalled my family members, who stepped up to cover my absence and to be brave.

I took these logistical actions as the matron, aware all the while that the mistress—the generally exhausted part of me who at that point just wanted to lie down when faced with matters related to Colombia—seemed particularly quiet. Peering at her from the periphery, I could see she was very still, as though perhaps immobilized in a freeze response. I let myself get quiet enough to turn directly to her, to tend. To ask her for the care instructions.[5] Within moments, she softened, and I softened. She rose with a pair of wings and fluttered over to my heart center and nestled in there. It was as though she had been waiting for me to acknowledge that going to Bogotá meant more than having the logistics squared away. Going to Bogotá meant going deep, softening into the heart space, letting spirit animate my actions, integrating joy.

It was the right instruction. In Bogotá, Daris met me in the heart space. Within minutes, she set the intention that we would need to establish connection first, to go to the other plane of existence to speak the truth at the level at which our mutual work demanded. Accordingly, of our two days in dialogue, we spent three-quarters of our time connecting (exchanging gifts and stories, chewing coca leaves, sharing meals, using the hotel spa). It was only in the final quarter that we turned to our "work" (looking squarely at the manuscript). Together, we created a container for holding both the stillness and the action. Alignment of our heart centers allowed the work to be clear in purpose, and swift. She called it a "historic debt" that we tended.

After the trip, I checked in with the mistress again and learned more. She was once again lying down, this time on a basement floor. It was the familiar exhaustion. By now, I knew that my job was not to try to reexperience, extinguish, or fix the exhaustion. My job was to tend it. To tend, I used my imagination to put a bed under her with silken sheets. I put a pillow. I added some light, emanating from the base of the bed. I just tended her and observed. Eventually she woke, stretched her arms overhead and to the sides, hands in little fists. She turned to sit on the edge of the bed. She looked around and was clear. She said, "Okay. Put me in, Coach."

She had experienced the things in my life that were not right or fair. She had spent years hustling to get needs met in indirect ways without directly confronting the sources of harm. She understood why she did that. I tended and observed. I could see that when given the space to rest, she is unafraid to say no to the harm. Her survival instinct is older than the harm. She is the one who knows—even before the question of safety intrudes—that it is her birthright to assert belonging. She is comfortable and unafraid to act from that instinct because she understands it as part of a collective need, a collective demand for space for wholeness, to "insist on our entire bandwidth," as Arundhati Roy would say.[6] She knows that getting individual needs met is part of the ability to be of service to the whole. She is playful and ready to play, available to the struggle from this source of play because she knows belonging like she knows her own skin. She knows it is the only game in town.

Once I could see that the source of her power is clarity from before the time of the earliest harm, I realized that she has been waiting for me there all along. I learned to create conditions for the matron to draw upon this inner clarity of purpose and lack of fear, so that I can possibly act with courage. I like to imagine that it is the place in which the U'wa women invite me to meet them. The place in which we are clear about that to which we are saying yes and that to which we are saying no, no more.

16

Muir Beach

I Found My Stance

It took me awhile to figure out how to approach Colombia's Truth and Recognition Chamber. The logistics were straightforward—everything would happen through email correspondence and Zoom. Harder for me was to discern how to navigate my feelings about participating. I felt skeptical that the process could deliver the outcome most basic to me, which was to unearth who was behind the murders, let alone facilitate transformation. Even to name and want these outcomes felt extremely vulnerable. Given the vast landscape of harms in the Colombian conflict and the Chamber's wide-ranging but limited charge, what were the chances that any process, no matter how skillfully pursued, could get to these outcomes?

To be of use, I had to figure out how to be available to the process at a protective emotional distance. To find a good balance, I experimented with my stance. My stance, or the way that I held my physical body, became a metaphor for the way that I held my emotional body.

To find this somatic stance, I looked to our relationships with nature, which in turn told me (again and again, as always) to look to the collective practice of interdependence.

The Somatic Stance of Standing Hips Square

First, I had to resolve my skepticism. How do we build the new when guns for hire of every stripe kill in cold blood to protect the old? The 1999 murders tore asunder the families of those who were killed and temporarily moved underground the momentum that several communities had been building to assert a new world. For me, the murders cracked open a fissure in the bedrock and exposed the instability of my foundational belief that we will win because we are good and right. Before the murders, believing that we would win was part of what made work for social change tenable. After the murders, I had to contend with the fissure in my belief system. The waters of grief were one thing. But learning balance as I walked on a cracked earth was another.

This fissure in my belief system also showed up as an ailment in my physical body. Shortly after the murders, walking itself became painful. My back was in a constant lock. To be pain-free, I had to relearn how to walk.[1] To reorganize the way the muscles gripped my spine. The desired outcome of this bodily reorganization was to let certain muscles relax. Resting muscles can recover. They can heal and gather strength. Gathering strength lets muscles remobilize for action in a new way, a way that doesn't cause more pain. To convince the muscles that it was safe enough to rest, I had to learn how to align my bones in a manner that would support the frame of my body in balance, so that the muscles no longer had to do the job of the bones. Through alignment, I could set the stage, but I could not control the outcome; I could not coax the muscles into resting. Paradoxically, letting go of the outcome was a key factor in allowing my body to settle into true alignment to prepare for healthy walking. When the muscles finally did relax of their own accord, I felt the ache of letting go. I could feel the muscles reorganize themselves toward healing. Relearning how to walk was a practice of faith. It was faith that, when I discerned the distinction between what I could and could not control, it was right action to attend diligently to alignment of the matters in my hands.

Similarly, I reorganized the way I related to hope. I came to understand that, for me, the belief that we will win could not be how I understood hope. It could not be the foundation for action. Too much grasping. Not enough conditions for relaxation and gathering strength. Hope had to be rooted in something else. To switch it up, I refocused on practices of alignment and gathering strength: together with others, we could envision the far horizon, and we could make the road by walking. We could create the conditions for winning, but we had to surrender the illusion that we could control the outcome. I developed a deep and abiding faith in the practices that build alignment and gather strength. I came to understand that walking with true stability toward our vision was possible.

Over time, walking this way also made it possible for me to understand hope as the "embrace of the unknown" that Rebecca Solnit urges, where it is within "the spaciousness of uncertainty" that we find the "room to act."[2] Uncertainty as the site of action felt playful, creative: If we don't know what's going to happen (which is always the case), we might as well put into the mix our most audacious visions for a transformed world and walk forward as though inhabiting that world now. As if it were already here. We undergird this practice of hope by walking in a manner that gathers strength, faithful to the integrity of the steps, a manner that adrienne maree brown describes as "moving towards freedom" even if we can't see the path or the outcome.[3] I could see how this stance could then become what the Hawaiians might call a "wanted obligation."[4] Beholden by choice.

I was experimenting with this stance when Colombia's Truth and Recognition Chamber invited me to participate in Case 001. I thought: *Of course* this invitation comes now, when, for the first time in twenty years, I have shaken loose the need to see the outcome of this story. And perhaps it was perfect timing. For the first time, I felt ready to approach the Chamber as my own fierce, bold, visionary, strategic, and humble self, standing with my hips square on the shoulders of giants and in the "full length of our dignity" as I made my truth demands.[5]

We Learn from the Bamboo an Ecological and Somatic Practice to Align with Interdependence

I was ready to prepare myself for the possibility that entering the Chamber could mean coming face to face with those who had done us harm. I had never turned myself squarely to face these figures. It felt like I was preparing to confront the heretofore theoretical and seemingly removed yet extremely personally threatening unknown other. I was eager to feel differently. I obviously had some work to do. For guidance, I summoned what I am learning from confronting within myself a boogeyman of a different ilk: climate change.

In the fall of 2018, as PG&E's fires swallowed the northern California woods, choking the region in what was in that moment the worst air pollution on the planet, I took my family to Muir Beach for fresh air. Muir Beach is a cove north of San Francisco where the long descent of the Green Gulch canyon empties out into the Pacific Ocean. Watching the kids, my mom and I burrowed our feet in the sun-kissed black sand and sat braced against the startling and brisk ocean wind.

Toward the end of our excursion, with the kids still at the water, I walked alone up into the canyon. In haste, I hiked into the foggy valley, cutting through Green Gulch Zen Center. The monks and nuns of the Zen Center have blanketed the valley with an acre of fruits, vegetables, and flowers. Winding my way through the farm, I passed a bamboo grove. Years earlier, my community came together in this grove as I prepared to birth Julian. We put blankets down and made a picnic. We sat in a ceremony called a seed circle, each friend witnessing the seeds, or intentions, that I nurtured as I turned myself toward the birth.[6]

Instead of continuing to scurry up the canyon, I stood in the grove to catch my breath. I watched the bamboo bend. I quieted enough to be naked before the giant grasses, stripped of haste. I had been racing in more ways than one. All day, I had been performing for my children my confidence in our safety from the fires even when I was not sure. With kids in tow, I could not confront the dystopic climate. But in the bamboo grove I stood still. I let my shoulders down. I allowed myself to touch the vein of collective panic. In disorientation, I wept.

When I was quiet again, I whispered, "Please." I was asking the bamboo for guidance. How do we hold our bodies in relation to the truth? How do we hold our children? How can our collective body move to recognize the truth? And act on it?

The bamboo answered. The birth of a child and the birth of a new world take the same kinds of focus and surrender. When my body is supple like bamboo, I can be a channel, open to let through my skills and creative attention in service to collective transformation. This answer resonated with me. As climate destabilization accelerates, I have noticed myself decelerating, stripping away what no longer serves, and clearing the decks—just as one does when preparing for birth. I have gravitated toward those who show us how to radically re-collectivize and vastly expand our circles of care—the moves one makes to fashion a safety net when ushering in new life. To respond to the changing climate at the scale and clip necessary requires us to be agile and attentive, with capacity to mobilize on many fronts at once, just as new mothers learn to do.

Standing there in the grove, I received the care instructions from the bamboo. In these times of climate destabilization, to focus means to deploy the mad skills we learned as part of (and despite) the extractive economy to now help midwife its obsolescence and transformation. At the very same time, to surrender, we need to grieve what is lost and what has been taken. To focus and surrender in alignment with what is true, we also need to go ahead and confront the self as the harmer.

To confront the self as the harmer is the hardest of these care instructions to follow. In writing this book, I have wrestled the most with my own interdependence with those who have hurt me. How can I balance the quest for truth about unspeakable injustice and the underlying reality that I am not separate from those who did the harm? To hold myself accountable, I need to be in circle with others, like trees in a grove. When in circle, my peripheral vision widens. I can see my own role and agency. I can look upon the brokenness of humanity and say not, "How could you do this to me?" but instead, "Geez, we've got a long way to go."

I realized then that awareness of interdependence *is* the island in the waters of grief. The state itself of remembering non-separation *is where* the refuge is; it is the location where it is safe for a heart in flight to land. Because what is the sea of grief without the perception of separation? Without the perception of separation, there is no sea of grief. There is just the state of being where the losses we experience fold back into the whole. There is nothing to chase, nothing missing, nothing lost; the form has just changed. Murder takes the body. Cancer takes the body. Unjust systems, accidents, time. They all take the body. Human-induced climate catastrophe. It is anguishing that the form changes. We rail against it; I rail against it. It can feel almost impossible to stay in relationship to the parts of the whole that may have caused the form to change. When we cultivate the capacity to hold this complexity, we are no longer adrift. We grieve the changes, yes, *and* we are not adrift; instead, we focus. The island we come home to is this state of being. It is present in our minds. It is also the same as the wholeness that is in the nature of our bodies and the earth itself.

Once I understood this continuity, I could see that our mercifully singular and therefore joyful job is to tend the temple. It is the temple of both the pelvic bowl and the heart center, both energetically and physically, inside the body, in community, and on the living earth. We light the candle and keep the altar fragrant. We fill the offering bowl. We sweep the steps and keep the pathways clear. We arrange the cushions and prepare the seat for sitting. This is us, creating the container for what happens next. Even if what happens next means confrontation with the parts that still feel separate.

Because we live in separate bodies and swim in the culture of separation, the truth of non-separation can elude us. Because it is elusive, it takes practice to find it again, and again. The practice, ironic in its simplicity, is to find refuge in the present moment. This is my experience of this practice:

> Get knocked off-kilter.
> Perceive the harm.
> Notice the sting of separation.
> Find the salve: walk it out, apply lip balm, take in the fragrance of the tea.
> Widen peripheral vision.
> Come back.
> Start over.
> Repeat. Repeat. Repeat.

The bamboo grove transmission seemed to be saying: Do this one thing. Again and again and again. It is simple but not easy. Strengthen this muscle, and your capacity to follow the rest of the care instructions will come into view. This is what is meant by alignment.

We Wield Diamonds in a Collective Practice of Non-Repetition

The Colombian Truth and Recognition Chamber invited victims to exercise our "right to non-repetition." According to the United Nations' universal instrument that describes basic principles and guidelines on the right to a remedy and reparation for victims of gross violations of international human rights law and serious violations of international humanitarian law, victims have the post-conflict right to adequate, effective, and prompt reparation. One basic form of reparation is the right to non-repetition. Guarantees of non-repetition are measures taken to help ensure that systemic human rights abuses do not recur. Measures to guarantee non-repetition might include strengthening civilian control over the military, or strengthening the judiciary and protections for journalists, human rights workers, and those in the helping professions.[7] This right is an essential component of reparation after violence because its measures contribute to prevention of future harms across the whole society.

When I first read the invitation to Julie and me to exercise our right to non-repetition, I laughed out loud. It read not as a measure to protect the whole society but rather as an individual measure to protect us from having the same harm happen again. Terence, Ingrid, and Lahe' had already been killed. I said to Julie, "Why, yes, let's make sure that doesn't happen again. Yes, absolutely, let's exercise that right." We laughed together.

It is a serious thing, how a society endeavors to guarantee non-repetition. We can build and strengthen institutions and structures. We can change behavior. On this particular guarantee, however, it seems as though the wheel of transformation turns on the extent to which we create deep and lasting fundamental change in hearts and minds.[8] We change hearts and minds through shifts in cultural norms and worldviews. At both the individual and collective scale, to avoid repetition of harm, we must reawaken our capacity for non-repetition of another, more essential, kind: non-repetition of the patterns that keep us separate from each other and distanced from our awareness of our interdependence with other species and the earth itself. Our perception of separation keeps us adrift in the face of loss. This very same perception of separation feeds notions of supremacy, domination, and dominion; notions that have been killing us for millennia. What happens when we design the institutions and structures of society to bolster our collective capacity to shift away from the illusion of separation? What can emerge from sacred governance for the whole?[9] Let's design for that.

To design society in a manner that guarantees the right of non-repetition of the illusion of separation, we must revive dormant tools: our imagination and our longing to understand each other in the same way that the right hand understands it cannot harm the left hand without harming itself.[10] Bodhisattvas, warriors of compassion, take on enormous projects of social transformation because they understand that there is nothing at stake for them as separate beings. And that everything is at stake for them as part of the whole. They refer to the "diamond that cuts through the illusion" of separation.[11] They wield the diamond as a way of teaching practices that can get us all free from the cycles of repetition. I am captivated by this idea. What becomes possible if we, too, wield this tool?

Some people extract diamonds, forged in the cauldron of the earth, to penetrate the earth for further extraction. Shortly after the 1999 murders, multiple legal, political, and direct action tactics had failed to prevent Occidental from sinking an exploratory well at Gibraltar. In the first half of 2001, Oxy probed 12,500 feet looking for the oil.[12] In response, the U'wa people did everything they could to make the oil hide, as they later told it. U'wa ancients evoked their cultural practices—practices designed to maintain the equilibrium between the world above and the world below the surface of the earth—and asked the oil to move through the ground to a different location, as oil, geologically, sometimes does. It is said that the oil company broke three diamond drill bits that season as it tried to break earth to find the oil before giving up. The diamond, with its ability to cut through anything, nevertheless did not yield the vein.

We must choose how to use our imagination. We must choose how to wield the diamond. I wrote as a practice to bring me into alignment with those who wield the diamond that cuts through the illusion of separation. And in that alignment, I turned to my truth demands.

Part 4

like a painting that I looked at
closely for a long time,
[...]
like the pitcher I use every day,
[...]
like a ship
that carried me
through the wildest storm of all.

—RAINER MARIA RILKE

17

A Puddle,
with Rainboots

In its first years, JEP initially prioritized seven macro-cases: kidnapping; assassinations and forced disappearances presented as combat deaths committed by state agents (the case of "false positives"); the use of children in armed conflict; the victimization of union members; and three territorial situations focused on the grave violations of the rights of Indigenous peoples, Afro-Colombians, campesinos, women, and LGBTI people in particular Colombian towns.

Our case was part of the macro Case 001, which encompassed kidnappings and involved hundreds of participating ex-combatants and thousands of recognized surviving victims. Among the surviving victims, Julie and I were the lone non-Colombians. Magistrate Julieta Lemaitre Ripoll, a beloved Colombian scholar and professor of human rights, presided over the case. She granted Julie and me status as special interveners and assigned her law clerk Ana María Mondragón Duque, yet another impactful human rights lawyer, to attend to us. Exactly twenty years after the murders, Ana María sent me a letter.

Witness This

Wednesday, February 27, 2019

Ana María Mondragón Duque
Magistrada Auxiliar
Jurisdicción Especial para la Paz - JEP
Carrera 7 No. 63-44, Piso 11
Bogotá, Colombia

Dear Abby,

. . . The Case 001 is [in] the first stages of the Truth and Recognition Chamber process. . . . This is an ongoing process in which we want to invite you and the families of Ingrid Washinawatok El-Issa and Lahe'ena'e Gay to get involved in if you are willing to do so. There are two ways to participate before the JEP, which are not mutually exclusive. The first one is to send a report to the Truth and Recognition Chamber in which you share with us your case and experience in your own words, as well as any documents or materials you might have and that can be useful for us in the search of truth and in the process of attribution of criminal responsibility to the former FARC guerrilla members. . . . The process of receiving reports from the victims and civil society organizations is key to do our work, because we need to build a dialogical process—as opposed to adversarial—in which the voice[s] of the victims are in the center of the process.

The second way to participate before the JEP is to request to be recognized as a victim in a specific Case in order to acquire the rights to intervene and effectively participate in all the stages of the process. In order to do so, the law says that you have to send (i) a request to be recognized as a victim; (ii) any mean[s] to prove your condition of victim (for example, press notes; judgments from different jurisdictions related with the case; lawsuits, etc.); and (iii) a report of the facts, specifying at least their time and date. In the case of the families of direct victims, they have to send (iv) proof of the family relationship. Last week we recognized the first 89 victims on Case 001 and we hope to continue this task in the following months.

Two weeks ago, the Chamber started the first round of voluntary versions of 31 ex-FARC members. These versions are closed hearings in which the ex-combatants have the opportunity to tell their version of facts related to the policy of kidnapping of the FARC, recognize their criminal responsibility and where the judges will ask them about specific cases, among other things. Recognized victims in the process have the right to send observations to these voluntary versions and also to participate in a subsequent hearing in which the ex-combatants can officially tell the truth and recognize responsibility or not. Depending on this, the judges have to decide if they can access the main benefit of the transitional justice system which is an alternative sanction—different [than] prison—or if they lose it. In this last case, an adversarial process would start in which ex-combatants would be prosecuted by our special prosecutor and they will have to defend themselves in trial.

You can send us the questions you have about your case—truth demands—so we can ask the ex-combatants about this in the context of the voluntary versions. When this first round of voluntary versions ends, you will have the right to access this information and send your comments, which will be taken into account to determine the truth of the facts. As the process moves forward, we will explain which are the next procedural moments in which you can participate and how.

. . . We are aware that this is a complex and new process to everyone and we are keen to explain as clearly as possible how the JEP works and which are the ways in which you can get involved and use your rights to truth, justice and non-repetition.

Warm regards,

Ana María

Monday, March 4, 2019

Dear Ana María,

I have conferred now with Terence's mom, Julie Freitas, about your February 27, 2019, email invitation. Julie supports my participation in the JEP process as a representative of Terence's family to the extent that I want to pursue it. With this email, I am communicating that yes, I want to participate in both ways you describe. It sounds like the documentation required would give me a formal way to establish both my connection to the harm and the ways in which I am representing Julie Freitas. . . . I am preparing now my submissions. . . . Twenty years ago today. It took twenty years.

Abby

Tuesday, March 5, 2019

Dear Abby,

Thank you for your answer and for communicating to us your will to participate in the Case. Today—twenty years after the painful and terrible events—we want to sincerely express how much we value your trust in the Special Jurisdiction for Peace and want to stress how important it is for the process to have the voice of the victims in the center. Thank you very much. . . .

Warm Regards,

Ana María

March 5, 2019. I receive Ana María's communication, but I find that I cannot respond. I feel once again like I am moving through molasses.

March 19, 2019

Dear Abby,

I am writing to follow up on our conversation with regards your interest to be recognized as victim in the Case 001. We understand per your last email that you expressed your will to participate in the process. Therefore, we have studied the case, and have concluded that given that the JEP already has several [forms of] documentation related to Terence Freitas case that we consider valid proof of the facts, we are ready to proceed with the judicial decision to recognize you and Julie Freitas as victims. This way you will acquire as soon as possible all your rights to participate actively in the process. . . . [W]e appreciate if you could send us . . . proof of your family relationship with Terence. . . .

All the best,

Ana María

March 19, 2019

Dear Ana María,

. . . For Julie's proof of family relationship with Terence, she can provide a copy of his birth certificate. But for my proof of family relationship with Terence, we just have love letters. We were 24 years old and were not married. What proof may I offer? . . . Thank you.

Abby

March 20, 2019. No one has ever asked for my truth demands before. For twenty years, I have held them, looking for some sturdy container to bear their weight. Somewhere to deposit them. I keep attempting to put them down. We preserve an argument in a court case over here, we entertain offers from peace brokers and film producers over there. I write the whole story out and tuck it away on my laptop. Julie has it down to twelve boxes. In my closet, there are six. Boxes that hold the memorabilia of his brief life. At the beginning, I furtively stuffed my questions into these boxes, too. I don't like to open the boxes—I can remember when his favorite t-shirt stopped smelling like him. Over time when my questions resurfaced, I would gingerly re-place them back in for safekeeping.

In the first year after the murders, when it was too much to bear, I dug a hole in the Tusas Mountains just north of the hole in the earth near the Jemez Mountains where we put his body. What trinkets I hadn't dropped into his grave I dropped into the earth in the Tusas: more silver and obsidian, other clay and feather, the remaining matter of our private shared language. Now they are asking for our truth demands and there is much to unbury. It is like starting over.

As before, I am stuck again on the corporeal:

Did you feed them during the eight days?

Were you hurting his body, or just at the end?

Were they bound the whole time, or just at the end?

Did he rest his body on the earth, ear to the ground, to find me way up north, where my body lay on the earth, with my ear to the ground, listening for him?

Did he speak my name?

Did you know my name?

March 21, 2019

Dear Abby,

Thank you very much for your answer. We will proceed now to build our judicial decision. With regards your questions: [For Julie, Terence's] birth certificate is the adequate means to prove her family relationship. In your case, we need to prove what the law names "direct and legitimate interest to be

recognized as a victim." Therefore, the love letters work. Also, you could send
us pictures and/or press notes or documents that helps us verifying that you
were Terence's girlfriend at the time of the facts. . . .

Best regards,

Ana María

March 27, 2019. To get to the birth certificate, Julie would have to open the boxes at her house.

Julie's not going to do that.

I ask her for her truth demands. She says: Why ten bullets, with four in the face? Why not just one bullet?

To find a love letter, I had to open the boxes at my house. Stupidly, I opened the first box at midnight. I was sitting in my closet. It was a wooden box. Under the heavy lid, a paper collage shielded me from the contents of the box. I must have made the collage within the last decade. The collage included an image of a woman in silhouette from the back, focused and victorious with arms raised, fists in the air.

Under the collage rested the eagle feather that Terence was given during a Sundance shortly before his murder. I was menstruating, so I wrapped the feather in a red cloth out of respect, as Nilak Butler had taught me to do shortly before her own death in 2002.

There was also a bone carving that Lahe' gave Terence from her homelands in Hawaii. There was a woven grass basket, U'wa-made and lined with silk that wrapped the bundles of Chumash white sage left over from his burial.

And there was a wool satchel tied tight. Inside, our written cor-respondence. His letters and mine. I had never opened this satchel. Someone at some point must have transferred my letters to him from some other box to this one. I read our entire story. Some of his letters were twenty pages long. I sat in my closet with the letters for the rest of the night.

Still, it was fleeting.

March 27, 2019

Thank you Ana María and hello Abby,

*. . . We have already identified two former guerrilla members who partici-
pated in the events; at this stage of the process we are also preparing a list of
questions victims want to ask perpetrators. It would be very helpful in your
reply if, in addition to the documents, you could express what you would want
us to ask the perpetrators and more generally what would justice mean for you
in this case. . . .*

Sincerely,

Julieta Lemaitre Ripoll
Magistrada

March 28, 2019
Magistrate Julieta Lemaitre Ripoll
*Sala de Reconocimiento de Verdad, de Responsabilidad y de Determinacion
de Hechos y*
Conductas
Carrera 7 #63-44 /Piso 9
Bogotá, Colombia

*Re: Request to be recognized from Julie Freitas and Abigail Reyes, Case 001
Kidnapping and Murder of Terence Unity Freitas, March 4, 1999*

Dear Magistrate Julieta Lemaitre Ripoll:

*Greetings from southern California. Please allow this letter to serve as the
request from Julie Freitas and Abigail (Abby) Reyes to be recognized in the
matter of Terence Unity Freitas in Case 001 of the Jurisdicción Especial para la
Paz (JEP). . . . We request to be recognized . . . not only as victims but also as
survivors. It is a semantic distinction, but one that is important to us, for dignity.*

*To establish the family relationship of Julie Freitas to Terence Freitas,
enclosed please find 1) a photograph of Julie with Terence and 2) a 1999
letter to the editor of the Washington Post from Julie shortly after the murders.*

*To establish the family relationship of Abby Reyes to Terence Freitas,
enclosed please find 1) an excerpt of a 1998 love letter from Terence to
Abby and 2) a 1999 open letter from Abby to then-Vice President Al Gore
reprinted in various news media outlets shortly after the murders.*

*Lastly, please allow this letter to document the request of Julie Freitas to
recognize Abby Reyes as her representative and agent in the JEP process. We
have established and agreed upon internal processes to facilitate our collaboration as the JEP process unfolds. . . .*

I enclosed the love letter excerpt. It was a printout I found in
my boxes of a 1998 email exchange between Terence and me. I had
emailed him from the ELAC office in Palawan, Philippines, where I
had just finished a board meeting and was about to head back home
to Brooklyn. He emailed me back from an internet café in Bogotá,
where he had just finished legal planning meetings with the U'wa
and right before boarding a local plane to U'wa territory.

Enclosure:

Subject: Re: board meeting is over i am energized
Date: Sat., 19 Sep 1998 06:34:28 PDT
From: "Terence Freitas" u——@hotmail.com
To: e——@pal-onl.com

Dear Abby,

. . . I am very tired from late night legal planning meetings, and insanity of the
last couple days, haven't had e-mail or fax access since I last wrote. . . . Maybe
I can call when I get back to Bogotá, on the 7th of October. We are one hour
behind NY since Colombians don't change their clocks. I would call in the evening, between 6 and 7:30 your time. I may also call you from Cubará sooner,
so let's just wait and see.

Must get on a plane in a few minutes, and silly internet café didn't open til 8:00 am.

Why will I so assuredly make it back. Aside from all the good reasons I have to stay alive long enough to continue doing such great work for various indigenous folk around the globe, I have a more compelling personal reason that I suspect will be able to get me through almost anything: you.

I think about you day and night, especially night when I get to lie down and think only of us being together—those are my most peaceful moments at present.

much love

Terence

>From: e——@pal-onl.com Fri Sep 18 09:15:55 1998

>Date: Fri, 18 Sep 1998 23:43:58 +0800

>To: u——@hotmail.com

>Subject: board meeting is over i am energized

>Hi Terry!

>

>so maybe you can tell me in brief, even though you just mailed it to me in New York, why you will be coming home safely, so assuredly now?

>

>It is midnight, friday night. Board meeting just ended. very very productive.

>

Justice

I asked Julie what justice more generally looks like to her. Without skipping a beat, she said, "Nothing can bring them back." In reply to the JEP, she continued, "Justice looks like the U'wa getting to live in peace, without interference from the oil companies, men with guns, and the state. Justice looks like the U'wa being able to recover their lands and waters, and to assert their traditional ways of life throughout their territory."

Justice in this case, for us, has never been about the petty agents of the extractive economy. It has been about making visible the lines between harm on the ground and the command centers, statehouses, and boardrooms that issue the often tacit orders to act. Justice looks like making those lines visible, following those lines all the way up and across institutions. Justice looks like inviting those who obfuscate their complicity to enter the chamber of truth and recognition as well. Those standing there, enmeshed in the web, and pretending not to be. Justice looks like the fossil fuel companies and state oil concerns paying for their environmental and other harms in U'wa ancestral territory, winding down their operations, and offering to shift all financial and material resources to U'wa-led efforts to reestablish the equilibrium.

Shortly after the murders, U'wa spiritual leaders said that Terence had come to them in a dream, with hand extended, holding a white spiraling shell, or caracol. They recounted that, in U'wa culture, the caracol represents a spiritual connection between the human part of experience and the cosmos. It is a symbol of the spiritual calling for defense of the territory. In the dream, Terence extended his hand. Justice looks like the rest of us adopting this stance in support of and deference to the leadership of communities like the U'wa that assert their sovereign right to govern through the transitions we, as humanity, need.

We Crafted Truth Demands with One Voice Missing

I submitted our truth demands. (See Appendix 1.) There were thirty-six of them. Demands worded as questions about facts. The demands were one part corporeal, three parts political. Julie and I both wanted to know what happened with his body—whether, how, and for how long he suffered. Together with the U'wa, the all-star team of lawyers and political scientists who helped us articulate our truth demands made sure that we also asked our investigative questions about the circumstances leading up to the murders. The lawyers from Earth-Rights, alongside whom I walked during almost a decade of board service, were now not only lawyers for the U'wa but some were also lawyers for Julie and me. They were whip-smart and fiercely protective of community-driven leadership in their cases. They were also an entire generation younger than me—one was born at Stanford the year before I began studying there as a student.

Our team also had two elders. One was Paul Hoffman, a human and civil rights lawyer who, over decades, had argued some of the most influential cases in the highest court of the land to seek corporate accountability for human rights abuses. I clerked for him during law school and was then his colleague at UC Irvine Law, where his clinical students worked on this case. The other elder was Dr. Terry Karl, a Stanford political scientist and specialist in the political economy of petroleum, the politics of war-torn countries, and the politics of Latin America. Terry was renowned for her expertise as a witness in case after case regarding, among other things, the role of US military and corporate operators in Latin American slaughter. She had worked with us significantly in the U'wa case, starting in 1999.

There was one person missing from our team. Terence's friend Dr. Leslie Wirpsa dedicated years of her life to this case, and to the restoration of Pueblo U'wa's dignity, sovereignty, and territory. She was an award-winning investigative journalist and a scholar. During the years of acute crisis and throughout our brief partnership in the U'wa Defense Project, Leslie's labor and love were the linchpin that kept us connected to the political realities on the ground and accountable to AsoU'wa. She was also broken by this work. She wrestled with survivor's guilt and our long-standing inability to seek the truth about the murders without putting more people in harm's way. On the eve of the twentieth anniversary of the murders, right as the truth and recognition process got underway, her neighbors found her body. She died in her bedroom alone.

Later that spring, on the birthday she shared with Terence, on the twentieth anniversary of Terence's burial, Julie and I traveled to Leslie's home in Colorado to speak at her memorial service. We said goodbye and helped Leslie's family transform her boxes into a research archive.

A Puddle, with Rainboots

Magistrate Lemaitre oversaw not only Ana María but a team of young Colombian lawyers who investigated the case. For two years, these young lawyers attentively anticipated and addressed the language barriers, cultural and historical context, national borders, and global pandemic that separated us from them. They translated our truth demands and prepared the investigatory magistrates to communicate the truth demands to the participating ex-combatants on our behalf. They sat with me and our lawyers on Zoom for hours fulfilling their constitutional charge to "transfer the voluntary versions" of the truth from the ex-combatants back to us. And they solicited our responses to the ex-combatants' versions.

The purpose of this part of the process was to enable the presiding magistrate to assess whether any given participating ex-combatants were telling enough of a truthful version to excuse them from facing criminal proceedings. If they were, such ex-combatants could avoid criminal proceedings and instead face five to eight years of restricted liberty and community service.

Because the process was designed to place the victims at the center, JEP lawyers asked participants like Julie and me to suggest ideas for the community-service sentence. Julie recommended that each ex-combatant be paired with a willing elder from their own community, a mother whose child or children were taken by the conflict, and who therefore faced her elder years, like Julie, without the support and help of her grown child standing by her side. Julie recommended that the men who had now put down their guns be of use to mothers of the slain.

At the beginning, the process overwhelmed me. Each request from the lawyers felt impossible to address. Even with everyone wearing kid gloves, I felt assaulted. I wanted to be present, but each time I approached the work, I worried that I was going to drown. Opening my inbox to a new correspondence from Magistrate Lemaitre could send a fresh wave of sobbing through me, stomach and lower back clenched. I knew the intense visceral feelings would pass and that I would survive. But invariably they left my body depleted and my mind scattered. My family could measure the waves by the number of table-height bruises I accumulated on my thighs during such periods. I bumped into the corners of furniture and dropped things in the kitchen.

I didn't, at this point, know much about resolving the trauma, but having had years of practice, I did know how to weather it, dissipate it, and regather myself. As the JEP process intensified, to regather myself, I rallied people around me. Jodie Tonita was the director of the Social Transformation Project and my friend. I described to Jodie the feeling of being submerged, of diving alone and too deep. Jodie offered a trauma reality check. She helped me see that when I felt like I was going under, I didn't face a bottomless ocean, but a puddle. She asked me to see if I could touch the bottom with my foot. I tapped my foot on the floor beneath my desk. She asked me to stomp my foot. I stood up and did. The depth of the trauma was actually a puddle.

The truth is that I'd always brought myself back. I'd never gotten lost in the puddle. I could stomp my foot and know that the bottom of the puddle was there. Soon enough, I only needed to tap my foot. This reframing markedly transformed my experience in this process from that of a victim to that of a survivor. With rainboots.

Jodie elicited my image of the matron and then helped me inhabit it. With the energy of the matron, I cleared my calendar, solicited help from law students and clinical colleagues, invested in regular bodywork, and called in a community of people to witness what was happening in the truth and recognition proceedings.

For the first time, I felt like I was in charge of the terms of engagement. I was in charge of what information, requests, energy, and people I let in the door. I didn't have to be run over by the freight train of other people's needs around the case. Jodie said, "Survivor's guilt says that, because you are still alive, you can't protect yourself by closing the door. But that is not true. You have the right to protect yourself. You have the right to say, 'Stop. It's too much.'"

18

Stowell Pond

I Walked into the Pond, Sundress and All

In the late 1990s, Rafael, whose real name was Reinel Guzman Flores, was the commander of the tenth front of the FARC, which operated on the outskirts of U'wa territory. Rafael had firsthand knowledge of the kidnapping and murders. And he was one of the ex-combatants participating in the Truth and Recognition Chamber.

In 2021, a JEP magistrate used our truth demands to interview Rafael in person in Colombia. Magistrate Lemaitre then arranged for me to view the recording of the interview over Zoom. The day before the viewing, my EarthRights lawyers helped manage my expectations by informing me that, while Rafael had been a participant in the killings, his interview would not add much to our understanding of *why* it happened, which was my core interest. He would just tell us more details of *what* had happened.

When I read my lawyer's email, I was in the living room of the tiny house I had rented for the summer in Vermont. I stood up from the desk, walked out of the cabin, and let the screen door bang shut. I walked barefoot through the clover, down the hill in front of the cabin to the edge of Stowell Pond. I wept. I continued walking into the pond, sundress and all. I floated there. When the shock of the cold water faded, my system reset. I climbed out and returned to the cabin.

I recognized the weeping—involuntary, fleeting. But I also noticed an unfamiliar discomfort. I felt invaded. The idea that someone out there knew some detail that I did not know felt too intimate, as though he was penetrating a world that had for so long been filled only with my questions and echoes of my questions, devoid of living people.

The JEP conducted the session the next afternoon. Magistrate Lemaitre called it a traslado, or transfer, of Rafael's version of the truth to me. This was an official proceeding. That morning, I wrote, which was my purpose in the cabin in the Vermont woods. I happened to be writing the part of this story that described the first time I met Terence, and I was immersed. When it was time for the traslado to begin, I realized that I was still in my exercise clothes and that my hair was still tied up in twin knotted buns that one might expect from a much younger version of myself. I set Zoom to soften my appearance and made sure the camera only caught my face. An Ansel Adams print of Yosemite's Bridal Veil Falls hung on the cabin wall behind me, forming a virtual background. I texted Jodie to let her know that I was going diving, as we had come to call it, and then I texted about ten other people the same thing. I was alone in the cabin, but I knew not to be alone in the process.

In the Zoom I was supported by my EarthRights lawyers, the JEP lawyers, a representative of the Colombian Inspector General's Office, and a Colombian political scientist who specialized in restorative justice practices. I asked the restorative justice expert for some tips during a traslado. She said to caress my own arms and to get a heavy blanket to put on my lap. She said to hold a stone or some other piece of the earth to help anchor me to the present as we talked about the past. She said to make tea.

I did those things.

She said to interrupt the video of the interview at any time.

I said I would.

Then she said to light a candle. At that point, all the Colombians on the screen held up to the camera the candle they each had lit next to them on their desks. The candle was supposed to represent our intention that the spirit of Terence, Ingrid, and Lahe' would be present with us during the traslado.

I couldn't get with that. It hadn't occurred to me until she said it that other people in other places also had the prerogative to invoke the presence of their spirits. It was an act that felt so private to me; it was not something that I could do with others. I declined with an easy out: I had no candles in the cabin.

They Gave the Orders: Mátelos / Cuídelos

Rafael stated that he gave the order to kill Terence, Ingrid, and Lahe'. Mátelos. Kill them. In the video, he described a timeline of events between the kidnapping and the executions that I had never heard before. It was a quick timeline that had them dead within three days of being kidnapped and five days before their bodies were found.

The morning of February 25, 1999, Terence, Ingrid, and Lahe' were riding in a pickup truck from U'wa territory to the airport in Saravena. Rafael said that his subordinates stopped the pickup truck and forced the three to change into FARC fatigues before placing them into a FARC vehicle. Although the subordinates were supposed to be operating under the direction of Rafael, at this point, they were not. These initial interactions with Terence, Ingrid, and Lahe' were not directed by Rafael. Rather, the FARC subordinates were following the orders of Germán Briceño Suárez, who went by the name Grannobles. Grannobles was a coordinator of the FARC military units in the Colombian states of Arauca, Boyacá, and Casanare. Grannobles's instruction to Rafael's team was to intercept Terence, Ingrid, and Lahe' and get them out of the region.

The next day, February 26, 1999, Rafael entered the scene as the FARC commander allegedly in charge of the front. Rafael said he was confused because Grannobles had broken rank to kidnap these three people without any instruction from Rafael. Rafael said that when he learned of the kidnapping, he radioed the bloque, or regional central command of the FARC, for instructions. The bloque said to wait. They were to drive the three to the Arauca River, which creates Colombia's eastern border with Venezuela. Get the three across the river and then wait.

On February 27, 1999, after Rafael received these instructions, his subordinates drove Terence, Ingrid, and Lahe' to the river. The next day, on February 28, 1999, the three were changed back into civilian clothes and put into a canoe. They crossed the river into Los Pájaros, a village in El Nula near the town of La Victoria in the Venezuelan state of Alto Apure.[1] From the accompanying report of the FARC central command to JEP, we know that the detainees' hands were tied with nylon rope the whole time.[2]

Rafael described the radio communications system between the front he commanded in rural eastern Colombia and his superior Mono Jojoy, the senior commander of the bloque, who was also Grannobles's brother. Rafael and Jojoy exchanged radio transmissions at 8 a.m. and 4 p.m. daily. They maintained a system that communicated the least amount of information possible to shield each other from implication in actions outside their own front. This is where the timeline became compressed in a way that was new to me.

Rafael said that on February 28, 1999, in his 8 a.m. radio communication, he asked Jojoy for instructions about what to do with the three kidnapped U'wa allies. Jojoy did not answer. At 4 p.m., Jojoy still had not answered. Rafael said that at 5 p.m., Grannobles radioed Rafael and told Rafael, "Mátelos." Kill them.

Rafael said he was still waiting for Jojoy to respond because Grannobles was out of rank to be giving an order to Rafael. Nevertheless, at 7 p.m., Rafael radioed his subordinates who held Terence, Ingrid, and Lahe' captive on the far side of the Arauca River. He repeated Grannobles's order. Mátelos.

Rafael said that, at 6 a.m. the next day, March 1, 1999, Rafael's subordinates radioed back to say, "It is done." They were killed with 9-millimeter pistols. He said that at 8 a.m., Jojoy radioed Rafael to say, "Wait. We are in a diplomatic situation. Hold them and take good care of them." Cuídelos. Take care of them.

Rafael then went on to recount that, upon learning of the executions, his own commander said to him, "Oh, what a failure. You are a failure."

At this point, I requested the JEP team to pause the video. I checked to make sure that I had shut the windows of my small cabin. And then I yelled at the screen. "You are a coward. You fucking coward! Why? Why not wait? Why on earth would you not have waited?"

I did not consider that Rafael may have been lying. His hapless demeanor and the ostensible lack of agency he hid behind struck me as cowardly.

If this one man could have slept on it, could have exercised forbearance over one night, our lives could have been so different. My life could have been so different.

I left the screen. I put on more water for tea. I walked outside the cabin into the summer rain. Dusk gathered. I hummed a low, guttural cry and caught my breath.

Back inside, I wondered out loud to the lawyers gathered, "Wait, if central command said on the morning of March 1, 1999, that they were in a 'diplomatic situation,' does that mean that we had made contact? Does that mean that the release efforts we were orchestrating from the American Indian Community House in New York had gained traction on the ground by the morning of March 1?"

The Colombians had no response.

We Faced a Gaping Hole in the Possibility of Truth

During the remaining recording of that first interview, Rafael's telling wildly contradicted contemporaneous evidence we had from the file of Colombia's own regular criminal investigation, which had taken place years before. In reviewing the thousands of pages of documentation, we had studied transcripts of intercepted FARC radio communications from that fateful week. Those transcripts told another timeline of events and threw Rafael's version of the truth into question.

Without finality, I hesitated to communicate Rafael's timeline to Julie. I did not intend to convey a jumble of uncertainty. We both knew how and when to titrate. This was one of those moments. If it was true that they were dead by the night of February 28 or the morning of March 1, this was three days earlier than what was stated in the coroner's reports. That would change Julie's imagination about the duration and character of Terence's suffering. And it would raise new questions: If Rafael had orders to cuídelos, or take care of them, once they were already slain, what did he order his subordinates to do with the bodies from March 1 to March 4?

Earlier in the JEP process, the FARC central command had already attested that after the murders, "the bodies were left on the Venezuelan side of the border and our units withdrew back to Colombian territory."[3] And on March 5, 1999, those of us gathered at the American Indian Community House in New York heard directly from the Venezuelan police that a Venezuelan farmer had found the bodies on March 4, bound and hooded, bled out, strewn across his rainy cow field.

Too many other inconsistencies remained. For example, one could interpret Rafael's assertion that he lacked instruction to kill from central command as a manipulation of the truth. FARC leadership delivered a mea culpa the week after the murders, maintaining that Grannobles acted alone without authorization from central command on the belief that the three were CIA agents. Twenty years later, this bad-apple theory remained the FARC leadership's party line in front of the JEP. But while Rafael may not have had timely instruction from FARC senior commander Mono Jojoy, Grannobles was Mono Jojoy's brother, and Rafael did have timely instruction from Grannobles. It was Grannobles's instruction that Rafael followed to give the order to kill. It is not a stretch to think that brothers in the highest echelons of the organization were talking to each other—there was some evidence of that shortly after the murders—and it is not a stretch to think that Mono Jojoy had told Grannobles to have them killed.[4]

Another inconsistency remained unaddressed. Rafael testified that Grannobles called the three detainees "indigenistas" from day one of the kidnapping. If this is true, it would corroborate Grannobles's girl-friend's characterization at the time that Grannobles orchestrated the kidnappings and murders because the three were "changing the policy of the U'wa Indians."[5] Whether Grannobles ordered them kidnapped because he thought (patronizingly) that the three were manipulating the U'wa into rejecting the oil company or because he thought the three were helping the U'wa achieve their own self-determination by resisting the oil company, both characterizations of Grannobles's state of mind suggest that he acted with awareness that the three were working with the pueblo, not with the state or the CIA. This orienta-tion matters. If Grannobles, a leader in the FARC, which was ostensi-bly aligned with the pueblo, ordered killings of supporters of Pueblo U'wa, it raises the question: With whom was Grannobles aligned? From whom was Grannobles or perhaps the FARC central command taking payments? Whose bidding might they be carrying out?

Who benefits from keeping these inconsistencies blurred? It could benefit many different actors and interests. It could benefit the oil company. How could we find out? Could JEP help us find out? The answer, unfortunately, was no.

In JEP, Colombia considered an oil company to be a "third party" to the armed conflict. Although investigation of the role of third parties had originally been part of the envisioned charge of the truth and recognition process, the judicial decision that finalized the investigatory scope of the JEP eliminated it. Business elites had ensured that third parties such as multinational resource extraction corporations were excluded from JEP investigation. The corpora-tions had thereby opened an exit for themselves: examination of the role of third parties in the internal armed conflict, such as Occiden-tal during its forty-year presence in Colombia, was beyond the reach of the truth and recognition process.[6]

So we faced a gaping hole in the possibility of truth. JEP permitted Julie and me, as special interveners in the process, to include questions about the role of Occidental in our truth demands, but to date, JEP has had the capacity neither to investigate the inconsistencies in FARC ex-combatants' testimony nor to compel ex-combatants to directly address our truth demands regarding Occidental. The result has been obfuscation.

Oxy's deflection of the facts at the time of the murders also contributed to obfuscation. Back in 2000, Oxy vice president Lawrence Meriage told Congress that the NGO working group that supported the U'wa served as de facto allies of the guerrillas—an inciting characterization that put the U'wa and their allies in mortal danger.[7] Meriage echoed Grannobles's characterization of NGOs as manipulating the U'wa people, who were "in no position to speak openly for themselves." He said the fact that NGOs focused their advocacy against Occidental without referring to the region's guerrilla and narcotics problems made him question "the real agenda of the NGOs."[8]

More recently, Oxy lawyers sought to question my own purpose. When we started the JEP process, I asked a federal district court in Texas, where Oxy had moved its headquarters, to compel Oxy to produce documents and communications for us for use in the JEP. Oxy argued that the court should not grant my request because of my "activist" commitments: providing rural environmental legal assistance in the Philippines, meeting with Colombian minister of the environment Juan Mayr, writing the letter to Vice President Gore, and granting an interview with a journalist about Terence's motivations for working with the U'wa. To Oxy, seeking justice for Terence was subversive.

The federal district court judge found that I had every right to ask for documents and communications from Oxy and compelled Oxy to produce them. Of the documents Oxy eventually handed over, the most important ones were highly redacted and fragmented. I found it curious that a company that had gone to Congress to complain that their contractors and workers were forced to pay the FARC kept no documents to this end.

We Contended with a Closing Window

According to ex-combatant Rafael, Grannobles gave him the order to kill. Rafael's testimony included no details about his understanding of Grannobles's rationale for stepping out of rank to order Rafael to give the order to kill.

FARC central command maintains that the 1999 murders happened in "a complex territorial situation in which an unfortunate mistake was made."[9] They maintain that the FARC's own internal justice process demoted and sanctioned Grannobles sufficiently while staying silent about the contradictory theories regarding Grannobles's motivation for the killings. In 2001, Colombia convicted Grannobles in absentia and sentenced him to forty years in prison for these three murders. In 2002, a US federal grand jury also indicted him for the murders.[10] But he has never been captured. Throughout all these proceedings, Grannobles himself has been nowhere to be found. Allegedly, he has been living in Venezuela since 2007.[11]

When Julie and I began participating in the JEP, neither the US nor Colombia had diplomatic relations with Venezuela. Grannobles was the most direct living source about the murders, and rumor had it that he was aging and ill, in hiding in Venezuela. I had always therefore considered Grannobles out of reach.

So I was utterly surprised when, in the middle of the JEP process, out of the blue, I received an email from a stranger I will call Vicente. Vicente was in Venezuela. He said that he knew where Grannobles was and how to find him.

Leads in this case have often turned out to be false or sinister, so I didn't think much of the email. But Vicente persisted. I eventually forwarded the email to my EarthRights lawyers so we could investigate the lead together. I was aware from my years serving on the EarthRights board as an advocate for increased security protocol that it would be a good idea to establish a secure and anonymous means of communication with Vicente. We tried. Nothing felt secure enough.

When we were out of options for going it alone, we acquiesced to contacting the FBI. At the time of the kidnappings, a new federal law had shifted authority to the FBI in cases such as ours involving US citizens in other countries. But during that fateful week in 1999, the FBI agents in Bogotá seemed hapless; without exception, every time I talked with one of them, I had more current information to share with them than they did with me. I was the one who informed the FBI agents that the bodies had been found.

In the twenty years since, I had not once considered reaching out to the FBI for help. But because we had no other options, and because we had strong counsel to do so, we did. It took little effort to get connected to the right person. The FBI special agent had had this case on her docket for years. We are the same age. She and I both entered our adult professional lives with this case running in the background.

When we talked to the special agent, we told her about the three related legal proceedings in which we were still participating: the JEP process, the Texas action, and the U'wa Nation's case against the government of Colombia before the Inter-American Court of Human Rights—a case involving a host of claims that go way beyond this narrow set of murders. We shared the questions we still carried.

The special agent updated us on the status of the 2002 federal grand jury indictment of Grannobles and five other FARC combatants. She told us that there was a 2018 notation in the file indicating that, procedurally, the Department of Justice was ready to close the case, with it having sat cold for so long, but then decided to keep it open anyway.

After contacting Vicente, the special agent reported back to us. She thought he was legitimate. Allegedly, Vicente had visited the Venezuelan agency that issued governmental identification which apparently had a side hustle to produce fake IDs. One day, Grannobles walked up and asked for a fake ID. When it was issued, a person who recognized Grannobles noted his new alias and Venezuelan contact information. To verify this information, during her next trip to Colombia, the special agent arranged to meet Vicente at the Colombia-Venezuela border.

When the appointed date arrived, however, Colombian public outcry about inequities exacerbated by the pandemic had reached a fevered pitch. Peoples' uprisings brought what seemed like the whole country out onto the streets. The meeting place at the border was inaccessible and the rendezvous was called off. The special agent came back to Miami with no new information.

She told us this news via email and we agreed to stay in touch for when another opportunity to contact Vicente arose. The next year, with a shift in diplomatic relations, the special agent came back to brief us about an additional opportunity she had had to corner Grannobles himself. The carefully planned operation involved multiple US, Colombian, and Venezuelan agencies, but it, too, had to be called off at the last minute.

Next to My Forbearance Sat Longing

When she told us, I felt a familiar forbearance. I was accustomed to keeping low expectations. I was accustomed to the glacial pace. I was accustomed to not knowing. But this time, when she came back empty-handed, I noticed that for the first time, next to my forbearance sat longing.

In 2002 when the US Department of Justice had indicted Grannobles for the murders, we responded to the US criminal proceedings by focusing on the macro picture. I had a harder time turning my attention to the matter of Grannobles and the five other individual men named in the indictment. I couldn't process information regarding these men. Consistently, I had this blurriness. It was like a fog, opaque and diffuse, stealing my focus. For many years, I would hear or read the details regarding these men over and over and over to try to grasp the information. I could not process it. The information had always felt too viscerally threatening. This kind of block is a common effect of trauma. The result was that I had not focused my ire, attention, or inquiry on these men.

But now, for the first time in all those years, I really, really wanted to talk with Grannobles. When it seemed as though the FBI was on the verge of verifying Grannobles's alias and whereabouts, I felt a quickening. It felt possible that the case was about to break wide open. But then it didn't. We were back at the glacial pace of legal proceedings regarding the murders. I steered myself away from the longing.

What might it take for me to be okay with never knowing? What if we did find Grannobles and he stuck to the party line and continued to allow himself to be the scapegoat by asserting that he acted alone? What if the JEP accepted the versions of the truth that these men provided and didn't ever require them to address the questions and contradictory evidence that we had presented in response? I was living in the gaping chasm of silence between these questions and their answers. Even as the rest of my life—mom, educator, organizer—continued apace, I also lived in the timeless liminality of this chasm.

19

Point Lobos

How to Unfold

In the JEP, I figured out how to demand truth without becoming attached to the idea that truth would emerge. Good thing. Depending on the extent to which one believes the traslados of testifying ex-combatants, the JEP process surfaced minor clarifications at best about the material circumstances of the kidnappings. Most of our demands for truth regarding the reasons for the kidnappings and murders remain unaddressed. My access to truth about what happened therefore remains fractured. I still hold only fragments.

I learned how to navigate waters replete with the hazards of ambiguity. In the murder investigation, the water remained murky where the truth remained elusive. In navigating a grief held by many, I felt that I had to tuck away fragments that are known but cannot be told to protect privacy, ceremony, or life. The waters therefore remained obscured. I felt constrained by these limitations, off-kilter, doubled over, muted. I resonated with Rilke's lament: "I want to unfold, because where I am folded, there I am a lie." I thought I could write my way through the obfuscation. If I could arrange the fragments of truth in the right way, I would emerge into clear waters. Everything would make sense. There would be resolution. I could unfold.

But writing my way into clear waters did not work. Our truth demands were not met. And some stories still need to remain private.

Here is the real lesson about unfolding. Unfolding becomes available when we see our own agency in the choices we make, including the choice about what we hold, what we put down, what stories we tell. Things happened. Some things can be told. Some things cannot be told. And some things will not be told. That's okay. Fragmented or whole, stories are not "the thing itself," as Virginia Woolf implores.[1] I am not my story. We are not our stories. Reality exists beneath the stories. In this way, I understand John Berger's assertion that "seeing comes before words."[2] Shaping experience into words is like a prayer at best, bounded, often, by our limited human capacity to comprehend the whole. The merit of the telling is in the effort. We must offer the effort back up to the waters. Freedom comes from recognizing agency in the effort and letting it go.

I Sensed a Mudra, A Seal of Sound

The day after I listened to Rafael's testimony, I went again to the small pond near my cabin. I swam its length. Back and forth between the tallest hemlock snag on one end and the boulder that interrupted the reeds on the other. When the first strong kick propelled my chest and arms high above the water's surface, I startled a duck who startled me.[3] It careened low and then high, pumping its wings with a rhythmic jut of the neck. The duck traced five wide circles around the pond before skidding back into home at the near end. I didn't see her again.

When I was done with butterfly, I rested on my back, floating. With my head tilted just so, ears submerged, I sensed a mudra, a seal of sound around my body. The sounds of the water, the bullfrogs, the songbirds, and the run of the creek upstream folded into the singular sound of the pounding of my heart in my ears. For a few minutes, I imagined that I was hearing the heart of the earth and that the lungs of the earth were keeping me afloat. I peered out through collective eyes, following the curve of the earth. I said hello in greeting as if welcoming a long-lost friend, rummaging in the drawer of memory, running my fingers over a necklace I hadn't realized was missing, but was actually still there, intact. I rested on the pond surface in a place of memory.

The Albatross Showed Me How to Walk out the Door

As I wrapped up a draft of this book, I tackled the one remaining box in my closet. This box was the repository for documents that I tagged as important to revisit. Post-It notes scribbled with marginal insights, related articles, JEP documentation, Terence's papers, court filings—any document that remained untreated or that I feared I would forget. I made my way through the box swiftly, lifting helpful citations, details, and corrections into this text. I hummed through the work. I watched for the familiar dissociative fog to begin. It didn't. I marveled at its absence, thinking I perhaps *had* made it solidly to the other side, to freedom.

I have.

This is how I know. The box contained a letter Terence wrote to me during a prior trip to the territory, a letter within the pages of his journal. A letter he had never sent or given to me. In this letter, he stated his belief that the FARC had gone full-bore in support of oil development and that he felt that he faced threats because of it.[4]

Over the past twenty-five years, in any forum possible, we have woven Terence's posthumous observations into our questions about what happened. I was familiar with the letter. But when I picked it up again from the box, I couldn't access my memory of those details. Instead, I experienced shock as though reading the letter for the first time. I was flooded with worry as though in a recurrent nightmare, one in which a missing key is revealed too late. That is how far my mind has buried pieces of this story that are the most threatening. In my shock, I called our team at EarthRights, worried that I had a new finding. They assured me that, yes, they knew this letter and had already integrated it into our work. I have no clear recollection of sharing the letter with them. Some past version of myself did, probably several times.

After talking to the EarthRights team, I felt relief and gratitude. My nervous system started to re-regulate. With balance restored, I reread the letter.

I observed something in Terence's writing. He wrote that even though he didn't plan to send me this letter, he had "all of these thoughts wanting to come out, to be written so that I can rest":

> Unfinished ideas that are screaming to become more whole. There, they are written. The way that I would say them if you were here. The way that I am saying them aloud to you now, so that you will comfort me in my sleep. . . . It feels strange saying that. I don't often feel the need to have someone else help me feel safe, moreover there are not many who could. You, your strength, makes me feel safe.[5]

I was struck that Terence turned to writing to unlock rest. I was familiar with choosing this pathway for myself, but I hadn't ever noticed that he did, too. A measure of the inadequacy of our support systems during those early years of walking alongside the U'wa, Terence, in essence, turned to his journal to stabilize his daily life on the ground.

His writing invited me to hold his words so that he could rest. In the normal course of things, this exchange—of words for rest— would be symbiotic. It would be an exchange that could expand into a community conversation. The burden would be shared. But our lives did not follow the normal course of things. He thought we had time. We did not. The murders stole time from us. I could see now that because this exchange happened only after he was already dead, it would go on to become, unbeknownst to Terence, the source of my own inability to rest for years to come. The clarity smarted. I gasped. Here was the source. I felt outraged.

At that moment, my husband Sunil walked into my office and sat back on the lounge chair. He started talking about his own work. I took off my reading glasses. I turned slowly from my desk to look at him, wide-eyed. I told him that I needed him to remove me from my desk and get me to the woods. He did. We walked it out. We talked it out. We hiked the hills surrounding our house. I kicked the stones and snapped the branches. I let myself feel angry at Terence. I let the anger have a place out there in the hills. I used the steps to dissipate, dissipate. Dissipation takes time; I gave it time.

Shortly thereafter I dreamt I stood inside an administrative building watching an enormous ocean bird that stood there, too, watching me. It was an albatross. Webbing, perhaps fishing line, thoroughly tangled the bird. In its beak, the bird held a large rectangular object, thin like a poster. The bird approached me, and it was clear that my role was to untangle the bird. I did. The bird moved away with the object in its mouth. I could then see that the object was a doormat. The bird placed the doormat at the threshold of an exit and exited. I walked across the doormat and the threshold, following the bird out the door.

I have grappled with Terence's words since I was twenty-five years old. To share the burden, I reshaped them into our truth demands and into this book. I have examined with care the exchange between words and rest. It is now twenty-five years later.

I let go of the words and I choose rest.

I Choose the Rest

In the summer of 2022, I listened to Elder Linda Eagle Speaker of the Blackfeet Nation of northern Montana talk about the practice of giving it over to the waters.[6] She talked about the discomfort and agitation that comes from awareness of that which cannot be changed, and witness of that which is changing at a pace too slow to prevent more harm. She said to wash it off in the water, to put it back in the waters where the grandmothers can handle it for you. Wash it off, let it go. Let the grandmothers take it, those who can handle it for you.

This giving over is not a tossing away. It is like the power of the river in Ingrid's territory, several Native nations to the east. The Mahwāēw River, also known as the Wolf River, or the one who howls. People give over at the water's edge. It is cyclical. It is healthy. It is necessary for continuing.

In the summer of 2023, I thought about Elder Linda's instructions. I was standing on a cliff overlooking the upended crags and sea stacks that form the southern end of Carmel Bay on California's central coast. Twenty-three years prior, Julie and my family were in the foothills behind this bay to plant a redbud tree in Terence's memory. After planting the tree, we traveled down the hills to this jagged coastline to let it go, to offer the effort up.

The Spaniards who centuries ago colonized this place likened the bark of the harbor seals to that of the wolves and named this place Point Lobos, or Wolf Point. The Pacific Ocean meets the land here in an unending churn of crash and retreat. Harbor seals navigate the turbulence with ease. In it they find their sustenance. In it they birth their young. And next to it, on the sun-kissed rocky shore, they rest.

I am in a constant and joyful practice of giving over. It is like swimming butterfly. Again and again and again. It is technique. It is sustenance. It is daily practice. It is freedom and it is hard won.

This unfolding allows rest. This unfolding allows the rest of the story to flow. This unfolding allows my gaze to refocus on what really matters.

I submitted our truth demands in Terence's case.

But there is so much more that the truth demands of all of us.

20

What the Truth Demands

To Inhabit the Voice of the Waters

The truth demands that we act from interdependence. That we inhabit the voice of the waters as a guiding means from our oldest remembering, from even before the harm, to seek justice and to paint the future that is porvenir—emerging and yet to come. (See Appendix 2.) The truth demands that we create conditions to remember and practice how to do that.

In August 2005, in the days and weeks following Hurricane Katrina, from her home in the drought-stricken Ojai Valley of southern California, Cuban American artist Carmen Abelleira watched the anguish pile up in the Superdome stadium, where a flooded New Orleans was funneling thousands of stranded and abandoned people. In response, Carmen painted *The Seamstress* on a salvaged scrap-wood pallet. In *The Seamstress*, a brown-skinned woman sits in rapt attention at the dress she is pinning and shaping. She has kicked off her shoes and moves with her feet planted and spine elongated. Her gaze is locked on the work of her hands, heart intact. At the same time, her peripheral vision holds the storm raging outside. Carmen painted in witness to Hurricane Katrina, a deluge that told the future.

When I first saw *The Seamstress* tucked away on the wall of Carmen's Ojai garage, I wept. Carmen said in one painting what has taken me twenty-five years to write with all these thousands of words. She painted *The Seamstress* to honor the work of the women of color who were navigating the waters and stitching life back together. The people who figure out what it takes to stop the harm, harness craft, repair the rips, and stay focused on creating anew, even when working with scraps. The people who assert the place of beauty and practice in the family of things, attentive all the while to the storm. The people whose actions call us into right relationship with our wanted obligation to make shelter from the storm for us all. People like my friend Colette Pichon Battle and her team whose approach to community lawyering in the Gulf South post-Katrina has by now come to offer a blueprint for the assertion of climate justice everywhere.[1]

In the painting, though, it was still 2005. The seamstress had not yet acquiesced to a future in which our world is at the mercy of ever increasingly violent storms. I wanted to intervene. Yes, I wanted to learn how to keep my hands steady like the seamstress even as I stayed attentive to the storm. Yes, I wanted to learn how to read the waters. But more—I wanted us collectively to remember how to inhabit the voice of the waters so that we might possibly take aim at transforming the source and course of the storm itself.

What We See from Standing on the Shore

A call to transform the source and the course of the storm is audacious. Yet the essence of this audacious vision animates many communities' efforts to address the root causes of climate change. Transformative social movements recognize that an audacious vision requires radical connection among the people who cultivate the vision and deep embodiment of the values underlying it. Only then is strategic navigation toward such a vision possible.[2] Together with dozens of others who recognize that we are in a moment of collective acceleration, I am learning about strategic navigation. The strategies come, no surprise, from studying water. We study how it moves and what its movements tell us about when it is time for us to move. This learning circle prompts me to ask what it would take for us to inhabit the voice of the waters as a method of strategic navigation. To get myself into right relationship with this inquiry, I first needed to take stock of what I had learned so far from standing on the shore.

I stand on this wretched shore: In the fall of 1996, I met the babies of Honda Bay, a barangay, or neighborhood, carved into the eastern edge of the island of Palawan. Honda Bay is the first community outside of my own with which I ever worked. There, families pushed out by commercial overfishing of their homelands in one part of the Philippines moved through the waters across the archipelago to resettle in Honda Bay in what seemed like the only available piece of land: a jetty built from the tailings of an abandoned American mercury mine. Upon learning the ways their children were being poisoned by playing on the earthen floor of their new abodes, the parents of Honda Bay looked at each other as if to say, But this is our home now. There is nothing left to eat where we were. We will adjust. We will fish farther out from the shore. We will lift our babies up. We have built our homes upon the source of the poison. *And* it is what we have. It is "a way out of no way."[3]

I also stand on this shore: In the winter of 1999, Terence, Ingrid, and Lahe' were taken by canoe across the Arauca River from Colombia into Venezuela and shot. The following winter, on the adjacent Cubují River, Pueblo U'wa and neighboring farmers barricaded the road with encampments in a multiweek, multi-location paro, or stop. Their bodies stopped the flow of labor and equipment at and on the road to Oxy's drill site. In solidarity, the countryside also briefly stopped in an economic strike. Colombian public forces and others escalated intimidation, harassment, and violence against U'wa protesters, attempting to disperse the encampments. To escape the violence, some U'wa mothers and their children chose the river. Moms carrying babies tied to their backs. Not everyone could navigate the strong current and at least one baby girl died. It was the news about the girl's drowning that prompted the anonymous Colombian civil servant to inform U'wa leadership about the continued existence of the colonial titles to their territory.

Another: In the winter of 2011, I helped scatter some of Fran Peavey's ashes into the Ganges at the river's bend in Varanasi. We met at Tulsi Ghat, a complex of river steps and buildings best known as the place where the sixteenth-century poet Tulsidas allegedly captured into written word the oral stories of the Ramayana, the Sanskrit epic poem and foundational Hindu text. When pilgrims to Tulsi Ghat pay homage to this spiritual and literary history, they also learn about the Swatcha Ganga, or Clean Ganges, campaign headquartered at Tulsi Ghat together with a water quality testing laboratory. Fran supported her colleague Dr. Veer Badra Mishra to establish both. From atop the ghat, the sun rises red over the beloved and polluted river; glistening orange water flows north at a clip. Sunrise sees thousands of the devoted pad their way down to the banks. Lips move with whispered prayers, palms joined, wrists touching forehead in an ancient gesture, generation after generation offering a continuously sustained prayer of gratitude for life, and devotion to the source of it. All day, people gather at the water's edge, to pray, bathe, wash clothes, vend, make offerings, gather sustenance. The source of life and the source of illness, one. The holy and the mundane, sacred and profane, jumbled together in the mix.

And another: In the fall of 2018, we gathered near the Mahwāēw River for encuentro between Santa Ana and Menominee community rebuilders. When we returned from the river, youth organizers from Santa Ana shared stories. Young people who've made a strong life together in the city, working urban lands to grow food for themselves and neighbors. Youth who, upon learning the soil they tilled may be heavy with lead, embarked on a multiyear investigation to understand and map the extent of the illness of the land and the people.

One young woman, Diana Luz, told the story of wanting to learn the word for *soil* in Purépecha, her root language, neither the colonial English nor Spanish. In the dispersal of diaspora, she did not have easy access to her root language or elders. When she gained some elders, as she put it, she learned that the word for soil in her root language translated to *mother soil*. As she told it, the words ushered in a sense of homecoming, of language finally reflecting her own understanding of the earth as being as alive as her grandmothers. She understood that the illness of the mother soil was of course reflected as illness in her grandmothers' children, children who had been cut off from the source of language and land. Children who were here getting by and growing food from land with water where there is no water. Where the dry riverbeds of the Santa Ana River watershed periodically surge with the makeshift homes of hundreds of people who have been pushed over the brink of houselessness. Making "a way out of no way." *Still/Here.*

Last: During the 2010 BP Deepwater Horizon oil spill in the Gulf of Mexico, I tried to hear what the manatees were saying. *Quiet your mind*, they said . . . *Draw toward stillness not from your despair but from your strength, and listen. Hear in the stillness our parting song. And make our song your own.*[4]

I stand here on the shore. Reading the waters. Listening. Learning. Mending. Calling in.

How to Use Our Two Hands

> Gate, gate, paragate, parasamgate, bodhi svaha /
> Gone, gone, way beyond, gone to the other shore.
>
> —THE HEART SUTRA'S CLOSING MANTRA

During law school, I took a semester off to work on the case of Winston Cabello, an economist under Chilean President Salvador Allende and a victim of General Augusto Pinochet's Caravan of Death.[5] Fearing for their own lives, Winston's surviving family members moved to the United States. They became aware that Pinochet henchman Armando Fernández Larios had also come to the States. Fernández Larios had pled guilty for his role in the 1976 Washington, DC, car bomb assassination of former Chilean foreign minister and ambassador to the US Orlando Letelier and his assistant Ronni Moffitt. After serving a short sentence for his role in the Letelier/Moffitt murders, Fernández Larios's plea agreement allowed him to remain in the US. The Cabello family recognized Fernández Larios as one of Winston's executioners—he was hiding in plain sight as a manager of an auto body shop in Miami. Twenty-six years after Winston's murder, his family found a way to bring civil suit in federal court for the henchman's participation. "Chile, your waters run red."[6]

I moved to Florida for the month of the trial. I was trying to understand what a US jury would do with facts like this, and how the courts might work with Terence's case. Of their legal victory, the Cabello family later said that the most important part of it all was having the chance to tell their story. Hearing that helped me understand why I needed to tell ours.

I told the story of our truth demands as a way of learning how to stand on this wretched shore. Doing so taught me how to navigate home. In the telling, I saw glimmers of how we navigate our collective hearts back home, too. I am clear that I do not stand on the shore alone.

There, in what Pueblo U'wa calls Kajka Ika, the heart of the world, the earth body and the bodies of earth rights defenders were slain.

Where did the hearts go? Did they fly away? Did they scatter to a far corner of the cosmos to regroup? Fossil fuel extraction, as a magnet for violence, creates conditions that invite the slaying of the body, but I do not believe that it can take the heart. For the collective heart to come back home after a lifetime spent in flight, we need to gather forces. To regroup. To rest. To strengthen and re-member strength. To purge the bitterness, salve the mortal wound. To begin again speaking the unspeakable. To tell the old stories, stitching the fragments freshly together with the new. This work transforms the wretched shore. It is necessarily collective work. To do it, we need to pivot toward each other and, together, toward the far horizon.

During the Vietnam War, after the bombing of Bên Tre, a US military representative said that the American forces had to destroy the village to save it. Upon hearing this absurd and barren rationale, Thich Nhat Hanh wrote his way through his anger. He wrote that he used his hands to hold his face and to prevent his soul from flying in anger.[7] His words were made into a folk song that I've known since high school.[8] But it wasn't until after the 1999 murders brought me to my knees that I understood the instruction in these words. As individuals, we can use our hands to try to keep our hearts from flying away so that we can stay where staying is needed. How can we apply this instruction in community?

We need a container that makes staying in community possible. We need a container where rest becomes possible because it is finally safe to rest. A container that welcomes the collective heart back home. In many social movements, people consider a community to be resilient when the people have what they need to create conditions to protect and nurture biological and cultural diversity even amid adversity, flux, and rapid change.[9] In our broken places, a community is resilient when it makes it safe for the earth to start growing life again. Removing the mercury and lead from the soil and the waters; without dispossession of people; with the language and presence of the ancestors. Growing ancestral foods, and community ownership, while shrinking urban heat islands. In tending the land (and walking alongside communities that tend the land), our hands do the work that helps us remember how to come home.

When we tend that which has been rendered unholy and broken, we may begin to recognize that the land itself is playing the same role in the community as the interior temple plays in the body. The tended earth can become an island refuge in the sea of harms that flows from our misperception of separation. To welcome our collective heart back home to the temple, we must light the candle, sweep the steps, and prepare the seat for sitting. Such actions are a reason to stay, a collective means of survival.

Beyond truth and recognition, this work is what comes to mind when I think about radical mending and reparation. When the hearts of a place find it safe enough to come back home, the community as a body has a chance of wading through the "uncomfortable middle," learning anew, or remembering, how to move together in ways that take and share responsibility for the whole going forward.[10] When the collective heart comes home, rest becomes possible. And with rest comes the possibility of stillness.

We need stillness to see the way forward. Zen teacher and Hakka-Native Hawaiian political strategist Norma Ryuko Kawelokū Wong teaches the collective acceleration intensive. She teaches that, in radical mending, we must "see whether the water in you is clear enough, calm enough for you to see . . . the reflection of the moon. [If] the shape of the moon is distorted, that is because the water is still tumultuous. The water needs to be calm to reflect the true shape of something."[11] Especially when the waters outside remain turbulent, stilling the waters internally is essential to generating the complex strategy needed to go beyond mending and recognition, toward justice and reconciliation.

To Leap

I am reminded of the story Terence told, writing from the cloud forest floor of the Colombian Andes. The story described the song cycle that his U'wa companions conducted to mark one U'wa girl's transition into adulthood. Days of continual singing of the stories of their people, of how the rivers got their names. It was a song with no end. Some would pick up the song where others left off. And then eventually silence, within which the song reverberated for hours in the earthen floor. The reverberating stillness is not unlike the aftereffect of the monks and nuns chanting the bodhisattva Avalokiteśvara's name at Plum Village. Of the U'wa song cycle, Terence's U'wa companion Daris later said that, while marking these life transitions, they sing about all the territory, including the rivers and mountains from Patagonia to Canada. She said the singing itself represents the equilibrium and sustainability of the planet.[12] They sing so that people can remember who they are, right where they are, through the words, mountains, and waters that shaped them. So that the parable of the choir can persist.[13] Terence wrote, "This is the reason we are doing this work, so that people can listen to singing."[14]

The U'wa say Terence, Ingrid, and Lahe' "aren't wandering in the river of the forgotten"; rather, their aka-kambra, or "word with spirit," persists.[15] After Thây died in 2022, Vietnamese American poet Ocean Vuong reminded the gathered and grieving community that language and sound are one of humanity's oldest ways to transmit knowledge. Vuong observed that the word *narrative* comes from the Latin word *gnarus*, meaning knowledge. Stories then, even fragmented, can be the translation of knowledge and a transmission of energy. This energy cannot die. "In this way," he said, "to speak is to survive, and to teach is to shepherd our ideas into the future, the text is a raft we can send forth for all later generations."[16]

The U'wa are known as the thinking people, the people who speak well. To speak well can take many forms. Whether the narrative is heard depends on the listener. In Terence's notebooks from March 1998, he meditated on the voice of silence in the U'wa people's resistance to oil extraction in their territory. "Where is the voice of silence? Of women? Of children? Of the communities that cannot speak publicly about opposition to petrol?" He wondered about the relationship between silence and fear. His final note regarded the silence of "the sound of the stumps cut during seismic line studies."[17] In U'wa territory, Terence contemplated the narrative that silence elicits.

Twenty years later, Colombia prohibited its post–civil war truth and recognition chamber from investigating the role of multinational fossil fuel extraction corporations during the internal conflict. In relegating corporations to third-party status, Colombia designed the chamber in a manner that restricted the range of stories that could be safely elicited. The narrative of silence was thus harder to hear. The sound of the stumps cut during seismic line studies did not ring out in the chamber. The earth itself was also rendered a third party, peripheral to the deliberations.[18]

Out here on the shore, we know better. We know how to listen for the silence of the stumps and the parting song of the manatees. We know how to listen for the reverberation of the songs of belonging and for "the ancestors' breath in the voice of the waters."[19] The practice of listening sharpens our other senses. Our vision is clear: the truth demands we move these so-called third parties—both the corporations and the voice of the waters—out of the periphery and into the center of our vision.

And when we do, we look carefully. We heed the voice of the waters. We take note of the momentum in the water, and the timing. We remember that water flows around boulders. And that boulders get worn away. We take note of who stands gathered with us. We ready ourselves to leap.[20]

EPILOGUE

The Water Pitcher

In the spring of 2023, my younger son, Julian, and I traveled to Santiago, Chile, to witness the hearing of Caso U'wa during the 157th regular session of the Inter-American Court of Human Rights. The Inter-American Court has jurisdiction over the national governments of twenty countries throughout Latin America.

At stake in this case is not just the righting of the U'wa Nation's grievances against the Colombian government. The decision will also have implications for the way all Latin American governments handle Indigenous peoples' right to self-determination. When it issues its ruling on Caso U'wa, the Court may further consolidate jurisprudence about what does and does not constitute consultation in a national government's obligation to obtain free, prior, and informed consent from Indigenous communities when seeking to construct and conduct projects in Indigenous ancestral territory. The Court may explain who decides in land use disputes involving Indigenous ancestral territory upon which a national government delineates a national park for recreation. The Court may explain the conditions under which an Indigenous nation can reasonably refuse a national government's demand for co-management of such lands and waters. And finally, the Court may take this opportunity to elaborate on the contemporary relevance of the colonial land titles issued by the King of Spain that are held not only by the U'wa Nation but also by other Indigenous peoples throughout the Americas—titles issued, in the case of the U'wa, before the formation of the modern nation-state of Colombia. Caso U'wa, filed twenty-five years ago, focuses us on what calls for landback mean in this moment in which climate change brings into relief the imperative of Indigenous and community-driven stewardship of land and waterways.

The night before the hearing began, the U'wa delegation reflected over dinner with Indigenous allies from Ecuador, Peru, and Chile. Berito, the dear friend of Terence's, was the eldest of the U'wa delegation. I presented Berito with the eagle feather that Terence had been given during a Sundance in the years prior to his murder. I told Berito that I had kept it in care all these years and it seemed right to give it to Pueblo U'wa before the hearing, with the hope that we could draw upon the vision of the eagle during the ensuing days.

The next morning, the delegation walked from the hotel to the administrative center of Santiago toward the courthouse. Across cobbled streets connecting a canyon of century-old edifices, members of the U'wa Indigenous guard wore blue vests and carried boldly colored ribboned staffs slung over their shoulders. Occasionally, one would jokingly hold the staff high above our heads, as though in procession.

Within a few blocks of La Moneda, the Chilean presidential palace, we arrived at the constitutional court. The Chilean court was hosting the Costa Rica–based Inter-American Court of Human Rights for the weeklong duration of its session. We filed into the courtroom and arranged ourselves for Day 1. The six judges filed in. Upon their signal, the room sat down.

Berito and a younger U'wa spiritual leader-in-training made their way to the bench and turned to those assembled in the courtroom. They offered a brief opening ceremony before the proceedings began. For Berito, the act served to open the channel and allow the right energies to flow. As he sang, he held in his right hand a beaded gourd, and in his left, several feathers, moving in a motion that drew up the energy from the earth toward the sky. In this way, the hearing began.

The hearing lasted two days. The decision from the court will take ages. The morning after the hearing concluded, over breakfast at the hotel, I had a final visit with Daris and Ebaristo, the two U'wa people who testified at the hearing, as well as Victor and Miguel, two additional members of the U'wa delegation. Daris and I were the first to arrive. When we sat down, Daris placed on the empty table a necklace. It was a beaded collar in the colors of the rainbow. "This is the necklace that was made for me to wear during the second day of the hearing," she said. "I am giving it to you. From my girls and from me and from the entire pueblo, we are grateful for your accompaniment, we are grateful that you are here, and you are always with us. The letter that Aura wrote yesterday to the international communities about this moment in our history, she wrote for you as an expression of gratitude from the U'wa Nation." I noted the beauty of the necklace and the honor I felt receiving it. I reminded Daris that it was not necessary to give it to me. She insisted. I said thank you.

When the others arrived, we talked about my work with the Community Resilience team at the University of California, Irvine. We talked about our work in Santa Ana, California, with Latine and Indigenous Latin American immigrant communities, who are asserting the very same rights to self-determination and community ownership, but who do so without a land base. We talked about the urban farms, land trusts, mercaditos, and worker-owned cooperatives that are emerging in response. We talked about the ten other community academic partnerships that we work with across California—partnerships that assert the same rights through community-driven participatory action research for relevant climate solutions. And about the trainings we offer to lawyers all over the United States, lawyers who have shifted—or are ready to shift—their legal practice to work alongside disinvested communities to assert these very same rights to a just transition in defense of their peoples, cultures, and the earth.

I got out the photos that Terence took during his prior trips to the territory. A photo of Ebaristo and Terence at Project Underground in Berkeley, California, when Ebaristo was so young. He said that the map Terence and Terence's dad made for the *Blood of Our Mother* report was the first map to attempt to show the full extent of U'wa territory and the proposed oil blocks therein. He called the map the true start of Caso U'wa, the case that culminated at the Santiago hearing. He noted Terence's necklace in the photo, an U'wa necklace comprised of the teeth of the guache and cusicusi animals found in the territory. I told them we buried Terence with that necklace. Miguel came over to sit next to me so that he could see the photos—photos taken in the territory when he was just a child. The sacred site at Shobar-kajka, still a mountain and a valley, that became the Gibraltar drill site and now a gas platform—a site at the center of Caso U'wa. Photos of families from across the territory. Photos of the building in which former Colombian environmental minister Juan Mayr came to meet with the U'wa, the time when they implored Minister Mayr to take Terence back to Bogotá with him in the helicopter. Photos of the water pollution flowing from the repeatedly bombed Caño Limón oil pipeline. A photo of Terence and U'wa elders and children standing outside of the thatch-roof house in which the ceremony took place for the Bocota girl who was becoming a woman. Ebaristo held this photo up to the group and said, "This is the photo that was missing from our slide presentation during the closing arguments at the hearing yesterday. This photo of Terry in the territory."

At this point, the U'wa delegation was soon due in the hotel lobby to depart for a day trip to the Chilean coast. To make haste, I started pulling things out of my bag. Earrings for the women to mark the significance that the U'wa delegation to the hearing included women at all. Three nursing shirts for Daris to take to Aura, whose baby was due the following week. Two beaded acorn necklaces with abalone made by a Native Californian Pomo artist that I'd bought in Berkeley a few weeks prior. I asked Daris to give one acorn necklace to the mother of the U'wa baby girl who was drowned in the February 2000 violence. The other acorn necklace I asked Daris to give to her own daughter,

Claudia. Claudia is training to become an U'wa spiritual leader and is also the one who, by now, had made for me three necklaces.

Then I pulled out the satchel containing items for Berito. While choosing the acorn necklaces, I had told the Pomo acorn artist about the U'wa story, and why I was buying the necklaces. A Chumash basket artist in the stall next door overheard the story. She came over and started to tell me the story of her own trip to Colombia, to visit the U'wa Nation with her film camera, in 1998, and the story of Terence, Ingrid, and Lahe'. I let her know that I was familiar with the story, yes, and I told her who I was. Our eyes met in mutual recognition. She told her story about being in the territory with Terence, about how her own elders had advised her not to go, but that she insisted. She told me that her elders cautioned that the effect of the visit would stay with her for life. And indeed, it has for her, in the sobering observation that the murders the following year could have included her. She remembered Berito and gave me one of her woven kelp baskets to give to him with a greeting of remembrance. I told Daris, Ebaristo, Victor, and Miguel this story and handed the basket to Daris for Berito.

My last satchel was a bandana that contained a bag of tobacco and around ten bundles of white sage. The sage bundles were from Terence's Chumash friend Red Star, who brought the enormous bag of the sage to New Mexico for the men to prepare Terence's body to go into the ground. The men had wrapped Terence's body in the sage. In the bandana, open there on the breakfast table at the hotel restaurant in Santiago, amid empty orange juice cups and half-eaten toast, were displayed the final bundles that remained left over from the burial. Ebaristo took the bundles to bring back to the territory, where the Werjayá would perhaps use them in the ayuno upon the delegation's return. In this way, the sage and tobacco would be put back in the earth, so that Terence can rest. I was so relieved. They knew what to do with the bundles. It felt like ancestral housekeeping, long overdue.

We parted ways. The U'wa delegation went to the sea. Julian and I went to the Museum of Memory, where Chile consolidates its telling of Pinochet's coup, the horrors of the dictatorship, and the findings of that country's truth and reconciliation process. Victor Jara's final stanzas grace the museum's exterior, as does the Universal Declaration of Human Rights. Julian listened to the scratchy recording of the six minutes of Chilean President Allende's final radio address and watched the faint footage from moments later of the bombing of La Moneda. He lingered before the glass cabinet that holds the brittle papers that, one by one, spelled the end of the rule of law in Chile. He ran his hand over the wall that inscribes the names of the 40,000 recognized victims of the dictatorship's torture, disappearance, killing, and political imprisonment. He took it in. We moved quickly through the museum when his pace picked up. We left when Julian felt it was time to leave.

During the hearings in Caso U'wa, my son had asked me two questions. First, he asked what elements a people would need to have in place to declare themselves their own nation-state. I told him. He wondered whether the U'wa Nation seeks to be recognized as such. I told him to ask the U'wa. Second, after we had listened to Colombia's expert witness assert that the development debate is simply a matter of balancing interests among stakeholders and that fossil fuel extraction can, by his account, be compatible with upholding a dissenting Indigenous people's rights, Julian whispered to me, "If it wanted to, couldn't the Colombian government instead bring a witness that just went ahead and agreed with the U'wa? And then the lawyer for the government could just also admit to the judges that she agrees, too? Maybe they'd both get fired, but couldn't they just agree with the U'wa?"

I responded, "Yes, that is entirely possible." Yes, my child, we are indeed on that cusp. *So be it. See to it.*[1]

There was one more item that I gave to my U'wa companions. It was a ceramic cup Terence had made. He was a ceramicist. He made a set of five simple teacups glazed in a deep brown and black, with shimmers of cobalt blue. To Terence, the set was a prized creation. In July 1998 we spent an afternoon bringing the teacups around to the houses of three of his mentors. We gave one cup in gratitude to each, including Kazuaki Tanahashi, the Japanese Zen brush mind artist. Terence then gave one cup to me and kept the final cup for himself. When he was killed shortly thereafter, it meant that I then had two cups, mine and his. My family has kept these cups in our tea cupboard all these years.

The week before going to Santiago, while bringing my other son, Kiran, home from volleyball practice, I was thinking about what I could possibly offer in greeting to the U'wa delegation, having just been with Daris in Bogotá a month earlier, where I had bestowed loads of gifts, sacred and mundane. Rounding the bend to our house, I thought of Terence's teacups. I gasped out loud. Startled, Kiran asked me what happened. I told him about the cups and my budding plan to bring the cups to Santiago. Kiran, with uncharacteristic assertion, said, "Mom, no, you can't bring them the cups. Those are special cups." I remarked that I was surprised he remembered the cups, let alone had feelings about them. I let him know I was paying attention.

The night before the trip, as I finished packing, I stretched to reach the cups down from the highest cupboard shelf. I brought both cups to my suitcase and examined them. On the bottom of one cup, next to Terence's inscription of his own initials, I saw Kiran's full name, written with a Sharpie in my handwriting. I was bemused and puzzled. Then I remembered that I had sent Kiran to kindergarten with this cup as his daily water cup—it was the perfect shape and durability for toddler hands. Kiran's name on the cup affirmed my own sense that indeed, this one was our cup to keep. It was also clear that the other cup, the cup that Terence had kept for himself, was not mine. I had taken care of it all these years, but it was not mine to hold. It belonged in the territory, a gift in greeting or parting, for his other mentors.

The morning after the hearing, I told Ebaristo and Daris the story of the five cups and gave them Terence's.

I told them that I could feel myself changing, could feel my life moving. I could see that this part of the accompaniment was also complete. I thanked them for taking the cup. They understood and thanked me, too. Ebaristo held the cup gingerly and said they would bring it back to the territory to put in the U'wa museum.

In tarot, cups are the suit of emotion. In the tarot deck I use, the card with the Two of Cups depicts two beloveds filling each other's cup, each drawing from the river. It is a card about fulfillment. I gave Terence's cup to my U'wa companions to bring to the territory.

I now hold one cup. Holding this single cup, I notice what has always been true: I am contained in my own container.

I am fully mine.

From the tarot deck, I draw, instead, upon the card that depicts the Priestess of Cups. In my tarot deck, the Priestess of Cups perches on the far shore, aware of the crumbling tower in the distance. In the card, there is no cup—the container is indistinguishable from the ocean itself. The Priestess sits breathing, paying attention. Clouds billow above. She presides. Her throat opens to join the song of the whales below.

⌒

Through the open door, I can hear my family making breakfast downstairs. Cutting apples. Filling the water pitcher. Sorting their backpacks for the day. With delight and a rush of lightness, I join them now.

On December 20, 2024, the Inter-American Court of Human Rights issued its decision in Caso U'wa.

We won.

APPENDIX 1

Thirty-Six Truth Demands

Date: April 3, 2019
Re: Truth Demands
Case 001 Kidnapping and Murder of Terence Unity Freitas,
March 4, 1999

Dear Justice Julieta Lemaitre Ripoll:

. . . Below please find my truth demands. I have gathered these questions together with Julie Freitas.

1. What were FARC members doing in the area when the three Americans were kidnapped? How did you know there were Americans in the area? Did you come across them by accident, or did you already know they were there?

2. If the FARC already knew the three Americans were in the area, how did the FARC come to learn that information? Did someone or some entity tell the FARC? Who?

3. In the weeks and months before the kidnapping, had the FARC heard about Americans coming and going from the area? When was the first time the FARC became aware of their presence in that area?

4. When you (the FARC) approached the vehicle from which you kidnapped the Americans, was anyone else present in or around the vehicle? If so, who? Did you go to the place where the three Americans were in the vehicle with the already-formed intention of kidnapping the Americans? When you decided to kidnap the three Americans, what happened to the other person(s) who were present at the time? Why did you decide not to kidnap this person(s) as well?

5. Did you know who the Americans were? If so, how did you know? Did you ask the Americans who they were? Did they explain why they were there? Did you believe them?

6. Why did you decide to kidnap them?

7. Did you at any point speak to the Americans about their travel to U'wa territory? What was the substance of those conversations?

8. Did you (the FARC) ask the three Americans whether they had been traveling to U'wa territory? What did they tell you?

9. Did your decision to kidnap the Americans have anything to do with their visit to U'wa territory? If so, what was the basis for that decision? Did anyone from or involved with the U'wa Nation discuss the Americans with you? If so, who? What did they say?

10. Did your decision to kidnap the Americans have anything to do with Pueblo U'wa's process of sanaemiento [territorial demarcation] in their territory? If so, what was the basis for that decision?

11. Do you know if any agency of the Colombian government was notified about the facts of the kidnapping while it was taking place? If so, what was their response? Did they take any action in response? If so, what action?

12. Did you ever consider requesting a ransom for the Americans? We know you kidnapped and threatened executives already, and we know you were being paid protection money. Why did you decide not to ransom them, or if you wanted to, why did you change your mind?

13. Was it your decision to kill them or someone else's? If someone else's, whose?

14. Were any Americans involved in this decision?

15. Did anyone ask you to kill the Americans? If so, whom? Why did they ask you to kill them?

16. Were you paid by someone to kill them? If so, by whom?

17. Did you have any conversations with any American companies or individuals about the Americans before you kidnapped them? If so, which companies or individuals? What was the substance of those conversations?

18. Did you have any conversations with any American companies or individuals about the Americans during the time you held them? If so, which companies or individuals? What was the substance of those conversations?

19. Did you have any conversations with any American companies or individuals about the Americans before you decided to kill them? If so, which companies or individuals? What was the substance of those conversations? Did you have any conversations with any American companies or individuals after the killings? If so, what was the substance of those conversations?

20. Do you know if anyone from the Colombian Government was involved in the decision to kidnap and kill the Americans? If so, from which sector of the government were they, and what was their role in those decisions?

21. Why did you decide to kill them? How did you feel about that at the time? Was everyone with you in agreement with this decision? How do you feel about this decision now?

22. Who else from FARC (or otherwise) was with you during the kidnapping and/or murders of the three Americans? What are their names? Where are they now?

23. When the FARC kidnapped the Americans, the U'wa Nation issued a comunicado begging the FARC to release the three Americans and informing the FARC that they were three indigenistas who had been accompanying the U'wa Nation. The comunicado specifically asked the FARC to release them. Did you see this communique? If you did see or hear of it, why did the FARC never take the U'wa Nation's communication or request into account, and on the contrary, proceed

to assassinate them? After U'wa leadership had clarified that the three Americans had been working alongside Pueblo U'wa, that they were U'wa allies, that they were helping Pueblo U'wa with its case, why did the FARC never take this into account to set them free?

24. When the dialogue with the FARC was initiated (including the dialogue in Havana), why was the U'wa Nation not included or taken into consideration? And why were the families of the three Americans not made to understand that this was a process that was later going to be taken up by the JEP?

25. During and surrounding the time of the kidnapping and murders of the three Americans, why why were we hearing reports that the FARC was regularly guarding Occidental Petroleum's machinery in the areas in and around U'wa territory? Why were they providing this service to Oxy, thus enabling Oxy's machinery to come into U'wa territory? Were you being paid for this service?

26. After the murders of the three Americans, did the FARC or anyone known to the FARC threaten, kidnap, murder, disappear, or otherwise intimidate and/or silence any person or persons who may have possessed information about the circumstances surrounding the kidnapping and murders of the three Americans? If so, who? And why?

27. Why, after all these years, has the FARC continued to persecute the U'wa leader, Berito Cobaria? We understand that FARC has also tried to assassinate him on multiple occasions. Why?

28. Before killing the three Americans, why had you crossed the river into Venezuela?

29. During the kidnapping, how did you move the three Americans from place to place?

30. During the kidnapping, where did the three Americans sleep? Did they sleep?

31. During the kidnapping, did the three Americans walk through the forest? Did they have shoes on their feet while walking? If they were barefoot, why?

32. During the kidnapping, to what extent did you feed them?

33. Were their bodies bound the whole time, or just at the end? Why did you bind them?

34. In the days leading up to the bullets, had you been hurting Terence's body? If so, tell us how. And, why?

35. Did he speak my name? Did you know my name? My name is Abby Reyes.

36. From Julie Freitas, Terence's mother: Why did you shoot him 10 times? Why 10 bullets?

APPENDIX 2

Two Emeralds

In addition to the Special Jurisdiction for the Peace (JEP), the 2016 peace accord also created a Commission for the Clarification of Truth, Coexistence, and Non-Repetition. Distinct from JEP, the Truth Commission sought not to attribute individual responsibility for crimes committed, but rather to shed light on the causes of the conflict, give public voice to the suffering and resistance, and restore victims' rights. Through oral history, one volume of the commission's final report aimed to capture the feeling of porvenir, or what is to come, by listening to survivors' experiences of the anticipation of the violence and the devastation that ensued—and also their visions of the emergent future that has not yet arrived but is expected to come, as though around the corner.

Colombian anthropologist Alejandro Castillejo Cuéllar, a lead commissioner, invited me to contribute to the commission's final report at the edge between the devastation and porvenir. See Abigail S. Reyes, "Dos Esmeraldas," *Hay Futuro Si Hay Verdad: Informe Final de La Comisión Para El Esclarecimientro de La Verdad, La Convivencia y La No Repetición*, ed. Alejandro Castillejo Cuéllar, 1st ed. (Bogotá: Colombia Comisión de la Verdad, 2022), 212–13 (testimonial stories in a volume subtitled "When the Birds Don't Sing"). Dr. Castillejo has read aloud from this essay when socializing the commission's work in public gatherings throughout the Colombian countryside. Edited excerpt reprinted below.

～

There is a place in the forest in my imagination. There on the eastern edge of Colombia along the wooded route from Cubará to the broad meanders of the Arauca River. There is a place in the pocket of forest where, during the kidnappings, he placed his body down. Him there, taken; me, not there, captive only to his absence and the absence of knowing. Belly down on the fertile earth. Claiming a moment in the blind chaos to pause. When I saw him, I, too, was between the trees— in the back of the community garden next to our Brooklyn apartment, sheltered from view from the street, belly down on the fertile earth, ear turned to the ground, listening for his presence. Scanning the curve of the earth with my mind's eye: *Where are you?*

In the days before he left New York for U'wa territory that last time, with the sounds of Union Street bustling outside our living room window, he surfaced an emerald cleaved into two pieces. It was a rough, cloudy emerald that a mine worker in rural Colombia had given to him. He pressed one piece into my palm and kept the other, burrowing it back into the interior of his belongings. When, after the US Department of State eventually delivered the pilfered detritus of his material estate to his mother's house in Los Angeles, I drew out a silver bracelet I had given him along with other trinkets, but the emerald was nowhere to be found. I remembered back to that night in the woods during the kidnapping. In my imagination, belly down on the earth, he paused to press his half of the emerald back into the mud for safekeeping. He paused in transition, in reorientation, in surrender to what was to come. The ground was receptive, enveloping.

The pause, belly to the earth, was never just about the kidnapping. We pause, prostrate, to communicate internally, collectively, that we are done with the blind chaos, the frantic hustle. The guns may dictate the external parameters of our movements, but we supplicate not to them. We supplicate to listen from a deeper source. When we "touch the earth," we pivot invisibly to reorient our breath to move in unison with the seeping silent flow of water, navigating underground in defiant and supple allegiance to future generations.[1] We touch the earth to breathe life into our backbody, to move in unison with our blood, chosen, and spiritual ancestors, the teachers who have gone before and who show us the way in this life.[2] We touch the earth to breathe life into the fullness of our wingspan, fingertip to fingertip, stretching out along the equator to encompass all our relations in community and solidarity. We touch the earth to breathe life along the stretch of the meridian of our earth body.

In this formation, there with our bellies on the earth, we call all our parts back home, we re-member the body, salvage it from the crush of the boot of extractive racial capitalist patriarchy. In this re-membering, we send what is precious underground, tuck it back into the earth for safekeeping. We rise realigned, our joints limber with tensile strength, knees slightly bent, weight in the balls of the feet, nape elongated, arms relaxed, palms facing up. With ancestors at our back, all our relations at our sides, we stand in the "full length of our dignity," tethered from earth to sky, attentive and allegiant to future generations who stand in front of us.[3] With or without the gun at our temple, we listen from a deeper place. We walk steadfast into that future. The way we walk is in balance, each step a sacred expression of our "wanted obligation" as "keepers of the equilibrium between the world above and the world below."[4] One step and then the next.

This is how we get where we are going: with each step in right relationship to the ancestors, the earth, our communities, and future generations. This action stands next to hope; it is faith. It is a kind of faith that strengthens with use. It is the faith that each step will rise and fall in time with the earth's own respiration, mirroring the alchemic work of the trees as they turn the gems that we buried at their roots into seeds that the fertile soil of the river valley knows how to grow.[5]

NOTES

Preface (pages xvii–xxii)

1 This book generally refrains from italicizing non-English words. See Khairani Barokka, "The Case Against Italicizing 'Foreign' Words," *Dialek: Dialect* (blog), Catapult, February 11, 2020, https://magazine.catapult .co/column/stories/column-the-case-against-italicizing-foreign-words -khairani-barokka. This book uses the Spanish word "p/Pueblo" interchange- ably with "p/People," "community/ies," and "Nation" when referring to a distinct Indigenous group that shares population, language, customs, terri- torial space, cultural conduct, government, and the ability to enter relations with other nations as a political entity; and "p/Peoples" when referring to a distinct society of Indigenous groups. See Gregory Younging, *Elements of Indigenous Style: A Guide for Writing By and About Indigenous Peoples* (Alberta, Canada: Brush Education, 2018), 65, 68; Leslie Wirpsa, "Oil Exploitation and Indigenous Rights: Global Regime Network Conflict in the Andes" (PhD diss., University of Southern California, 2004), 141, n. 57. See also Sandra Álvarez, "'Their Shadows Still Walk with Us': Mapping a Decolonial Cartography of Struggle with Ingrid Washinawatok El-Issa," *Lectora* 22 (2016): 103 (quoting Ingrid Washinawatok El-Issa's husband as noting, "Ingrid, she fought since 1977 until her death for the letter S" at the end of "Peoples.").

2 Sandra Cristina Álvarez, "Intercultural Sovereignty: The Theory and Prac- tice of Indigenous Social Movements" (PhD diss., University of California, Santa Cruz, 2012), 123, https://escholarship.org/uc/item/1zq3r3rf (quoting Gilberto Cobaria).

3 Arundhati Roy, *War Talk* (Cambridge, MA: South End Press, 2003), 75.

4 See Charles Sepulveda, "Our Sacred Waters: Theorizing Kuuyam as a Decolonial Possibility," *Decolonization: Indigeneity, Education & Society* 7, no. 1 (2018): 40–58.

5 Thich Nhat Hanh, *For a Future to Be Possible: Buddhist Ethics for Everyday Life* (Berkeley, CA: Parallax, 2007); Carolyn Forché, ed., *Against Forgetting: Twentieth-Century Poetry of Witness* (New York: W. W. Norton, 1993).

6 Thich Nhat Hanh, "The Island of Self; The Three Dharma Seals" (Dharma talk, Plum Village, France, July 28, 1998).

7 The observation regarding oral tradition emerged in discussion with Adriana Aldana and Alana LeBrón at Mesa Refuge, March 11, 2023.

8 Sun Tzu, *The Art of War*, translated by Samuel B. Griffith (High Falls, NY: Blue Heron Books, 2006); see also Norma Wong, *Peace Is Dynamic and Must Be Waged in Order to Become* (Oahu, HI: Art of Waging Peace Across Generations in Collective Acceleration, February 2021) (describing "all under heaven intact" as Sun Tzu's central strategy from which all other strategies emanate of moving toward the far horizon of wholeness).

9 Alexis Pauline Gumbs, *Undrowned: Black Feminist Lessons from Marine Mammals* (Chico, CA: AK Press, 2020), 153.

Prologue (pages xxiii–xxviii)

1 The prologue sources biographical information for Ingrid Washinawatok El-Issa, Lahe'ena'e Gay, and Terence Unity Freitas from media briefing materials and memorial service missives prepared by the bereaved families in 1999 from the author's private collection. With care, this book refrains from further describing the rich lives and works of Ingrid and Lahe' out of deference to their families.

2 Ellipses within quoted material generally indicate omission of words, phrases, or sentences for readability; ellipses do not indicate redaction of classified information. Please see chapter 17 for excerpts of author's 2019 correspondence with the Truth and Recognition Chamber.

3 Leslie Wirpsa introduced me to the description of an oil pipeline as a magnet for armed violence. See also Terry Lynn Karl, *Paradox of Plenty: Oil Booms and Petro-States* (Berkeley: University of California Press, 1997).

Chapter 1. The Escalante River (pages 3–4)

1 Mary Oliver, "Wild Geese," in *Dream Work* (Boston, MA: Atlantic Monthly Press, 1986).

Chapter 2. The Sulu Sea (pages 5–20)

1 John Berger, *Into Their Labours: A Trilogy* (London: Granta Books, 1992).

2 John Berger, Sven Blomberg, Fox Chris, Michael Dibb, and Richard Hollis, *Ways of Seeing: A Book* (London: British Broadcasting Corporation, 1977), 11.

3   Phil Dickson, "US $2 Billion Camago-Malampaya Project Will Transform the Philippines," *Oil and Gas Online*, n.d., https://oilandgasonline.com/doc /us-2-billion-camago-malampaya-project-will-tr-0001 (describing Occidental and Shell's original partnership in the Camago-Malampaya Project off the coast of Palawan Island in the territory of the Philippines' South China Sea).

4   The U'wa leaders were, of course, not the first community to advocate for this solution; they were the first community *I* heard state it so plainly. In the twenty years since, "keep it in the ground" had coalesced as an advocacy demand to world leaders from over 400 civil society organizations from 60 countries, a demand formally delivered shortly after the 2015 Paris Agreement. See, e.g., "End New Fossil Fuel Development," #KeepItInTheGround, March 20, 2018, https://keepitintheground.org.

5   Terence Unity Freitas and Anonymous, *Blood of Our Mother: The U'wa People, Occidental Petroleum and the Colombian Oil Industry* (Berkeley, CA: Project Underground, 1998), 6. When first published, all authors of this report remained anonymous. Posthumously, Project Underground recognized Terence Freitas as a lead author.

6   *Blood of Our Mother*, 1, 14.

7   See, e.g., Convention Concerning Indigenous and Tribal Peoples in Independent Countries (ILO no. 169), 72 ILO Official Bulletin 59, entered into force September 5, 1991, ratified by Colombia on September 18, 1991 (recognizing the distinctive cultures, traditions, and rights of Indigenous and tribal peoples, and seeking to ensure their full and effective participation in decision-making processes that affect them in areas including land rights, employment, education, and cultural preservation); American Convention on Human Rights, Treaty Series, No. 36, Organization of American States, 1969, entered into force July 18, 1978, ratified by Colombia on May 28, 1973; United Nations Declaration on the Rights of Indigenous Peoples (UNDRIP), adopted by UN General Assembly September 13, 2007 (reinforcing ILO Convention 169 by recognizing the right of Indigenous peoples to give their free, prior, and informed consent (FPIC) before adopting measures that may affect their lands, resources, or cultural heritage); CIDH, Informe No. 116/19, Caso 11.754. Fondo. "Pueblo Indígena U'Wa y sus Miembros. Colombia." 28 de Septiembre de 2019 ("Regarding the State's argument, the IACHR emphasizes that the obligation to carry out free, prior and informed consultation is derived from the American Convention itself, in a joint reading of the rights established in Articles 13, 21 and 23, which have been binding on the Colombian State since the ratification of the instrument." trans.

Wyatt Gjullin); see also *Mayagna (Sumo) Awas Tingni Community v. Nicaragua*, Judgment of August 31, 2001, Inter-Am. Ct. H.R., (Ser. C) No. 79 (2001) (first Inter-American case to recognize Indigenous communal title); *Saramaka People v. Suriname*, Judgment of November 28, 2007, Inter-Am. Ct. H.R., (Ser. C) No. 172 (2007) (strengthening consultation and consent requirements).

8   *Blood of Our Mother*, 3.

9   *Blood of Our Mother*, 1; see also *Working to Be a Good Neighbor in Colombia*, pamphlet (Bakersfield, CA: Occidental Oil & Gas Corporation, 1998), 2, author's private collection; Evan King, "The Dirty War for Oil in Colombia," *North American Congress in Latin America*, August 25, 2022, https://nacla .org/dirty-war-oil-arauca-colombia.

10   See, e.g., Alexei Barrionuevo and Thaddeus Herrick, "Wages of Terror: For Oil Companies, Defense Abroad Is the Order of the Day—Occidental Fends Off Rebels in Colombia, Nurturing Delicate Ties to Military—Hearing Shots in the Night," *Wall Street Journal*, February 7, 2002, sec. A1 ("When it was discovered in 1983—then with an estimated one billion barrels of reserves— Cano Limon was seen as a field that would transform Occidental. But as oil royalties began gushing into Arauca, the ELN frequently bombed the pipe-line and shook down local repair crews. Occidental acknowledged gifts of money, food and transportation to the guerrillas. 'We take care of the local population,' said Occidental's late founder Armand Hammer in 1985. 'It has worked out so far.'"); see also *Hearing on Colombia, before the United States House of Representatives Government Reform Subcommittee on Criminal Justice, Drug Policy and Human Resources*, 106th Cong. (2000) (statement of Lawrence P. Meriage, vice president of executive services and public affairs, Occidental Oil and Gas Corporation).

11   See, e.g., AsoU'wa, "The U'wa Indigenous People of the Departments of Boyaca, Santander, Norte de Santander, Arauca and Casanare, We Denounce before the National and International Public Opinion," Public communique, January 31, 2000, author's private collection ("We condemn all support by Colombians in favor of the interests of the multinational oil company Oxy. Thus, we strongly reject the collusion of the Colombian State, through its military forces, the FARC, the multinational Oxy and the subcontractor Rocas del Llano, to protect and safeguard vehicles, equipment and machinery of the transnational Oxy, from the municipality of Pamplona to the Samoré Block, as it is evident the close coordination to fulfill such purpose.").

12   The second follow-up meeting with Pueblo U'wa that the government of Colombia points to as consultation took place *a few weeks after* the government issued Occidental the permit.

13 *Blood of Our Mother*, 3.

14 John Vidal, "A Tribe's Suicide Pact," *Guardian* (UK edition), September 20, 1997; Leslie Wirpsa, "Indians Threaten Mass Suicide to Safeguard Oil-Rich Land," *National Catholic Reporter*, 1997, 32.

15 *Blood of Our Mother*, 4.

16 *Blood of Our Mother*, 21, 26.

17 See Wirpsa, "Oil Exploitation and Indigenous Rights."

18 Álvarez, "Intercultural Sovereignty," 95, 141.

19 Wirpsa, "Oil Exploitation and Indigenous Rights," 149.

20 See Joanna Macy, *World as Lover, World as Self: Courage for Global Justice and Ecological Renewal*, 30th anniv. ed. (Berkeley, CA: Parallax Press, 2021).

21 *Men with Guns*, dir. John Sayles (New York: Sony Pictures Classics, 1997). After the murders, Julie Freitas published a letter in the *Washington Post* assailing congressional efforts to use Terence's murder as a rallying cry to fund more "men with guns," a reference to this film. See Julie Freitas, "The Meaning of My Son's Murder," letter to the editor, *Washington Post*, May 22, 1999, A18. In the ensuing years, director John Sayles exchanged written correspondence with Julie, reflecting on Terence's work to stop the harm of men with guns. Author's private collection.

Chapter 3. The East River (pages 21–38)

1 *Ingrid Washinawatok Memorial Service*, missive (New York: Cathedral of St. John the Divine, May 22, 1999), author's private collection.

2 *Blood of Our Mother*, back cover.

3 Terence Unity Freitas, personal notebook dated March 11, 1998, 10, author's private collection.

4 See Rosa González, *Spectrum of Community Engagement to Ownership* (Oakland, CA: Facilitating Power and Movement Strategy Center, 2019); Rosa González, *Community-Driven Climate Resilience Planning: A Framework* (Oakland, CA: Facilitating Power in affiliation with National Association of Climate Resilience Planners, 2020).

5 *Blood of Our Mother*, 2 (describing the U'wa right to self determination as encompassing their right to decide, even if that decision is, in some case, to welcome some form of energy development on their ancestral territory).

6 *Blood of Our Mother*, 14.

7 *Blood of Our Mother*, 14.

8   Taj James and Beloved Communities Network, "Building Transformative Movements: Deep Democracy and Beloved Community," in *Practicing Liberation: Transformative Strategies for Collective Healing and Systems Change,* edited by Tessa Hicks and Hala Khouri (Berkeley, CA: North Atlantic Books, 2024), 200 (describing strategies for releasing the lie of our inherited story of separation, supremacy, scarcity, and singularity and returning to the reality of intersectionality, interdependence, and interbeing); see also Julie Quiroz and Kristen Zimmerman, *Leading with 100 Year Vision: Transforming Ourselves, Transforming the Future* (Oakland, CA: Movement Strategy Center, 2020), https://movementstrategy.org/resources/leading-with -100-year-vision-transforming-ourselves-transforming-the-future (describing Movement Strategy Center's 2014–2019 transitions gatherings that brought together movement leaders under the guiding question: How do we transition from a world of domination and extraction to a world of regeneration, resilience, and interdependence?).

9   Since 1999, an entire domestic sector of training for transformative leadership in progressive social movements has emerged. Eight months after the murders, André Carothers, Robert Gass, and others piloted the first Rockwood Art of Leadership training featuring tools and practices for starting to orient toward the slow work in what we would soon call "leading from the inside out." The pilot tested the curriculum on invited environmental grant makers and activists, including me. In 2008 Jodie Tonita and Robert Gass formed the Social Transformation Project to develop tools to bring transformative leadership and organizational development practices to social change organizations and coalitions. In 2010 Kristen Zimmerman, Neelam Pathikonda, Brenda Salgado, Taj James, and the Movement Strategy Center chronicled the journey "out of the spiritual closet" taken by many people who animate contemporary progressive social movements and described multiple sources upon which various communities draw to integrate the slow work. Over the years, each of these starting points evolved to meet the moment, joining a river of already existing and additionally emerging methodologies, frameworks, and approaches to what many now call the "depth work" that makes social transformation possible.

10   T. S. Eliot, "Burnt Norton," *Collected Poems, 1909–1935 of T.S. Eliot* (New York: Harcourt, Brace, 1936). Shortly after the murders, Janice Rous introduced me to Eliot's description of the still point.

11   Terence Unity Freitas, email message to Steve Tribbeck, October 20, 1998; see also *Terence Unity Freitas Memorial Service,* missive (Los Angeles: Highland Hall Waldorf School, March 21, 1999), author's private collection.

12 Julie Freitas, Debrief with U'wa representatives after the murders, hand-written simultaneous transcription of dialogue between U'wa leaders and representatives from the bereaved families (Malibu, CA: April 1999), 11, author's private collection.

13 *Good Neighbor in Colombia*, Occidental Oil & Gas Corporation, 9.

14 Álvarez, "Intercultural Sovereignty," 140.

15 Álvarez, "Intercultural Sovereignty," 148; see also *Biography of Lahe'ena'e Gay* (Pahoa, HI: Pacific Cultural Conservancy International, 1999) ("In December 1998, seventeen U'wa communities proposed to reject Colombia's national education system and close down all government schools located on their reservation lands. It was at that time that the Traditional U'wa Authority requested Lahe'ena'e's assistance [with a] traditional Indigenous education model.").

16 Roy, *War Talk*, 75.

17 Terence Unity Freitas, email message to author, December 1998, author's private collection.

18 Terence Unity Freitas, personal notebook dated October 9, 1998, author's private collection.

19 To underscore: The contemporaneous consensus among Latin Americanists was that this communications irregularity was not likely to have contributed in any way to the kidnappings. And from my small perch in midtown Manhattan that fateful week, this was the sequence of events I experienced. Chapter 7 discusses how I processed this experience.

Chapter 4. The Arauca River (pages 39–50)

1 Julie Freitas, Debrief, 17.

2 Abigail S. Reyes, notes dated February 27, 1999, Brooklyn, NY, author's private collection (during the first conference call among the three families during the kidnapping).

3 Mem Fox, *The Goblin and the Empty Chair* (Camberwell, VIC: Penguin, 2009), 14.

4 *Ingrid Washinawatok Memorial Service,* missive (New York: Cathedral of St. John the Divine, May 22, 1999), author's private collection.

5 Abigail S. Reyes, notes dated Monday, March 1, 1999, Brooklyn, NY, author's private collection.

6 Portions of this segment were originally published in Abigail S. Reyes, "Mercy," in *Women Working for Change Newsletter* (New York, 1999), 46–47 (remarks during Terence Unity Freitas's memorial service), author's private collection.

Chapter 5. The Rushes at the Water's Edge (pages 51–56)

1 One of the women was Nilak Butler, the Inuit human rights and environmental activist and actor, and/or Tonya Gonnella Frichner of the Onondaga
Nation, a lawyer and activist known widely for her collaboration with Ingrid
and others to push through the United Nations' Declaration on the Rights of
Indigenous Peoples. During the kidnapping, Nilak and Tonya were integral to
the families' mobilization.

2 Portions of this segment were originally published in *Women Working for
Change Newsletter*, 46–47.

3 Terence Unity Freitas, letter to the author, February 7, 1999, author's private
collection.

4 Norma Wong, *We Stand with Ancestors for Descendants Yet to Be* (Oahu, HI:
Art of Waging Peace Across Generations in Collective Acceleration, February 2021), 3–4.

Chapter 6. The Frozen Earth at Gavilan Ranch (pages 57–70)

1 Sat Santokh S. Khalsa co-created Creating Our Future, the social action
training organization for high school students, together with initial board
members Jerry Garcia, Bob Weir, Ram Dass, and Joanna Macy. Singer-
songwriter Betsy Rose, co-counselor Rita Archibald, and social change
worker Fran Peavey were some of the adult trainers. Singer-songwriter
Snatum Kaur Khalsa and YES! co-founder Ocean Robbins were two of the
youth trainers. André Carothers, Claire Greensfelder, Marianne Manilov,
and others who were then based at large national environmental organizations provided additional adult allyship to young people in this crew.

2 Fran Peavey, *Heart Politics Revisited* (Annandale, NSW: Pluto Press, 2000).

3 Peavey, *Heart Politics Revisited*, 147–67.

4 Fran Peavey, *Strategic Questioning: An Experiment in Communication of the
Second Kind*, handbook (San Francisco: Crabgrass, 2001).

5 Portions of this segment were originally published in Abigail S. Reyes, "My
Milk Lets Down," in *Celebrating the Life of Terence Unity Freitas: May 27, 1974–
March 4, 1999*, eds. Atossa Soltani et al. (Berkeley, CA, 2009) (reflections by
Terence's friends and colleagues on the ten-year anniversary of the murders).

6 Mark Levine, "Epitaph for a Crusader: Terry Freitas Lived for a Cause, a
Place, a People. But He Died for No Good Reason at All," *Outside*, May 1999,
www.outsideonline.com/outdoor-adventure/epitaph-crusader.

7 Fox, *Goblin*, 14.

8 Poet and friend Timothy Bradford offered me Rainer Maria Rilke's first elegy shortly after the murders. First Elegy from *Duino Elegies*, trans. Stephen Mitchell (Boston: Shambhala, 1992), 18. At a 1999 Rainforest Action Network gala, when asked to speak publicly about the murders for the first time, the words I could muster were from this poem.

9 Portions of this segment were originally read during opening remarks preceding a spoken-word benefit by John Trudell for the Colombian Pueblo U'wa at the San Francisco Women's Building, March 6, 2001.

10 Aya de Leon, "Sacrifices," unpublished poem (2000).

11 Joan Didion, *Year of Magical Thinking* (2005; reis., New York: Vintage Books, 2007), 75 ("I seemed to have crossed one of those legendary rivers that divide the living from the dead, entered a place in which I could be seen only by those who were themselves recently bereaved."). Kate Hallward reminded me of Didion's apt description of the bereaved.

Chapter 7. Two Ponds in the Tusas Mountains (pages 73–82)

1 By 2000, Leslie Wirpsa and I, together with AsoU'wa and the Colombian and US-based lawyers on our team, had articulated UDP's mission statement as: "In full consultation with the U'wa Traditional Authorities, U'wa Defense Project provides legal, community development and research support to the Colombian Indigenous U'wa people as they strive for self-determination over their lives and culture through defense of their ancestral territory and environment, bringing their knowledge about ecological and people-centered development into the global debate." Letter from author to friends, August 30, 2000, 2, author's private collection.

2 Hari Dass, *The Yoga Sūtras of Patañjali: A Study Guide for Book I Samādhi Pāda*, ed. Dayanand Diffenbaugh (Santa Cruz, CA: Sri Rama Publishing, 1999), 5–8.

3 See Kaira Jewel Lingo, *We Were Made for These Times: Ten Lessons on Moving through Change, Loss, and Disruption* (Berkeley, CA: Parallax Press, 2021) (describing lessons learned during Kaira Jewel's journey at Plum Village and beyond).

4 Chan Khong, *Learning True Love: How I Learned and Practiced Social Change in Vietnam* (Berkeley, CA: Parallax Press, 1993).

Chapter 8. The Cubujón River (pages 83–92)

1 See, e.g., Julie Freitas, "The Meaning of My Son's Murder" (denouncing the congressional cry for war in response to her son's murder).

2 King, "The Dirty War for Oil in Colombia" (describing historical ecocide and genocide caused by actions of multinational corporations that were protected by US-trained military personnel in Arauca).

3 Paul D. Coverdell, "Starting with Colombia," editorial, *Washington Post*, April 10, 2000, A21.

4 See, e.g., Colombia's letter of intent to the International Monetary Fund, [Minister of Finance and Public Credit] Juan Camilo Restrepo Salazar and [General Manager of the Bank of the Republic] Miguel Urrutia Montoya, Letter to Michel Camdessus, Managing Director of the International Monetary Fund, December 3, 1999, www.imf.org/external/NP/LOI/1999/120399.HTM (outlining proposed economic policies for 1999–2002 in compliance with IMF structural reform, pledging to increase private sector oil investment enough to remain a net exporter of oil).

5 *Hearing on Colombia,* Meriage statement.

6 *Hearing on Colombia,* Meriage statement.

7 Portions of this segment were originally prepared and read as opening remarks preceding a public talk by U'wa president Roberto Pérez at the San Francisco Women's Building, December 11, 2000. Leslie Wirpsa edited the opening remarks. Author's private collection.

8 Terence Unity Freitas, personal notebook dated March 17, 1998, 8, author's private collection (describing U'wa contemplation of landback strategies).

9 Petition to the Inter-American Commission on Human Rights for Precautionary Measures on Behalf of the U'wa People of Colombia, Case No. 11.754 – *Pueblo U'wa*, February 11, 2000, 3.

10 See, e.g., https://landback.org (describing history and contemporary pursuit of landback strategies).

11 Petition to the Inter-American Commission on Human Rights, Case No. 11.754 – *Pueblo U'wa*, 3, n.6.

12 Petition to the Inter-American Commission on Human Rights, Case No. 11.754 – *Pueblo U'wa*, 3; "Se revive debate por pozo en bloque Gibraltar," *El Tiempo* (Bogotá), January 21, www.eltiempo.com/archivo/documento /MAM-1277497; "El Ejército Impide Paso de Indigena U'wa," El Tiempo (Bogotá), January 25, 2000, www.eltiempo.com/archivo/documento /MAM-1272474; see also U'wa Defense Working Group, "The U'wa Struggle Continues: A Chronological Update as of October 2000," October 2000, 2, author's private collection (noting that the Colombian Embassy in Washington, DC, claimed that 250 soldiers were present, while a military spokesman in Bogotá put the number at 500, and U'wa witnesses and participants on the scene claimed 5,000).

13 AsoU'wa, "Invasion and Eviction of the U'wa People," public communique, January 25, 2000, author's private collection.

14 AsoU'wa, public communique, January 26, 2000, in petition to the Inter-American Commission on Human Rights, Case No. 11.754 – *Pueblo U'wa*, Appendix 7; John Vidal, "Battle for the Sacred Oil," *Guardian* (UK edition), February 9, 2000 (describing tense standoff in which Colombian military forcibly removed twenty-six U'wa people by truck and helicopter); see also "U'wa Defense Project, Fact Sheet – Colombia Pipeline Protection," April 17, 2002, author's private collection; Declaration of Professor Terry Karl Regarding the Impact of Petroleum Development in the Samoré Area of Colombia, Submitted for the Nullification Action against Occidental Petroleum's Environmental License before the Colombian Council of State, July 2000, 34–35, author's private collection (further describing that on July 12, 2000, a judge ruled that the January eviction had been made in error; that the full acreage needed to be rightfully returned to the U'wa; and that the state had forty-eight hours to implement without procedural error the original eviction order from the four hectares, noting that the four hectares in contention made up Occidental's proposed well site).

15 AsoU'wa, "The U'wa Indigenous People of the Departments of Boyaca, Santander, Norte de Santander, Arauca and Casanare, We Denounce Before the National and International Public Opinion," public communique, January 31, 2000, author's private collection (declaring a civilian strike to begin February 1, 2000); AsoU'wa, "Communique to the General Public," February 21, 2000, author's private collection.

16 "U'was dicen que darán la pelea," *El Tiempo*, June 26, 2000, www.eltiempo .com/archivo/documento/MAM-1242722; "Paro Armado del ELN en Arauca," *El Tiempo*, June 27, 2000, www.eltiempo.com/archivo/documento/MAM -1239507; see also U'wa Defense Working Group, "The U'wa Struggle Continues," 2 (describing police violence against U'wa protesters on June 24 and 25, 2000, at the road blockade on a bridge over the Cobaria River near the town of Cubará wherein violence included use of tear gas, beatings, threatening with guns, and the arbitrary detention of thirty-three people, with at least one protester treated for a gunshot wound; describing riot police violence against U'wa occupants of the Bella Vista and Santa Rita farms on August 23, 2000, wherein violence included threat of rape and landmines, and removal; describing military cutoff of U'wa people from the Bella Vista and Santa Rita farms on September 8–11, 2000, prompting the U'wa to travel through the mountains to enter the farms via an alternative route).

17 AsoU'wa, public communique, January 31, 2000 ("We reiterate our noble intention to continue fighting peacefully for the defense of our ancestral and

traditional territorial rights, and we do not share the actions carried out by the National Liberation Army ELN, by destroying machinery and equipment of the transnational oil company OXY, because actions like these only aggravate the conflict.").

18   AsoU'wa, public communique, January 31, 2000 ("We condemn all support by Colombians in favor of the interests of the multinational oil company Oxy. Thus, we strongly reject the collusion of the Colombian State, through its military forces, the FARC, the multinational Oxy and the subcontractor Rocas del Llano, to protect and safeguard vehicles, equipment and machinery of the transnational Oxy, from the municipality of Pamplona to the Samoré Block, as it is evident the close coordination to fulfill such purpose" and denouncing "the strong militarization carried out on the 19th of this month in Cedeño on land that is our property where U'wa brothers were cordoned off by members of the army and the Norte de Santander anti-riot police, who physically and psychologically mistreated the Indigenous comrades who were there, destroying goods and belongings that were ours.").

19   "Disturbios en Desalojo a U'was," *El Tiempo* (Bogotá), February 12, 2000, www.eltiempo.com/archivo/documento/MAM-1237734; Petition to the Inter-American Commission on Human Rights, Case No. 11.754 – *Pueblo U'wa*, 3-4; see also AsoU'wa, public communique, June 29, 2000, author's private collection (describing the more than thirty equipment trucks working for Oxy and the National Army's more than six war tanks loaded with heavy artillery "as if it were a conventional war").

20   Petition to the Inter-American Commission on Human Rights, Case No. 11.754 – *Pueblo U'wa*, 9. Note: The 2000 petition for precautionary measures followed a 1997 petition to the Inter-American Commission on Human Rights filed on behalf of the U'wa Nation by the Association of Cabildos Mayores of the U'wa Nation, National Indigenous Organization of Colombia, and the Coalition for Amazonian Peoples and Their Environment. Inter-American Commission on Human Rights, Report No. 146/19, Case 11.754, Background, "Pueblo Indígena U'Wa y sus Miembros. Colombia," September 28, 2019, 2, n.1; see also *Blood of Our Mother*, 24.

21   "U'wa Indigenous People v. Colombia," EarthRights International, www .earthrights.org/case/uwa-indigenous-people-vs-colombia; see also Inter-American Commission on Human Rights, Report No. 146/19, Case 11.754. Background, "Pueblo Indígena U'wa y sus Miembros. Colombia," September 28, 2019, 7, 17–20 (incorporating Pueblo U'wa's allegations of physical violence against U'wa protesters by state forces in 2000 as facts of

the case and citing the existential threat to the U'wa posed by Colombia's armed conflict in holding Colombia responsible for violating Pueblo U'wa's human rights).

22 Letter from Representative Sam Farr et al. to Colombian President Andrés Pastrana, July 26, 2000, author's private collection.

23 Cynthia McKinney, "Big Oil Finds Big Surprise in McKinney Office," news release, March 31, 2000.

24 Decision of the 11th Circuit Court of Bogotá, March 30, 2000 (issuing injunction); U'wa Defense Working Group, "The U'wa Struggle Continues," 2 (noting that Superior Court of Bogotá overturned injunction on May 15, 2000).

25 U'wa Defense Working Group, "U'wa Leaders Present the Colombian Government with Proof of 'Royal Land Titles' Granted by the King of Spain: Colonial Titles Could Negate Occidental & the Government's Sub-surface Rights," press release, September 15, 2000; Briefing by U'wa legal representative Ebaristo Tegria to international press, transcription, September 15, 2000, author's private collection.

26 Reyes, Women's Building Opening Remarks; U'wa Defense Working Group, "The U'wa Struggle Continues," 2 (stating that by September 28, 2000, an estimated 700–1,000 Colombian troops occupied the Saravena-Cedeño highway leading to the drill site; stating that by October 1, 2000, more than 80 trucks carrying drilling equipment, including components of the drilling tower, arrived in U'wa territory protected by thousands of troops; stating that, by October 2, 2000, more than 40 U'wa representatives met Oxy's convoy of trucks, maintaining the trucks outside of the Gibraltar 1 drill site).

Chapter 9. The Gulf of Siam (pages 93–102)

1 *Hearing on Colombia,* Meriage statement.

2 See Karl, Declaration, 7–21 (describing oil crisis syndrome, in which exporting oil can diminish the common good, and Colombia's demonstration of the syndrome).

3 See Karl, Declaration, 23–25 (describing oil war syndrome in Colombia which, among other things, enabled oil companies to deploy the strategy of subsidizing any armed force that will protect their investment, thereby creating conditions to crush local opposition to oil development).

4 Thich Nhat Hanh, "Thây's Poetry / Please Call Me by My True Names (Song & Poem)," Plum Village, July 16, 2020, www.plumvillage.org/articles/please

-call-me-by-my-true-names-song-poem; Thich Nhat Hanh, *Call Me By My True Names: The Collected Poems of Thich Nhat Hanh*, new ed. (Berkeley, CA: Parallax Press, 2022).

5 Portions of this segment were originally published in an open letter from the author to Minister Juan Mayr, October 4, 1999, author's private collection.

6 Editorial, *Wall Street Journal*, September 29, 1999.

7 See Franz Douglas, "The 2000 Campaign: The Vice President; Gore Family's Ties to Oil Company Magnate Reap Big Rewards, and a Few Problems," *New York Times*, March 19, 2000, A33; Ken Silverstein, "Gore's Oil Money," *Nation*, May 3, 2000, www.thenation.com/article/archive/gores-oil-money.

8 Abigail S. Reyes, "Mr. Gore—Get Rid of Those Oil Holdings—Do It for Terence," *Marin Independent Journal*, February 12, 2000; Abigail S. Reyes, "Dear Vice President Gore: A Challenge to the Man Who Would Be President: Get Out of Dirty Oil," *Adbusters*, 2000.

9 Letter from Representative Barbara Lee to Vice President Al Gore, April 4, 2000; Letter from Vice President Al Gore to Representative Barbara Lee, April 13, 2000; Letter from Representative Cynthia McKinney to Vice President Al Gore, March 30, 2000; Letter from Vice President Al Gore to Representative Cynthia McKinney, April 13, 2000; Letter from Vice President Al Gore to Abigail Reyes, May 23, 2000, author's private collection.

10 See Silverstein, "Gore's Oil Money," *Nation*, May 3, 2000.

11 *US v. Fuerzas Armadas Revolucionarias de Colombia, Briceno Suarez, El Marrano, Jeronimo, Bocota Aguablanca, Vargas Rueda, Dumar*, Indictment, April 30, 2002 (DDC).

12 "Rueda de prensa del secretario de Justicia de E.U. John Ashcroft," *El Tiempo* (Bogotá), April 30, 2002; Dan Eggen and Karen DeYoung, "Colombian Rebels Are Indicted as Terrorists," *Washington Post*, May 1, 2002; "U'wa Defense Project, Fact Sheet" (stating that the 2003 Foreign Operations Appropriation request included $98 million of foreign military financing to provide military protection to the Caño Limon pipeline and that the 2002 Supplemental Request included $6 million to "jump-start" this program. Requested aid included helicopters, training, and equipment for Colombia's 18th Brigade, based in the Arauca Department, and a new 5th mobile brigade), author's private collection.

13 Freitas Family press release, May 1, 2002, author's private collection.

14 See, e.g., Christopher Marquis, "6 Colombian Rebels Indicted in '99 Killings," *New York Times.* May 1, 2002, A4 ("The father and girlfriend of Terence Freitas released a statement today accusing the administration of exploiting

his killing 'to justify further U.S. military aid to the Colombian armed forces.'"); Amy Goodman, "Attorney General John Ashcroft Indicts the Revolutionary Armed Forces of Colombia for the Killing of Three Americans—Relatives Say He's Using the Murders to Drum Up Support for Increased U.S. Military Aid to Colombia," *Democracy Now*, New York, WBAI, May 2, 2002 (interview with Julie Freitas and the author).

15 Freitas Family statement, April 23, 2003, author's private collection (regarding Colombia's agreement to extradite accused killer).

Chapter 10. Tomales Bay (pages 103–112)

1 Portions of this segment were originally delivered in a TEDx talk. Abigail S. Reyes, "How to Come Home," TEDx UC Irvine, May 14, 2016.

2 Within a few years, international delegations slowly resumed, with the community's self-organized Indigenous guard on high alert.

3 Álvarez, "Intercultural Sovereignty," 155.

4 Soltani et al., *Celebrating the Life of Terence Unity Freitas*.

5 Álvarez, "Intercultural Sovereignty," 181, n. 91 (describing fear held by some U'wa community members that external education of U'wa women could lead to dilution of the U'wa population).

6 David Hill, "Colombian Tribe Scores 'Historic' Victory versus Big Gas," *Guardian*, March 26, 2015, www.theguardian.com/environment/andes-to-the-amazon/2015/mar/26/colombian-tribe-scores-historic-victory-versus-big-gas.

7 Co-petitioners included the National Indigenous Organization of Colombia, AsoU'wa, the José Alvear Restrepo Lawyers Collective, and EarthRights International.

8 See Álvarez, "Intercultural Sovereignty."

9 While attribution for this ubiquitous invitation is unclear, the author recalls first receiving it in the context of social movement mobilizations for Indigenous-led environmental protection.

Chapter 11. The Mahwáéw River (pages 113–120)

1 One handwritten letter is a "message from the people of the Sovereign Dineh Nation" that states, "We are thankful for what Terence Freitas has done for us and people in struggle. We appreciate and are thankful for how brave he was. . . . What was done to him should not be tolerated and we want you to

know we stand with you and support you." The letter is signed by twenty-three members of the Dineh Nation, including three signatures by thumb stamp. Another letter from the Indigenous Women's Network, of which Ingrid was a founding co-chair of the board at the time of her death, states, "I hope it will give you consolation to know how highly respected your son was and is within the Indigenous community, nationally and internationally. Our struggle for land rights and dignity is strengthened by the selfless work of people like Terence and we want you to hear that from us." Author's private collection.

2 See, e.g., Jenny Pearce, "Oil and Armed Conflict in Casanare, Colombia: Complex Contexts and Contingent Moments," in Mary Kaldor, Terry Lynn Karl, and Yahia Said, ed., *Oil Wars* (New York: Pluto Press, 2007), 225–73 (describing Colombian and foreign oil companies' protection payments to guerrillas in Arauca and Casenare in the mid-1990s); see also King, "The Dirty War for Oil in Colombia" (describing ongoing practices in Arauca, especially involving Occidental).

3 *Hearing on Colombia,* Meriage statement.

4 Fredy Mora Gámez, "Colombian Truth Commission Final Report (2022): Challenges and Opportunities for Social Sciences," *Acta Colombiana de Psicología* 26, no. 1 (epub February 19, 2023), 5–8, https://doi.org/10.14718/acp.2023.26.1.1 (describing story collection as a technology of memory).

Chapter 12. A Tangle of Frozen Bramble, Glistening (pages 121–130)

1 See, e.g., Climate Justice Alliance, "Jemez Principles for Democratic Organizing," December 30, 2019, https://climatejusticealliance.org/jemez-principles (republishing the principles as drafted by environmental justice advocates in Jemez, New Mexico, at a 1996 meeting hosted by the Southwest Network for Environmental and Economic Justice).

2 See UCI Community Resilience, "Encuentro: Land and Freedom," blog post, February 20, 2020, https://communityresilience.uci.edu/encuentro-land-freedom (describing the encuentro).

3 Terence Unity Freitas, personal notebook dated March 17, 1998, 36, author's private collection.

4 Terence Unity Freitas, personal notebook dated March 22, 1998, 43, author's private collection.

5 The observation regarding the impact of this cultural norm emerged in discussion with Taj James.

Chapter 13. Shell Beach (pages 133–142)

1 Portions of this segment were originally published as an essay in a poetry journal. Abigail S. Reyes, "Parting Song: Reflection on the Gulf Oil Spill," *Interim: The Eco-Issue* 29 (2011): 368.

2 Letter from the author to Daris Cristancho and Aura Tegria dated May 3, 2018; Letter from Daris Cristancho and Aura Tegria dated May 22, 2018; Julie Freitas, Debrief, 2 (describing Berito's invitation to the families immediately following the murders), author's private collection.

Chapter 14. Bloodletting (pages 143–148)

1 Thomas Merton, *Conjectures of a Guilty Bystander* (Garden City, NY: Image Books, 2014). First published 1965 by Doubleday Religion.

2 Maggie Nelson, *The Red Parts: Autobiography of a Trial* (Minneapolis, MN: Graywolf Press, 2016), 129. First published 2007 by Free Press.

3 Portions of this segment were originally delivered in a TEDx talk. Abigail S. Reyes, "How to Come Home," TEDx UC Irvine, May 14, 2016.

4 Fox, *The Goblin and the Empty Chair.*

5 Joanna Macy and Molly Young Brown, *Coming Back to Life: The Updated Guide to the Work That Reconnects* (Gabriola Island, BC: New Society Publishers, 2014) (describing the truth mandala practice); see also Aryeh Shell, Abigail S. Reyes, and Rachel Pennington, *Student Leadership Institute for Climate Resilience Curriculum Manual*, 2nd ed. (Irvine, CA: UCI Community Resilience, 2018), 118–20 (adapting Joanna Macy's truth mandala practice for use with university student leaders, as shown to us by Youth Lead the World in Australia and SERES in Guatemala).

Chapter 15. Ma Ganga (pages 149–160)

1 Jumana Sophia, "Break the Grip of Past Lovers," DailyOM, n.d., accessed August 16, 2023, www.dailyom.com/courses/break-the-grip-of-past-lovers.

2 Thich Nhat Hanh, "Breathing In, Breathing Out," song (Loubès-Bernac, France: Plum Village Song Library, July 13, 2021), www.plumvillage.org/library/songs/breathing-in-breathing-out (song describing inner awareness as being solid as a mountain, firm as the earth, and free).

3 David Whyte, "The House of Belonging," in *River Flow: New and Selected Poems, 1984–2007* (Langley, WA: Many Rivers Press, 2012), 6–8.

4 Peavey, *Strategic Questioning*, 8.

5 Angelina Star Cheney and Megan Coulter taught me this method of asking for the care instructions.

6 Arundhati Roy, "An Evening with Arundhati Roy: *The Ministry of Utmost Happiness*" (discussion in conversation with Héctor Tobar, ALOUD Library Foundation of Los Angeles, Los Angeles, June 29, 2017) (observing it as a form of resistance to demand space for our joy and reflecting that, in working with the poorest people in the world who stand up to the most violent actors such as the mining companies, she saw joy there, too, and understood the importance "for us to insist on our entire bandwidth").

Chapter 16. Muir Beach (pages 161–170)

1 Janice Rous (www.bodydialogues.com) and Jean Couch (www.balancecenter .com) retaught me how to walk pain-free.

2 Rebecca Solnit, "'Hope is an Embrace of the Unknown:' Rebecca Solnit on Living in Dark Times," *Guardian*, July 15, 2016, www.theguardian.com/books /2016/jul/15/rebecca-solnit-hope-in-the-dark-new-essay-embrace -unknown; see also Rebecca Solnit, *Hope in the Dark: Untold Histories, Wild Possibilities* (Chicago: Haymarket Books, 2004).

3 Elvis Mitchell, "Actress Stephanie Hsu on Writer adrienne maree brown," *The Treatment*, KCRW, Los Angeles, June 17, 2023, www.kcrw.com/culture /shows/the-treatment/cheryl-pawelski-terry-mcdonnell-stephanie-hsu /stephanie-hsu-adrienne-maree-brown-emergent-strategy (Hsu para- phrasing brown's reflection on Harriet Tubman's decision to keep walking: "[There's] something amazing about being grounded down to the speed of walking and to know that if you continue to walk, because you have no other choice other than to move towards freedom, then you're okay.").

4 Norma Wong, "Collective Acceleration" (lecture, Collective Acceleration Intensive, September 30, 2020) (describing the Hawaiian practice of hon- oring kuleana, or our wanted obligations and the contemporary imperative to acknowledge our kuleana as our response-ability to pivot and step into renewed forms of sacred governance); see also Wong, *We Stand with Ances- tors*, 3 (describing kuleana as "a philosophical and operational purpose that also guides your choices of where to put effort, and where to support, and where to stand aside").

5 Staci Haines, "Centering Practice with Staci Haines" (video, Strozzi Insti- tute, March 15, 2021), www.youtube.com/watch?v=77EJgznvqLc (describing the Strozzi Institute and generative somatics practice of centering energy in

a way that allows us to stand in "the full length of our dignity"); see also Staci Haines, *The Politics of Trauma: Somatics, Healing, and Social Justice* (Berkeley, CA: North Atlantic Books, 2019).

6 See Abigail S. Reyes, "How to Do a Seed Circle," June 30, 2011. Sat Santokh Singh Khalsa taught me how to do a seed circle in 1989.

7 See "Basic Principles and Guidelines on the Right to a Remedy and Reparation for Victims of Gross Violations of International Human Rights Law and Serious Violations of International Humanitarian Law," General Assembly Resolution 60/147, adopted December 15, 2005, www.ohchr.org/en/instruments-mechanisms/instruments/basic-principles-and-guidelines-right-remedy-and-reparation.

8 See Robert Gass, *What Is Transformation? And How It Advances Social Change* (Boulder, CA: Social Transformation Project, 2014), 19 (describing the "wheel of transformation").

9 The Resonance Network convenes people who are designing into these questions through #WeGovern. See www.we-govern.org.

10 Taj James introduced me to this example, which comes from engaged Buddhism. See, e.g., Eliza Barclay and Phap Dung, "A Buddhist Monk Explains Mindfulness for Times of Conflict," interview, Vox, November 22, 2016. ("The thing is that left and right were never separate. Your right hand maybe has done a lot of awful things—like smashing trees, destroying the forest. But when the right hand gets hurt, your left hand comes to its assistance, grabs and holds it without hesitation. This is the way we engage in politics—we try not to see other as separate from us; they are us. We get out there and try to heal but we don't cause more harm.")

11 See, e.g., Thich Nhat Hanh and Anh Huong Nguyen, *Diamond That Cuts through Illusion* (Berkeley, CA: Parallax Press, 2010) (describing the Diamond Sutra from the Mahayana tradition).

12 Wirpsa, "Oil Exploitation and Indigenous Rights," 306.

Chapter 18. Stowell Pond (pages 189–200)

1 See also *US v. Fuerzas Armadas,* indictment (stating that the bodies were found at kilometer marker 56).

2 Jurisdicción Especial para la Paz, *Las Versiones Voluntarias en el Marco del Caso No. 01*, 2019, 13, author's private collection (informal translation of "Annex 2: Cases in Clarification of Part of the Former Eastern Bloc of the FARC-EP").

3 Jurisdicción Especial para la Paz, *Las Versiones Voluntarias*, 14.

4 See, e.g., "¿Orden Del 'Mono Jojoy'?" *La Semana* (Bogotá), March 15, 1999, 880 edition.

5 Jurisdicción Especial para la Paz, *Auto 19*, 2019, para. 465, author's private collection (describing 2001 published interview with Grannobles's former girlfriend Narda Patricia Cabezas).

6 "Occidental Petroleum Sells Onshore Colombian Assets to the Carlyle Group," Leaders League, October 8, 2020, www.leadersleague.com/en/news /occidental-petroleum-sells-onshore-colombian-assets-to-the-carlyle -group (describing Occidental's more than forty-year presence in Colombia upon the 2020 sale of its onshore Colombian assets).

7 *Hearing on Colombia,* Meriage statement.

8 *Hearing on Colombia,* Meriage statement.

9 Jurisdicción Especial para la Paz, *Versiones Voluntarias*, Annex 2, 3.

10 *US v. Fuerzas Armadas*, indictment; "U.S. Indicts Colombian Rebel Group," *New York Times*, April 30, 2002; "US Grand Jury Indicts Colombians," Associated Press, May 1, 2002.

11 Aadriaan Alsema, "FARC Leader Orders Commanders to Return to Colombia: El Tiempo," *Colombia Reports*, April 19, 2011, www.colombiareports .com/amp/farc-commander-orders-commanders-to-return-to-colombia (restating an *El Tiempo* account from April 19, 2011, describing Grannobles's alleged habitation in Venezuela since 2007).

Chapter 19. Point Lobos (pages 201–206)

1 Virginia Woolf, *Moments of Being* (1976; reis., Boston: Mariner Books Classics, 1985), 72. Adriana Aldana, Alana LeBrón, André Carothers, and Taj James helped me arrive at this understanding of how to unfold.

2 Berger, *Ways of Seeing*, 33.

3 Annie Dillard, *Teaching a Stone to Talk* (New York: Harper & Row, 1982), 12 ("I startled a weasel who startled me").

4 Terence Unity Freitas, personal notebook dated October 9, 1998, author's private collection.

5 Terence Unity Freitas, personal notebook dated October 9, 1998, author's private collection.

6 Linda Eagle Speaker-Pierce, "Collective Acceleration" (presentation in conversation with Norma Wong, The Art of Waging Peace Across Seven Generations for Collective Acceleration Intensive, June 10, 2022).

Chapter 20. What the Truth Demands (pages 207–216)

1 See https://taproot.earth (describing the work of Colette Pichon Battle and team) and https://justtransitionlawyering.org/details (describing the work of Colette Pichon Battle, Angela P. Harris, Jacqui Patterson, Dorcas Gilmore, Kaaryn Gustafson, Amy Laura Cahn, Rosa González, Dean Spade, Judith LeBlanc, the author, and many others in piloting the Just Transition Lawyering Institute as one way to proliferate the patterns these many seamsters /seamstresses set into motion through their work).

2 Movement Strategy Center, *Practices of Transformative Movements* (Oakland, CA: Movement Strategy Center, 2016).

3 See, e.g., Martin Luther King, Jr., "Where Do We Go from Here?" (speech, Atlanta, GA, 11th Annual Southern Christian Leadership Conference Convention, August 16, 1967) (lifting up the popular African American expression).

4 Portions of this segment were originally published as an essay in a poetry journal. Reyes, "Parting Song," 368.

5 See Abigail Reyes, "Estate of Winston Cabello, et al. v. Armando Fernández Larios: Aiding and Abetting and Conspiracy under the Alien Tort Claims Act and the Torture Victim Protection Act," *ACLU International Civil Liberties Report*, 2003, 167–72.

6 Sweet Honey in the Rock, "Chile, Your Waters Run Red Through Soweto," track 17 on *Breaths*, Flying Fish Records, 1988, compact disc.

7 Thich Nhat Hanh, "For Warmth," *Call Me by My True Names: The Collected Poems of Thich Nhat Hanh*, new ed. (Berkeley, CA: Parallax Press, 2022).

8 Betsy Rose, "In My Two Hands," song on *In My Two Hands*, Parallax Recordings, 1988, cassette tape.

9 See Movement Generation, *A Framework for Just Transition: From Banks and Tanks to Cooperation and Caring* (Berkeley, CA: Movement Generation, 2017), https://movementgeneration.org/justtransition.

10 Transformative justice facilitators Haewon Asfaw and Sara Briseño Torres elucidated to me that, in their approach to transformative justice, it can be useful to cultivate a conscious practice of moving into and through the "uncomfortable middle" in which the process itself begins to embody the future that we seek to create, with culture following suit. Haewon Asfaw and Sara Briseño Torres conversation with author, March 29, 2023.

11 Norma Wong, "The Art of Waging Peace across Generations in Collective Acceleration" (lecture, Collective Acceleration Intensive, June 9, 2022). See also www.collective-acceleration.org.

12 Daris Cristancho, discussion with the author, March 4, 2023; see also *Blood of Our Mother*, 5–6 ("For the U'wa, the purpose of life is to 'maintain this equilibrium and give rise to the unwrapping of chance, correcting the processes that have a place inside the universe by means of the celebration of the myths, songs, and life for a time of equilibrium and harmony.'").

13 The parable of the choir is that "a choir can sing a beautiful note impossibly long because singers can individually drop out to breathe as necessary and the note goes on," a method instructive to social justice work. Source unknown.

14 Terence Unity Freitas, email message to Steve Tribbeck, October 20, 1998; see also *Terence Unity Freitas Memorial Service*, missive (Los Angeles: Highland Hall Waldorf School, March 21, 1999), author's private collection.

15 AsoU'wa, "Our History of Life Is the Resistance of the U'wa Ancestral People, but Their Deaths Strengthened the Roots of Life and Resistance Even Stronger for the Future of our Next Generations," public communique, March 4, 2024, author's private collection.

16 Ocean Vuong, "Planting Seeds of Compassion," *Thich Nhat Hanh Foundation*, February 17, 2022, https://thichnhathanhfoundation.org/blog/2022/2/17/a-love-letter-for-our-community-by-ocean-vuong.

17 Terence Unity Freitas, personal notebook dated March 11, 1998, 16–18, author's private collection.

18 This insight emerged in discussion with Alejandro Castillejo Cuéllar and doctoral student Sara Mejia in Bogotá, March 4, 2023.

19 Sweet Honey in the Rock, "Breaths," track 1 on *Breaths*, Flying Fish Records, 1988, compact disc (adapting a Biago Diop poem). Those gathered at Terence's memorial service in Los Angeles on March 22, 1999, sang this song during the service.

20 Norma Wong, "Strategy in Waging Peace in Collective Acceleration" (lecture, Collective Acceleration Intensive, September 22, 2023).

Epilogue (pages 217–224)

1 Octavia E. Butler, Notes on Writing, "I Am a Bestselling Writer," 1988, "Octavia E. Butler: Telling My Stories," exhibition, Huntington Library, Art Collections and Botanical Gardens, 2017.

Appendix 2 (pages 233–236)

1 Thich Nhat Hanh and Rachel Neumann, *Teachings on Love* (Berkeley, CA: Parallax Press, 2007) (describing the Buddhist practice of touching the earth).

2 See Haines, "Centering Practice with Staci Haines" (describing this practice of centering energy in a way that allows us to stand in "the full length of our dignity"); see also Haines, *Politics of Trauma*.

3 Haines, "Centering Practice."

4 Wong, *We Stand with Ancestors*, 2 (describing kuleana as "a philosophical and operational purpose that also guides your choices of where to put effort, and where to support, and where to stand aside"); Pueblo U'wa, time imme-morial (teaching U'wa cosmological practice of maintaining equilibrium between the world above and the world below).

5 Las Zapatistas, mid-1990s (reviving the insight on buried seeds).

ACKNOWLEDGMENTS

Thank you: Sunil Gandhi, for being my safe harbor; Betsy Reyes, for *staying where staying was needed*;* and Polly Howells, for accompanying me. Thank you: Julie, Kian, and Jennifer Freitas, for sharing Terence; and Daris Cristancho, Ebaristo Tegria, and Berito Kuwar'U'wa, for accompanying him.

Thank you: Nadinne Cruz, Janice Rous, André Carothers, Angelina Star Cheney, Taj James, Caroline Laskow, Kaira Jewel Lingo, Philippa Scarlett, Nicholas Thompson, and Alexa Wesner; Kaki Bernard, Karin Boyd, Nilak Butler, Susan Cordero, Ram Dass, Polly and Suresh Diffenbaugh, Claire Greensfelder, Patty and Michael Gold, Danny Kennedy, Carolyn Laub, Marianne Manilov, Elizabeth Martin, Fran Peavey, Jason Reyes, Nelson Reyes, Emily Schaffer, Katie Tinto, Steve Trebbeck, Ben Vigoda, Leslie Wirpsa, Alexi Wright, and Erika Zavaleta. Together with Betsy Reyes and Polly Howells, these people were the *ship that carried me through the wildest storm of all*. Thank you: Jodie Tonita, Megan Coulter, Hope Mohr, Sara Weinberg, Mariabruna Sirabella, Alana LeBrón, and Adriana Aldana for ensuring that I didn't *stay folded*.

For publishing, thank you: Tim McKee and the skillful team at North Atlantic Books. For editing, expertly, thank you: Sunil Gandhi, Susan Griffin, Kate Hallward, Terry Karl, Shayna Keyles, Nicola Kraus, Hope Mohr, Janelle Ludowise, Margeaux Weston, and Matthew Hoover. For reading, reflecting, redirecting, and more, thank you: Celia Alario, Adriana Aldana, Sandra Álvarez, Sean Authors, Amy Laura Cahn, André Carothers, Donna Chavis, Daris Cristancho,

---

* Italicized phrases in the acknowledgments are attributable to Fox, *The Goblin and the Empty Chair*, and Rilke, "I Am Too Alone."

Nadinne Cruz, Keith Donnell Jr., Julie Freitas, Kian Freitas, Wyatt Gjullin, Naomi Glassman-Majara, Taj James, Terry Karl, Danny Kennedy, Alison Knowles, Caroline Laskow, Alana LeBrón, Kaira Jewel Lingo, Joanna Macy, Marianne Manilov, Grizelda Mayo-Anda, Ana María Mondragón Duque, Astrid Puentes Riaño, Aryeh Shell, Marco Simons, Heber Tegria Uncaria-Kambrayo, Juan Gabriel Jerez Tegria-Kuanakuvo, Nicholas Thompson, Jodie Tonita, Martin Wagner, Alexi Wright, Marissa Vahlsing, and people who wish to stay anonymous. All errors are mine.

For sharing expertise, thank you: Celia Alario, Lluvia Cardenas, Sean Desmond, Abigail Everdell, Naomi Glassman-Majara, Melody González, Sekita Grant, Terry Karl, Sara Mejia, Astrid Puentes Riaño, Ian Rosenberg, Marissa Vahlsing, Gabriela Valentín Díaz, and Norma Wong. For accompanying the U'wa, thank you: Juliana Bravo Valencia for leading the EarthRights legal team together with Wyatt Gjullin, Naomi Glassman-Majara, Milena Mazabel, Laura Posada, and Marissa Vahlsing; Paul Hoffman and the students of the UCI Law International Human Rights Clinic.

For financial and/or in-kind support of this writing, of my survival immediately following the murders, of the U'wa Defense Project's *first* pivots following the murders, and of my legal education, thank you: Polly Howells and Eric Werthman, foremost; André Carothers, Alexa Wesner, Marisa Arpels, North Atlantic Books, and the Jeannette Pontacq Investigative Journalism Fellowship at the Mesa Refuge Writers' Residency; the collective of Polly and Eric's friends who paid my Brooklyn rent after the murders, Rose Boyle, Betsey Johnson, Annie Prutzmann, Janice Rous, Mount Madonna Center, and Peace Development Fund; Chela Blitt, Tom Burt, Henry and Kathleen Chalfant, Leonardo DiCaprio, Michael Freund, Sting and Trudie Styler, the Fetzer Institute, the Funding Exchange, Social and Environmental Entrepreneurs, the Furthur, Goldman, Pachamama, Rainforest, and Threshold Foundations, the collective of people who supported the purchase of the farms, among others, and people who wish to stay anonymous; Victoria Ortiz, former dean of students, Berkeley Law; and the Davis-Putter, Letelier-Moffitt, and Amnesty International Patrick Stewart scholarship funds.

For the storytellers who remain anonymous, thank you. For the people who moved into and traversed the uncomfortable middle with me to arrive here on the other side with grace, thank you.

For the land that helped me write, thank you: Mesa Refuge, Point Reyes Station, California; Los Colibris, Todos Santos, Baja California Sur, Mexico; the cabin at Stowell Pond, Norwich, Vermont; Fat Sheep Farm, Windsor, Vermont; Plum Village Lower Hamlet, Loubès-Bernac, France; Mount Madonna Center, Watsonville, California; Vallecitos Mountain Retreat Center, Tierra Amarilla, New Mexico; and the Garden of Union, Brooklyn, New York. For Kajka Ika, the heart of the world in U'wa territory. For the waters, thank you, full stop.

This book is in memory of Terence Unity Freitas, Lahe'ena'e Gay, and Ingrid Washinawatok El-Issa.

ABOUT THE AUTHOR

Photo by Jamie Grenough

Abby Reyes, JD, cut her teeth doing rural environmental legal assistance in the Philippines, her father's homeland, and walking alongside the Colombian U'wa Indigenous pueblo for dignity against big oil, work for which Barnard's Scholar and the Feminist Conference once named her a "model of resistance." She now directs community resilience at the University of California, Irvine, where she supports leaders from climate-vulnerable communities and their academic partners to accelerate community-owned just transition solutions. A graduate of Stanford University and UC Berkeley Law, Abby co-chaired the board of EarthRights International and is an advisor to the National Association of Climate Resilience Planners. She is a Mesa Refuge alumna and recipient of the 2018 Jeanette Pontacq Investigative Journalism Fellowship. This is her first book.

Abby can be reached at abbyreyes.org.

ABOUT
NORTH ATLANTIC BOOKS

North Atlantic Books (NAB) is an independent, nonprofit publisher committed to a bold exploration of the relationships between mind, body, spirit, and nature. Founded in 1974, NAB aims to nurture a holistic view of the arts, sciences, humanities, and healing. To make a donation or to learn more about our books, authors, events, and newsletter, please visit www.northatlanticbooks.com.